NUCLEAR WEAPONS LAW

This book examines the law relating to the possession, threat or use of nuclear weapons. By addressing in logical sequence the law regarding sovereignty, the threat or use of force, the conduct of nuclear hostilities, neutrality, weapons law and war crimes, the book illustrates the topics that an effective national command, control and communications system for nuclear weapons must address. Guidance is given on intractable issues, such as the responsibilities of remote submarine commanders. The continuing relevance of the ICJ's Nuclear Advisory Opinion is assessed, and the prospects for the Treaty on the Prohibition of Nuclear Weapons are discussed. The book has been written in an accessible style so that it will be equally useful to lawyers and practitioners, including relevant commanders, politicians, policy staffs and academics. The objective is to state the law accurately and to explain its implications and provide practical guidance in this most sensitive area. This book is also available as open access.

William H. Boothby is an Honorary Professor at the Australian National University. He retired from the RAF in 2011 as Deputy Director of Legal Services in the rank of Air Commodore.

Wolff Heintschel von Heinegg is the Chair of Public Law, in particular Public International Law, European Law and Foreign Constitutional Law, at Europa-Universität Viadrina in Germany.

Nuclear Weapons Law

WHERE ARE WE NOW?

WILLIAM H. BOOTHBY
Geneva Centre for Security Policy

WOLFF HEINTSCHEL VON HEINEGG
Europa-Universität Viadrina Frankfurt (Oder)

CAMBRIDGE
UNIVERSITY PRESS

CAMBRIDGE
UNIVERSITY PRESS

University Printing House, Cambridge CB2 8BS, United Kingdom

One Liberty Plaza, 20th Floor, New York, NY 10006, USA

477 Williamstown Road, Port Melbourne, VIC 3207, Australia

314–321, 3rd Floor, Plot 3, Splendor Forum, Jasola District Centre, New Delhi – 110025, India

103 Penang Road, #05–06/07, Visioncrest Commercial, Singapore 238467

Cambridge University Press is part of the University of Cambridge.

It furthers the University's mission by disseminating knowledge in the pursuit of education, learning, and research at the highest international levels of excellence.

www.cambridge.org
Information on this title: www.cambridge.org/9781316511428
DOI: 10.1017/9781009052634

First published 2022

A catalogue record for this publication is available from the British Library.

ISBN 978-1-316-51142-8 Hardback

Contents

A

Introduction to the Book

This book examines the legality of the threat or use of nuclear weapons from a variety of legal perspectives and from a viewpoint grounded in the 2020s. Some things should be stated from the outset. Nuclear weapons are the most awful kinds of weapon known to humankind. Their use would put at risk humanity's very existence and must, in most if not all circumstances, be seen as not only unlawful but also morally repugnant. The expression 'most if not all circumstances' is used advisedly. In an Advisory Opinion given in 1995, the International Court of Justice (ICJ) could not conclude that such use would be unlawful in all circumstances. Moreover, a number of States are known to possess them, including the five States that are permanent members of the UN Security Council. Furthermore, certain other States are believed to possess them or to have active nuclear weapon development programmes. In such circumstances, to talk of a customary rule prohibiting the possession and use in any circumstance of nuclear weapons would seem to be at variance with perceptible reality. Nevertheless, it is clear that the use of such a weapon in all but the most exceptional and serious of circumstances will generally be regarded as an unlawful act of the utmost gravity. The emotive sentiments that any use of such a weapon would be bound to unleash have no place in a strictly legal analysis. Hence, in the following Sections of this book, the complex legal issues associated with nuclear weapons are explored in as objective and clinical a manner as possible.

Section C's discussion of the rules of *jus ad bellum* as they would seem to apply to nuclear weapons use should not, however, be misunderstood as implying that the use of such a weapon would likely be considered by the international community in the same light as a use of force or armed attack involving conventional weapons. A nuclear use of force or armed attack would undoubtedly be seen for what it almost certainly would be – namely, an outrage, probably attracting global action against the perpetrator, including forceful action, in response. Similarly, the articulation of the principles and rules of *jus in bello* and an explanation of how they would likely apply in the nuclear context should not be misinterpreted as in any way suggesting that the employment of a nuclear weapon can sensibly be equated with the conduct of conventional hostilities. It cannot. To resort to using a nuclear weapon will, in virtually all circumstances, be regarded as a most serious breach of international law, and the precautionary nuclear command, control and communications (NC3) measures discussed in Section L must be rigorous, robust and secure enough to ensure that such use will not occur outside the most exceptional, compelling and strictly lawful of circumstances. This is one area in which the global community will never forgive a mistake. NC3 measures must be designed with that ultimate truth in mind. In the opinion of the present authors, a globally recognised taboo is developing that prohibits any resort to nuclear weapon use. That taboo must be reinforced and respected, and nothing in this book is intended in any way to undermine it. Rather, the principles and rules set out below seek to articulate the additional legal constraints that apply to any use of nuclear weapons.

It is unclear, at the time of writing, how nuclear weapons may be expected to develop in the future. The possibility is that limited-yield nuclear weapons that have comparatively restricted areas of effect may emerge. How restricted those areas might become is unclear. It is therefore appropriate in the following pages to consider not just the rules that apply to strategic-level bombardment but also those that apply in the case of tactical-level engagements. Moreover, this book tackles the law as it applies in several distinct contexts.

For example, it addresses the law as it applies when a nuclear weapon is used, or when a threat of such use is made, before an armed conflict occurs. The book also addresses the law applicable to the use, or threatened use, of such a weapon during an armed conflict. Thirdly, the book considers the law that governs the use of conventional force to target a nuclear weapon, nuclear-propelled platform or nuclear installation. All of these, and other, situations are considered to come within the scope of nuclear operations, and thus to be regulated by the legal rules discussed in this book.

A.1 THE EMERGENCE OF LAW RELATING TO NUCLEAR WEAPONS

The modern law that applies to the conduct of hostilities really started to emerge in the middle of the nineteenth century. The immediately following paragraphs are not intended to provide a comprehensive history of the adoption of each legal provision that is relevant to the subject of this book. Rather, in this short overview an attempt will be made to pick out a few of the key legal developments that help to explain, in broad terms, how the body of law that we have today came into being. Accordingly, only what are thought to be the most significant of these developments will receive a brief mention. In 1861, Dr Francis Lieber of Columbia University wrote a lengthy and authoritative statement of the laws of land warfare as they then existed – a text that was issued to the army of the Union side in the American Civil War. Among the many observations made by Dr Lieber were an acknowledgement of the necessity of those measures that are indispensable for securing the ends of the war and lawful according to the modern law and usages of war, and an appreciation that there are limits to what military necessity should permit. Specifically, he opined that it should not permit of cruelty, such as the infliction of suffering for the sake of suffering or for revenge, nor the use of poison.[1]

In 1868, a Declaration was agreed among States in St Petersburg, the operative provisions of which do not need to trouble us. In the preamble to the Declaration, however, the participating States recognised the following:

> That the only legitimate object which States should endeavour to accomplish during war is to weaken the military forces of the enemy;
>
> That for this purpose it is sufficient to disable the greatest possible number of men;
>
> That this object would be exceeded by the employment of arms which uselessly aggravate the sufferings of disabled men, or render their death inevitable;
>
> That the employment of such arms would, therefore, be contrary to the laws of humanity . . . .[2]

The modern formulation of that principle prohibits the employment of weapons, projectiles and material and methods of warfare of such a nature as to cause superfluous injury or unnecessary suffering. This principle applies to nuclear weapons in the manner explained in Section G.

After drawing attention to the military necessity principle, the Lieber Code noted 'the distinction between the private individual belonging to a hostile country and the hostile country itself, with its men in arms. The principle has been more and more acknowledged that the unarmed citizen is to be spared in

[1] Instructions for the Government of Armies of the United States in the Field, US Army General Order No. 100, 24 April 1863 (Lieber Code), Articles 5, 6.

[2] Declaration Renouncing the Use, in Time of War, of Explosive Projectiles under 400 Grammes Weight, St Petersburg, 11 December 1868 (St Petersburg Declaration), preamble, paras. 3–6.

person, property, and honor as much as the exigencies of war will admit.'[3] That principle evolved over time to become the principle of distinction, which is the central pillar of the law of targeting and which is explained in Section E. As law evolved during the latter part of the nineteenth century, the focus tended to remain on prohibiting destruction not imperatively demanded by the necessities of war.[4]

In 1923, jurists developed some draft rules for the conduct of air warfare. The results of their labours were never adopted by States in legally binding form, but the draft rules remain an authoritative assessment of the state of the applicable law at the relevant time.[5] As far as bombardment from the air was concerned, the jurists concluded, inter alia, that, in cases where lawful targets 'cannot be bombarded without the indiscriminate bombardment of the civilian population, the aircraft must abstain from bombardment'.[6] In the next paragraph, the jurists proposed: 'In the immediate neighbourhood of the operations of land forces, the bombardment of cities, towns, villages, dwellings or buildings is legitimate provided that there exists a reasonable presumption that the military concentration is sufficiently important to justify such bombardment, having regard to the danger thus caused to the civilian population.'[7] These were early formulations of ideas that in due course were to become the prohibition of indiscriminate attacks and the rule on proportionality, both of which are discussed in Section E.

The law on the resort to the use of armed force is largely set forth in the United Nations Charter. That document was signed in San Francisco on 26 June 1945. Determined 'to save succeeding generations from the scourge of war',[8] the negotiators produced a text that places the maintenance of international peace and security at its core and which prohibits the use or threat of force subject to two limited exceptions. This is the body of law that is discussed in Section C.

The law of war had traditionally applied exclusively to situations of war existing between States, and the term 'war' was the subject of differing legal

3 Lieber Code, Article 22.

4 Consider, for example, Regulations Concerning the Laws and Customs of War on Land, Annex to Hague Convention IV Respecting the Laws and Customs of War on Land, The Hague, 18 October 1907 (Hague Regulations), Article 23(g). Note that Article 27 listed kinds of building regarded as protected.

5 General Report on the Revision of the Rules of Warfare, part II, Rules of Aerial Warfare, adopted unanimously by the Commission of Jurists, 19 February 1923 (Draft Hague Rules of Aerial Warfare).

6 Draft Hague Rules of Aerial Warfare, Article 24(3).

7 Ibid., Article 24(4).

8 Preamble to the UN Charter.

interpretations. In 1949, with the adoption of the four Geneva Conventions of that year, the scope of application of the law was extended to situations of inter-State armed conflict. 'Armed conflict' was an altogether different notion to 'war', as the determination of whether an armed conflict is occurring involves a factual assessment of what is taking place. Some limited provision was also made in 1949 with regard to armed conflicts that are internal to a State. Then, in 1977, two treaties were adopted, both of which are described as being additional to the Geneva Conventions. The first of these, Additional Protocol I or API,[9] applies to armed conflicts that are international in nature, meaning that they take place between States. The second, Additional Protocol II or APII,[10] is a somewhat shortened version of API and applies to non-international armed conflicts, meaning conflicts internal to a State which take place between government armed forces and rebel forces of specified kinds that fulfil particular conditions. API included important rules on the law of targeting in Articles 48–71, and these rules remain the core of the law of targeting. The more limited rules in APII, though restricted in application, are of legal significance and have been much supplemented by the customary law rules that emerged beforehand and in the decades following the adoption of these treaties.

The fate of cultural property during warfare was a matter of particular and enduring concern. There had been specific provision in this regard in a number of the important treaties that were adopted during the 1899 and 1907 Peace Conferences held in The Hague. It was not until 1954, however, that a comprehensive convention on the protection of cultural property was adopted.[11]

If, in recent years, environmental protection has become a global priority, early law of armed conflict treaties made little or no reference to the natural environment. Arguably, the first significant provision of that kind was a prohibition on the use of the environment as a weapon. This was in the context of forest and crop destruction operations by the United States during the Vietnam War and reported attempts by the same State during the same conflict to influence weather to its own advantage. The UN Environmental Modification Convention[12] plus the provisions within API

[9] Protocol Additional to the Geneva Conventions of 12 August 1949, and Relating to the Protection of Victims of International Armed Conflicts, Geneva, 8 June 1977.

[10] Protocol Additional to the Geneva Conventions of 12 August 1949, and Relating to the Protection of Victims of Non-International Armed Conflicts, Geneva, 8 June 1977.

[11] Convention for the Protection of Cultural Property in the Event of Armed Conflict, The Hague, 14 May 1954.

[12] Convention on the Prohibition of Military or Any Other Hostile Use of Environmental Modification Techniques, adopted at New York, 10 December 1976.

aimed at prohibiting high levels of incidental environmental damage during armed conflict[13] are considered in Section E and, to the extent relevant, in Sections G and H.

The law relating to weapons has been the focus of much of the development in the law of armed conflict, at least as far as the adoption of new treaties is concerned, since 1977. Following a unilateral decision by the United States government to renounce the use of such weapons, a treaty was adopted that comprehensively prohibited most kinds of activity associated with biological weapons.[14] It was followed by similarly comprehensive prohibitions covering chemical weapons,[15] anti-personnel landmines[16] and cluster munitions.[17]

The Diplomatic Conference that led to the adoption of API and APII[18] recommended the convening of a separate conference to reach agreements on prohibitions and restrictions on the use of certain conventional weapons. At its second session, that later conference adopted the Conventional Weapons Convention.[19] Under the auspices of that Convention, protocols were adopted addressing certain fragmentation weapons;[20] mines, booby-traps and other devices;[21] incendiary weapons;[22] and blinding laser weapons.[23] They included more detailed provisions in respect of mines, booby-traps and other devices.[24] All of these developments, in so far as they have relevance to nuclear weapon operations, are reflected in Section G below.

An often-neglected issue relates to States that are not parties to an international armed conflict. The law of neutrality was codified in the 1907 Hague

13 API, Articles 35(3), 55.

14 Convention on the Prohibition of the Development, Production and Stockpiling of Bacteriological (Biological) and Toxin Weapons and on Their Destruction, opened for signature at London, Moscow and Washington DC on 10 April 1972.

15 Convention on the Prohibition of the Development, Production, Stockpiling and Use of Chemical Weapons and on Their Destruction, Paris, 13 January 1993.

16 Convention on the Prohibition of the Use, Stockpiling, Production and Transfer of Anti-Personnel Mines and on Their Destruction, Oslo, 18 September 1997.

17 Convention on Cluster Munitions, opened for signature at Oslo on 3 December 2008.

18 Diplomatic Conference on the Reaffirmation and Development of International Humanitarian Law Applicable in Armed Conflicts, Geneva, 1974 to 1977.

19 Convention on Prohibitions or Restrictions on the Use of Certain Conventional Weapons Which May Be Deemed to Be Excessively Injurious or to Have Indiscriminate Effects, Geneva, 10 October 1980.

20 Protocol on Non-Detectable Fragments (Protocol I), Geneva, 10 October 1980.

21 Protocol on Prohibitions or Restrictions on the Use of Mines, Booby-Traps and Other Devices (Protocol II), Geneva, 10 October 1980.

22 Protocol on Prohibitions or Restrictions on the Use of Incendiary Weapons (Protocol III), Geneva, 10 October 1980.

23 Protocol on Blinding Laser Weapons (Protocol IV), Geneva, 13 October 1995.

24 Amended Protocol on Prohibitions or Restrictions on the Use of Mines, Booby-Traps and Other Devices (Amended Protocol II), Geneva, 3 May 1996.

Conventions V[25] and XIII,[26] which continue to be the main authoritative sources.[27] Interestingly, the law of neutrality does not address the protection of neutral States against the damaging effects of the use of conventional weapons by the parties to an international armed conflict. In respect of the potential use of nuclear weapons, or of conventional weapons used against platforms either carrying nuclear weapons or that are nuclear-propelled, it is an open question whether and to what extent the protection of neutral States against the effects of such attacks is to be assessed in the light of the law of neutrality or general public international law.

It would be a mistake to think that treaty-making constitutes the only mechanism whereby the law that needs to be considered in connection with nuclear weapons has been clarified. In 2004, the International Committee of the Red Cross published an extensive assessment of the customary rules of international humanitarian law.[28] In 1995, the San Remo Manual on International Law Applicable to Armed Conflicts at Sea, produced by an international group of experts, was published. In 2010, an international group of experts prepared an international manual addressing the international law that applies to air and missile warfare,[29] and similarly produced international manuals on cyber warfare law and on the law relating to cyber operations more generally have followed.[30]

In the related field of international criminal law, ad hoc tribunals were established to deal with, inter alia, war crimes, genocide and crimes against humanity committed during the armed conflicts in the former Yugoslavia[31] and in Rwanda.[32] A framework for the more global, and less ad hoc, prosecution of genocide, crimes against humanity, war crimes and, in time, aggression

25 Convention (V) Respecting the Rights and Duties of Neutral Powers and Persons in Case of War on Land, The Hague, 18 October 1907.

26 Convention (XIII) Concerning the Rights and Duties of Neutral Powers in Naval War, The Hague, 18 October 1907.

27 The expert manuals referred to in notes 29 and 30 below address the law of neutrality but are mainly reflective of the two 1907 Hague Conventions.

28 International Committee of the Red Cross, *Customary International Humanitarian Law*, vol. 1, ed. J.-M. Henckaerts and L. Doswald-Beck (Cambridge University Press, 2005).

29 *Manual on the International Law Applicable to Air and Missile Warfare*, Program on Humanitarian Policy and Conflict Research at Harvard University, March 2010.

30 *Tallinn Manual on the International Law Applicable to Cyber Warfare*, ed. M. N. Schmitt (Cambridge University Press, 2013); *Tallinn Manual 2.0 on the International Law Applicable to Cyber Operations*, ed. M. N. Schmitt and L. Vihul (Cambridge University Press, 2017).

31 Statute of the International Criminal Tribunal for the Former Yugoslavia, UN Security Council Resolution 827, 25 May 1993.

32 Statute of the International Criminal Tribunal for Rwanda, UN Security Council Resolution 955, 8 November 1994.

was established with the adoption of the Rome Statute of the International Criminal Court.[33]

In the mid-1990s the International Court of Justice was asked to give an opinion on the legality of the threat or use of nuclear weapons. Its resulting Advisory Opinion will be considered at some length in Section J. More recently, a treaty prohibiting nuclear weapons was adopted in 2017.[34] Following the deposit of the fiftieth instrument of ratification, the treaty entered into force on 22 January 2021. Clearly, the text is of great potential relevance to the topic of this book and will therefore be specifically addressed in Section K.

Although none of the treaties and expert manuals referred to above explicitly addresses nuclear weapons, the law on arms control and disarmament does, of course, regulate, on a multilateral level, the (non-)proliferation of nuclear weapons[35] (together with a safeguards regime[36]) and even the prohibition of nuclear weapons.[37] At a bilateral level, the United States and the Russian Federation (formerly USSR) agreed on the reduction of strategic,[38] intermediate- and shorter-range missiles[39] and anti-ballistic missiles systems,[40] and these agreements were supplemented by regulations on confidence-building measures. In the light of the current position of the Russian Federation and the United States vis-à-vis bilateral agreements on nuclear arms reduction, and because of the reluctance of, for instance, the People's Republic of China to become part of such a regime, nuclear disarmament and arms control will most

33 Rome Statute of the International Criminal Court, Rome, 17 July 1998.

34 Treaty on the Prohibition of Nuclear Weapons, New York, 7 July 2017.

35 Treaty on the Non-Proliferation of Nuclear Weapons, London, Moscow and Washington DC, 1 July 1968.

36 The safeguards system under the responsibility of the International Atomic Energy Agency (IAEA) consists of safeguards agreements between States and the IAEA.

37 Treaty on the Prohibition of Nuclear Weapons, New York, 7 July 2017.

38 Strategic offensive arms are nuclear weapons with a range exceeding 5,500 kilometres and their reduction is regulated in a series of bilateral treaties between the Russian Federation and the United States. The last of those bilateral treaties is the Treaty between the United States of America and the Russian Federation on Measures for the Further Reduction and Limitation of Strategic Offensive Arms (New START), Prague, 8 April 2010. The duration of New START was limited until 5 February 2021. In January 2021, the parties agreed on an extension for a further five years.

39 Treaty between the United States of America and the Union of Soviet Socialist Republics on the Elimination of Their Intermediate-Range and Shorter-Range Missiles (INF Treaty), Washington, 8 December 1987. Because of the United States' withdrawal, the INF Treaty expired on 2 August 2019.

40 Treaty on the Limitation of Anti-Ballistic Missile Systems (ABM Treaty), Moscow, 26 May 1972. The United States withdrew from the ABM Treaty, thus terminating the treaty as of June 2002.

likely be governed only by the Treaty on the Non-Proliferation of Nuclear Weapons, the Treaty on the Prohibition of Nuclear Weapons and, occasionally, by UN Security Council resolutions. Disarmament and arms control law is dealt with in Section K.

A.2 THE PURPOSE OF THE BOOK

As the preceding paragraphs demonstrate, the development of the bodies of law that are of relevance to nuclear weapons has not been linear. Some treaties have been a response to particular events, while others have followed national initiatives. There are undoubted gaps in the law, but the purpose of the present book is to examine the lawfulness of nuclear weapons, their possession, their use and deterrence policies associated with them, and the fulfilment of that purpose requires an objective consideration of the law we have. The book will focus on treaty law, on certain stated positions of States, on international court judgments of greatest relevance, on influential international manuals that have been the product of collective expert authorship and on other sources of similar standing. The views of individual commentators will not generally be addressed.

The objective in tackling the topic in this way is to seek to identify the duties that States must fulfil in the command and control of, and in communications relating to, nuclear weapons.

This will be the topic of Section L, and it will extend to considering deterrence and use of nuclear weapons, as well as operations that target nuclear weapons and capabilities. It is hoped that the method of analysis will amply justify the conclusions reached and that the whole book will bring clarity to a topic where, in the view of the authors, such clarity is of the utmost importance.

A.3 A SECTION-BY-SECTION DESCRIPTION OF THE BOOK

Accordingly, after this introductory Section A, certain important preliminary legal matters that are of relevance to any discussion of nuclear weapon issues will be reviewed in Section B. Thereafter, the law pertaining to the resort to force, specifically nuclear force, will be examined in Section C. In Section D the important distinction between international and non-international armed conflict is made, with the vital characteristics of each being detailed. It would seem likely that the use of nuclear weapons is a more realistic, though no less unacceptable, prospect in the former class of conflict, but the undertaking of military operations against a nuclear weapon facility, which is also included within our notion of nuclear operations, cannot be excluded as a possible feature of the latter class of conflict.

Section E seeks to show how the law pertaining to the conduct of hostilities that applies when use is made of conventional weapons is also applicable in respect of nuclear operations. In a similar vein, Sections F and G consider the application of, respectively, neutrality law and the law relating to weapons in relation to nuclear operations. No book of this nature would be complete without considering international criminal law and its potential application to the topic. Indeed, given the widespread revulsion, a nuclear attack is likely to occasion, a wish to pursue criminal charges is highly foreseeable. The possible options are laid bare in Section H. States do not generally say a great deal about their nuclear policies or, for that matter, their views on how the law applies to nuclear weapon activities. What little material the authors have been able to access is summarised in a short Section I.

The International Court of Justice considered the legality of the threat or use of nuclear weapons a quarter of a century ago and reached conclusions that, to put it kindly, did not secure universal admiration from commentators. The interesting question to consider is whether, if the question were re-submitted to the Court, the somewhat changed circumstances twenty-five years on might be expected to cause the Court to reach a significantly different conclusion. That is the topic addressed in Section J. As was noted earlier, the Treaty on the Prohibition of Nuclear Weapons has since been adopted, in 2017. Section K addresses the provisions of that arms control treaty article by article, discusses its likely impact on the subject of this book and briefly examines the prospects of arms control law.

Tentative conclusions on the implications to be drawn from the analyses in the different Sections of the book will be brought together in Section L with a view to identifying the important features that an NC3 mechanism must have if it is to be fit for purpose. In brief, the purpose of such a mechanism should be to ensure that nuclear weapons are only ever used as an absolutely last resort; that every possible step to prevent and avoid their use is taken; that systems are in place to ensure that those steps are indeed as likely as possible to successfully prevent the resort to nuclear weapons; that confusion, ambiguity, uncertainty, miscommunication and any other source of reduced clarity are, as far as possible, weeded out of such systems; and, finally, that all nuclear weapon-armed States have the best possible NC3 systems and that they benefit from mutual assurance that other similarly armed States also possess such efficient systems. If global peace is still a long way off, global security in respect of nuclear weapons ought to be given the highest international priority.

Readers will note that Sections C, D, E and F follow the Tallinn Manual approach in terms of the sequencing of topics, the black letter rule and associated commentary layout and, to a degree, the legal perspectives set forth in the Commentaries and Rules. This is hardly surprising given the authors' central, though shared, roles in the development of that Manual.

That said, the Rules and Commentaries prepared below reflect the characteristics and contexts specific to nuclear weapons. The authors nonetheless wish to place on record their appreciation of the scholarship of the Tallinn experts.

A.4 THE INTENDED READERSHIP

This book will be of interest to anyone who is involved with, or interested in, the development of nuclear weapons; the maintenance of nuclear deterrent capabilities; the generation and updating of nuclear weapon-related policies; or any aspect of the law as it applies to the development, possession and use of nuclear weapons and deterrence policies relating thereto. It will also interest academics, members of think-tanks, policy advisors and others in the legal and policy communities whose responsibilities require them to understand the current law applying to nuclear weapons.

A.5 CERTAIN TERMS AND ABBREVIATIONS

The following abbreviations have the meanings given below:

AMW Manual: *Manual on the International Law Applicable to Air and Missile Warfare* (Program on Humanitarian Policy and Conflict Research at Harvard University, March 2010).

API: Protocol Additional to the Geneva Conventions of 12 August 1949, and Relating to the Protection of Victims of International Armed Conflicts, Geneva, 8 June 1977.

APII: Protocol Additional to the Geneva Conventions of 12 August 1949, and Relating to the Protection of Victims of Non-International Armed Conflicts, Geneva, 8 June 1977.

API Commentary: International Committee of the Red Cross, *Commentary on the Additional Protocols of 8 June 1977*, ed. Y. Sandoz, C. Swinarski and B. Zimmermann (Martinus Nijhoff, 1987).

Canadian Manual: Office of the Judge Advocate General, *Law of Armed Conflict at the Operational and Tactical Levels*, Doc. B-GJ-005–104/FP-021 (2001).

CCW: Convention on Prohibitions or Restrictions on the Use of Certain Conventional Weapons Which May Be Deemed to Be Excessively Injurious or to Have Indiscriminate Effects, Geneva, 10 October 1980.

Commentary on GCI (2016): International Committee of the Red Cross, *Commentary on the First Geneva Convention*, ed. K. Dörmann, L. Lijnzaad, M. Sassòli and P. Spoerri (Cambridge University Press, 2016).

Galić Trial Chamber Judgment: *Prosecutor* v. *Stanislav Galić*, International Criminal Tribunal for the Former Yugoslavia Case IT-98–29-T (Trial Chamber Judgment of 5 December 2003).

GCI: Geneva Convention I for the Amelioration of the Condition of the Wounded and Sick in Armed Forces in the Field, Geneva, 12 August 1949.

GCII: Geneva Convention II for the Amelioration of the Condition of Wounded, Sick and Shipwrecked Members of Armed Forces at Sea, Geneva, 12 August 1949.

GCIII: Geneva Convention Relative to the Treatment of Prisoners of War, Geneva, 12 August 1949.

GCIV: Geneva Convention Relative to the Protection of Civilian Persons in Time of War, Geneva, 12 August 1949.

Hague Convention V: Convention Respecting the Rights and Duties of Neutral Powers and Persons in Case of War on Land, The Hague, 18 October 1907.

Hague Convention XIII: Convention Concerning the Rights and Duties of Neutral Powers in Naval War, The Hague, 18 October 1907.

Hague Regulations: Regulations Concerning the Laws and Customs of War on Land, Annex to Hague Convention IV Respecting the Laws and Customs of War on Land, The Hague, 18 October 1907.

German Manual: Federal Ministry of Defence of the Federal Republic of Germany, *Humanitarian Law in Armed Conflicts: Manual*, ZDv 15/2 (1992).

ICJ Corfu Channel Judgment: *Corfu Channel Case (United Kingdom* v. *Albania)* (Judgment of 9 April 1949) [1949] ICJ Rep. 4.

ICJ Genocide Judgment: *Application of the Convention on the Prevention and Punishment of the Crime of Genocide (Bosnia and Herzegovina* v. *Serbia and Montenegro)* (Judgment of 26 February 2007) [2007] ICJ Rep. 43.

ICJ Nicaragua Judgment: *Military and Paramilitary Activities in and against Nicaragua (Nicaragua* v. *United States)* (Judgment of 27 June 1986) [1986] ICJ Rep. 14.

ICJ Nuclear Opinion: *Legality of the Threat or Use of Nuclear Weapons* (Advisory Opinion of 8 July 1996) [1996] ICJ Rep. 226.

ICJ Oil Platforms Judgment: *Oil Platforms (Iran* v. *United States)* (Judgment of 6 November 2003) [2003] ICJ Rep. 161.

ICJ Tehran Hostages Judgment: *United States Diplomatic and Consular Staff in Tehran (United States* v. *Iran)* (Judgment of 24 May 1980) [1980] ICJ Rep. 3.

ICRC Customary Law Study: International Committee of the Red Cross, *Customary International Humanitarian Law*, vol. 1, ed. J.-M. Henckaerts and L. Doswald-Beck (Cambridge University Press, 2005).

NIAC Manual: International Institute of Humanitarian Law, *The Manual on the Law of Non-International Armed Conflict*, ed. M. N. Schmitt, C. H. B. Garraway and Y. Dinstein (2006).

Oslo Manual: *Oslo Manual on Select Topics of the Law of Armed Conflict*, ed. Y. Dinstein and A. W. Dahl (Springer, 2020).

Rome Statute: Rome Statute of the International Criminal Court, Rome, 17 July 1998.

San Remo Manual: International Institute of Humanitarian Law, *San Remo Manual on International Law Applicable to Armed Conflicts at Sea*, ed. L. Doswell-Beck (1995).

Tadić Appeals Chamber Judgment: *Prosecutor* v. *Tadić*, International Criminal Tribunal for the Former Yugoslavia Case IT-94-1-A (Appeals Chamber Judgment of 15 July 1999).

Tallinn Manual 2.0: *Tallinn Manual 2.0 on the International Law Applicable to Cyber Operations*, ed. M. N. Schmitt and L. Vihul (Cambridge University Press, 2017).

UK Manual: UK Ministry of Defence, *Manual of the Law of Armed Conflict* (Oxford University Press, 2004) as subsequently amended.

US DoD Law of War Manual: US Department of Defense, *Department of Defense Law of War Manual* (June 2015), as subsequently amended.

For the purposes of this book, the term 'nuclear operation' covers all activities involving the use, or threatened use, of nuclear weapons, nuclear deterrent activities and all actions whose purpose is to target nuclear weapons and nuclear equipment as such, including their command, control and communications systems.

A.6 WHAT ARE NUCLEAR WEAPONS?

A nuclear weapon is a device designed to release energy in an explosive manner due to nuclear fission, nuclear fusion or a combination of those processes. Fission weapons are also referred to as atomic weapons or, more usually, atomic bombs. Fusion weapons are also called thermonuclear bombs or hydrogen bombs. The explosive blast energy is usually measured in terms of a comparison with the quantity of conventional TNT explosive that would be required to produce an equivalent amount of energy. The measures used are the kiloton, equivalent to 1,000 tons of TNT, and the megaton, equivalent to 1,000,000 tons of TNT.

In very broad terms, the process of nuclear fission consists of the bombardment of certain isotopes of uranium and plutonium by neutrons, causing them to split into atoms of lighter elements. In addition, free neutrons are emitted in the fission process and explosive energy is generated. Nuclear fusion consists of the joining or fusing of the nuclei of two atoms to form a single, heavier atom. Such a process, performed at particularly high temperatures and involving the use of isotopes of hydrogen, can cause the release of large amounts of energy. In those high temperatures, the energy associated with the movement of the nuclei causes them to get close enough together for what is called the strong force to attract and fuse the nuclei. The necessary temperatures and the density of the fusion materials are both achieved by a fission explosion.

The blast from a nuclear weapon produces a shock wave, vast amounts of heat and ionising radiation. Radioactive debris can be thrown high into the atmosphere, later falling to the Earth's surface as radioactive nuclear fallout.

The use of a nuclear weapon is likely to have catastrophic effects: very large numbers of persons are likely to be killed; areas of the Earth's surface would be rendered unfit for human habitation or use; and there would likely be serious illness among those affected by the fallout. While the earliest nuclear weapons were air-delivered, in more recent times nuclear weapons have more usually employed ballistic missiles. Tactical nuclear weapons may use artillery, landmine, depth-charge, torpedo, cruise missile or ballistic missile technology.

The United States, the Russian Federation, France, the United Kingdom and China all have significant numbers of nuclear warheads. Israel, India, Pakistan and North Korea are all also known to have nuclear weapon capabilities. Yet other States are believed to have nuclear weapon development programmes.

Enhanced radiation warheads, or neutron bombs, consist of low-yield (approximately one kiloton) thermonuclear devices, so designed as to intensify the production of lethal fast neutrons and thereby increase the numbers of fatalities while limiting damage to structures. Such technology might be employed in anti-ballistic missiles, short-range ballistic missiles and artillery shells, for example.

The very large amounts of energy they generate, the extreme levels of heat they produce and the radiation their explosions cause mark out nuclear weapons from conventional weapons. Factors that will determine the nature and extent of the impact of a nuclear weapon include whether it is a fission or fusion weapon and the yield; whether the explosion takes place in the air, on the surface, subsurface or under water; the meteorological and environmental conditions; and whether the location of the explosion is urban, rural or military in nature. The consequences of a nuclear explosion are a fireball, a shock wave (air blast), heat and radiation.[41]

Discussion of low-yield nuclear weapons is far from academic. Russia is believed to be investing heavily in such technologies. Reportedly, a new nuclear warhead requested by, and designed and produced for, the US government was deployed aboard the USS *Tennessee*, a submarine, at the end of 2019. The W76-2 is said to be a low-yield variant of the nuclear warhead more usually used in the Trident missile.

> Official U.S. nuclear-warhead yields remain classified, but experts estimate that the new W76-2 would explode with a yield of about 6.5 kilotons, whereas the full-size W76-1 explodes with a yield of roughly 90 kilotons. By comparison, the warheads the U.S. military used on Hiroshima and Nagasaki, Japan, in 1945 exploded with about 15 and 20 kilotons of force, respectively.[42]

Clearly, though described as 'low yield', the W76-2 remains a most potent weapon, likely to cause very numerous casualties, widespread devastation and very damaging fallout, while also either triggering or constituting the response to other nuclear strikes – perhaps proportionate perhaps not – by the adversary. It remains to be seen whether very much smaller-yield nuclear weapons will be developed and fielded in future years. If, however, a trend of reducing yields can be identified, it seems sensible not to limit the present discussion to strategic, very large-scale strikes. Accordingly, the law as it applies to targeted attacks will be considered to the extent that it appears relevant.

41 This brief description of nuclear weapons draws heavily on the *Encyclopaedia Britannica* entry 'Nuclear weapon' by T. B. Cochran and R. S. Norris, www.britannica.com/technology/nuclear-weapon (viewed 13 February 2020).

42 P. Sonne, 'U.S. military arms its submarines with new "low-yield" nuclear warheads', *Washington Post*, 4 February 2020; A. Mehta, 'Trump's new nuclear weapon has been deployed', *Defense News*, 4 February 2020.

B

Important Legal Preliminaries

Sovereignty

Rule 1

Sovereignty consists of the right of a State to exercise State functions to the exclusion of other States.

1 States enjoy sovereignty over the nuclear weapons and facilities that are located on their territory and over any activities that are connected with such weapons and facilities. It is essentially a territorial notion, from which notions of jurisdiction (Rule 2 below), mutual recognition of immunities by States (Rule 4) and the requirement to exercise due diligence[1] derive. Accordingly, irrespective of the location from which nuclear weapon operations are conducted or where they have their effects, the persons involved will be subject to the jurisdiction of one or more States.

2 A State enjoys sovereign authority in relation to nuclear and other weapons and associated equipment, persons and activities that are located on its territory, subject to international legal obligations.[2] This gives the State the right to apply the measures it sees fit in respect of nuclear weapon-related equipment, personnel and activities on its territory, subject to international law rules. It may enact and enforce laws and regulations concerning such equipment, persons and activities; it may protect such equipment; and it may safeguard relevant activities. This means that a State has the sovereign right and, arguably, responsibility to enact legislation to prescribe which nuclear weapon-related activities are prohibited, to criminalise prohibited activities, to provide for the arrangements that are needed to secure nuclear weapon sites and equipment and the

[1] On due diligence, see Commentary accompanying Rule 5 below, para. 1.

[2] There are legal limits on interference by a territorial State with diplomatic activities and personnel. Rights of innocent passage, archipelagic sea lanes passage and transit passage rights limit the territorial State's sovereignty in such areas; see UN Convention on the Law of the Sea, Montego Bay, Jamaica, 10 December 1982 (UNCLOS), Articles 17–19, 37–8, 52, 53.

information related to nuclear weapons and to implement other necessary arrangements. In short, it will be pursuant to a nation's sovereign rights and responsibilities that NC3 procedures will be developed, applied and enforced.[3] Clearly, a military operation undertaken against nuclear weapons, equipment or systems in another State and which causes damage will violate that other State's sovereignty unless, as is unlikely, the military operation is undertaken with the consent of the territorial State.

Jurisdiction

Rule 2

Subject to certain international obligations, a State may exercise its jurisdiction over persons engaged in nuclear operations on its territory, over nuclear weapons and associated equipment located on its territory and, outside of its territory, as permitted by international law.

1 The opening words of this Rule – 'subject to certain international obligations' – acknowledge certain limitations on the exercise by a State of territorial jurisdiction.[4]

2 There are criminal, civil and administrative aspects to the notion of jurisdiction. The notion extends to prescribing applicable rules, to enforcing those rules and to determining whether the rules have been breached. The physical or legal presence of a person or of an object on the territory of a State gives that State, respectively, *in personam* or *in rem* jurisdiction. *In personam* jurisdiction gives the State the right to create laws and regulations dealing with what persons on its territory may or may not do in respect of nuclear weapons and associated systems. It can also regulate the activities of private companies registered within its jurisdiction. The *in rem* basis for jurisdiction allows the State to pass laws dealing with the nuclear weapons and equipment as such. It is the physical presence of the person or object that is central to notions of territorial jurisdiction.

3 Territorial jurisdiction can be subdivided as follows. Subjective territorial jurisdiction applies where an event is initiated within the territory of a State but is completed somewhere else. Accordingly, if a cyber hacking operation against a nuclear command and control network were to be initiated within State A, but the targeted network belongs to and is located within State B, State A would have subjective territorial jurisdiction, even though the hacking operation has no effect within State A. That jurisdiction will extend to the right to prescribe applicable

3 See Rule 2 below and accompanying Commentary.

4 Consider combatant and diplomatic immunities and notions of a primary right to exercise jurisdiction provided for in certain status of forces agreements.

laws and regulations, the right to enforce those laws and regulations and the right to determine whether they have been breached. Alternatively, objective territorial jurisdiction grants a State jurisdiction over persons where an event was directed against persons or objects within that State from outside the State and has a substantial connection or impact on the State seeking to exercise jurisdiction. In the example given earlier in this paragraph, if the operation initiated from State A has a substantial impact on State B's nuclear command and control system – say, by breaking the communications link between superior commanders and an operational unit – that substantial connection with and impact on State B would be the basis on which State B might exercise objective territorial jurisdiction against the persons responsible for the operation, wherever they are located.

4 Jurisdiction claims may also be based on the nationality of the person undertaking an operation; the nationality of the victim; the threat that the operation creates to the national security of the State; or on the universal jurisdiction attaching to certain crimes, such as grave breaches of the Geneva Conventions. So, non-trivial interference with a State's nuclear command and control system would likely amount to a threat to its national security and would form the basis for a claim to jurisdiction based on the third ground listed earlier in this paragraph.

5 It follows from the above that more than one State may have concurrent jurisdiction in relation to a particular nuclear weapon- or nuclear system-related event. Imagine, for example, that a team of hackers located in State A intrudes into the computer system that controls the launching of State B's nuclear missiles. They manage to launch a missile that flies for a short distance before falling to Earth and exploding on the territory of State C near its border with State D. The blast wave causes deaths and damage in States C and D to nationals of both States and generates nuclear fallout that falls to Earth in States E and F, rendering many of their nationals sick, some with fatal consequences. State A's claim to jurisdiction would be on the basis that the operation was initiated in that State. States B, C and D would seem to have jurisdiction on the basis of objective territorial jurisdiction, and States C, D, E and F on the basis of passive personality (i.e. the nationality of the victims).

Jurisdiction on Ships, Aircraft and Other Platforms

Rule 3

If a nuclear weapon and/or associated equipment is located on a ship, aircraft or other platform on the high seas, in international airspace or in outer space, it is subject to the flag State's or State of registration's jurisdiction.

1 High seas, for the purposes of this Rule, are considered to be sea areas beyond the outer limit of the territorial sea of a coastal or archipelagic State and, due to

its general international character from the perspective of sovereignty, include the Exclusive Economic Zone.[5] International airspace is the airspace above the high seas.[6] Outer space, for the present purposes, refers to locations at a greater altitude than 100 km.[7]

2 Nuclear weapons, nuclear command, control and communications systems and associated equipment may be located on ships, aircraft, offshore installations or space vehicles, including satellites.[8] The flag State principle governs jurisdiction rights with regard to ships carrying such weapons, systems and equipment, whereas the State of registration is the determinant with regard to aircraft and space objects. For offshore installations, applicable jurisdiction will be based on exclusive sovereign rights of the coastal State or on nationality.[9] Moreover, flag- or registration-State jurisdiction does not exclude the possibility that other States may have jurisdiction on other grounds.[10]

Sovereign Immunity

Rule 4

Interference by a State with nuclear weapons, nuclear command, control and communications systems and associated equipment located on a ship, aircraft or other platform that enjoys sovereign immunity violates the sovereignty of the flag or registration State irrespective of where the ship, aircraft or other platform may be.

1 A sovereign ship, aircraft or other platform and all persons and things that are on it are immune from the exercise of jurisdiction over the ship, aircraft or platform by another State. Warships and ships that a State owns or operates and that it uses exclusively for government, non-commercial service[11] enjoy

5 UNCLOS, Article 86.
6 Ibid., Article 2.
7 UK Manual, para. 12.13; AMW Manual, Commentary accompanying Rule 1(a), paras. 4, 5.
8 Note that the stationing of nuclear weapons in orbit or on celestial bodies is prohibited by Article IV of the Treaty on Principles Governing the Activities of States in the Exploration and Use of Outer Space, including the Moon and other Celestial Bodies, London, Moscow and Washington DC, 10 October 1967 (Outer Space Treaty).
9 *Tallinn Manual on the International Law Applicable to Cyber Warfare*, ed. M. N. Schmitt (Cambridge University Press, 2013) (Tallinn Manual 1.0), Commentary accompanying Rule 3, para. 3.
10 See Commentary accompanying Rule 2 above, para. 5.
11 Consider Tallinn Manual 1.0, Commentary accompanying Rule 4, para. 6, citing Convention on Jurisdictional Immunities, Article 5.

immunity from the jurisdiction of any State other than the flag State.[12] State aircraft also enjoy sovereign immunity.[13] Objects in outer space that are operated for non-commercial government purposes are also considered to enjoy sovereign immunity.[14]

2 To enjoy sovereign immunity, the relevant system or equipment must be devoted only to government purposes. In the unlikely event that a network is used partly for a State's nuclear weapons-related communications or control purposes and partly in support of commercial activities, the network will not benefit from sovereign immunity because of the commercial, non-governmental usage.

3 If an object benefits from sovereign immunity, any interference with it breaches international law. Prohibited interference might involve damaging the object or adversely affecting its performance to a significant degree. The mere fact that a platform, such as a military aircraft, enjoys sovereign immunity does not exempt it from the obligation to comply with international law rules, such as the requirement to respect the sovereignty of other States. If, for example, a military aircraft, whether nuclear-armed or not, enters the airspace of a foreign State without permission, the intruded State has the right to take necessary action to secure its sovereign rights, which may include the use of force. Consider, for example, a situation in which a warship belonging to State A, while located in the territorial sea of State B, fires missiles against nuclear weapons facilities located in State C. Because such activities by the warship do not comply with the restrictions that apply to innocent passage through territorial waters, State B may, notwithstanding the warship's sovereign immunity, take action to prevent its non-innocent passage.[15]

4 During periods of armed conflict, the rules as to sovereign immunity and inviolability cease generally to apply in the relations between the parties to the armed conflict, and objects that would ordinarily enjoy such immunity or inviolability may become the object of attack as military objectives (Rule 34 below) or may be liable to seizure as booty of war.[16]

12 UNCLOS, Articles 95, 96.

13 UK Manual, para. 12.6.1; AMW Manual, Commentary accompanying Rule 1(cc), para. 6.

14 Tallinn Manual 1.0, Commentary accompanying Rule 4, para. 2, citing Convention on Jurisdictional Immunities, Article 3(3).

15 UNCLOS, Articles 19, 25(1), 32; consider also Rule 5 below and accompanying Commentary.

16 AMW Manual, Rule 136(a) and accompanying Commentary. Note, however, that diplomatic archives and communications are protected under the Vienna Convention on Diplomatic Relations, Articles 24, 27.

Acts Adversely Affecting Other States

Rule 5

A State must not knowingly allow the nuclear weapon capabilities, including nuclear command, control and communications systems and associated equipment, that are located in its territory or under its exclusive governmental control to be used for acts that adversely and unlawfully affect other States.

1 Nuclear weapons, nuclear command, control and communications systems and associated equipment that are located on a State's territory, or that are located elsewhere but over which it exercises control, are covered by this Rule. The Rule reflects the view that, as '[b]etween independent States, respect for territorial sovereignty is an essential foundation of international relations' and the appreciation that a State is under an obligation 'not to allow knowingly its territory to be used for acts contrary to the rights of other States'.[17] This translates into an obligation ('obligation of due diligence') to take suitable steps to protect those rights of other States.[18] The Rule extends to acts that potentially or actually inflict serious damage on persons or objects that are protected by the target State's sovereignty.

2 So the Rule applies to all unlawful acts adversely affecting another State's territory or objects that are protected under international law. The adverse effect will not necessarily consist of damage. Accordingly, if State A allows a hacking group that is located on its territory to use computer equipment that is located there to hack into and corrupt a nuclear communications system located in State B, this Rule will have been breached. If State A was unaware of the activities of the hacking group but had been notified, either by officials from State B or from another State, that the interference and corrupting activities were taking place and failed to take reasonable action to stop the activities, the Rule will also have been broken. Similarly, the Rule will also apply if, in the example set forth in this paragraph, the hacking group is using computer equipment that is located outside State A territory but that is subject to State A's exclusive control (e.g. by virtue of an agreement or arrangement between State A and the host State or, for example, because the equipment is located on a platform on the high seas or in international airspace).

3 The 'suitable steps' referred to in paragraph 1 may consist of action taken either by State organs – such as members of the armed forces, security service or intelligence officials – or by private undertakings. The requirement is that

[17] ICJ Nicaragua Judgment, para. 202; ICJ Corfu Channel Judgment, 22.

[18] ICJ Tehran Hostages Judgment, paras. 67–8.

all means at the disposal of the relevant State be used to put an end to the acts that constitute breaches of this Rule.

4 A State will be regarded as having knowledge for the purposes of this Rule if State organs become aware of the activity, whether directly or by being given reliable information that the activity is taking place.

5 In the example given in paragraph 2, if State A has knowledge of the activity that is adversely affecting State B and fails to take suitable steps as required by this Rule, State B may have the right to take proportionate action in response. Depending on the relevant circumstances, such action may take the form of countermeasures,[19] the use of force in self-defence (Rule 11 below) or, during an armed conflict, the use of force under the law of neutrality (Rule 67 below).

State Responsibility

Rule 6

A State bears international legal responsibility when conduct (an act or omission) is attributable to that State under international law and if the act or omission consists of a breach of an international legal obligation of that State.

1 This Rule is based on the Draft Articles on State Responsibility, [20] Articles 1 and 2. An act or omission is internationally wrongful if, for example, it consists of a use or threat of force in breach of Article 2(4) of the UN Charter (Rule 8 below), a breach of the law of armed conflict prohibition on making civilians the object of attack (Rule 28 below), an unlawful intervention in the internal affairs of another State, a violation of the sovereign immunity rights of another State (Rule 4 above) or a breach of Rule 5 above. There are numerous other examples of activities that constitute breaches of international law.

2 For an act or omission to come within this Rule, three elements must be present. There must be an act or a failure to act; the act or failure must be attributable to a State; and the act or failure to act must constitute a breach of an international law obligation.

3 Acts or omissions by an organ of a State are always attributable to the State.[21] Organs of a State include armed forces, internal security, customs,

[19] See Commentary accompanying Rule 7.

[20] International Law Commission, Responsibility of States for Internationally Wrongful Acts, Annex to UNGA Resolution 56/83, 12 December 2001 (Draft Articles on State Responsibility).

[21] Ibid., Article 4(1).

intelligence and State agencies.[22] Irrespective of whether the organ was acting in accordance with or outside its instructions, or indeed without any instructions, if the organ is acting in an apparently official capacity, attribution will be automatic.[23] So, ultra vires acts or omissions by an organ will attract attribution, whereas purely private conduct will not. For example, if in peacetime a senior military commander of State A threatens to order an air strike against the armed forces headquarters of State B, this threat in breach of Article 2(4) of the UN Charter would be attributable to State A even if the commander were acting outside or contrary to his or her instructions. It would be unlikely that such a threat could sensibly be regarded as having been purely private conduct.

4 Acts by a person or group of persons 'shall be considered an act of a State under international law if the person or group of persons is in fact acting on the instructions of, or under the direction or control of, that State in carrying out the conduct'.[24] The instructions or direction or control – any one of the three suffices – must relate to the relevant conduct. The ICJ has stated that a State has responsibility for the acts, and presumably for the omissions, of non-State actors if it has 'effective control' over the actors.[25] The International Criminal Tribunal for the Former Yugoslavia decided that, when determining the nature of an armed conflict in connection with criminal proceedings, 'overall control' suffices for the activities of a non-State actor to be regarded as those of the controlling State.[26] While a distinction can be drawn between the test for determining whether an international or non-international armed conflict is taking place and the test for allocating State responsibility,[27] under the less demanding criterion of 'overall control' something more than financing and equipping of the armed group would be required, with involvement in planning and supervision of the group's military operations also being looked for.[28] If the attribution of acts of individuals or groups not organised into military structures is being considered, an overall or general level of control will not suffice. There must have been specific instructions or directives aimed at the commission of specific acts, or there must have been public approval of

22 Persons or organisations authorised under a State's domestic law to exercise governmental authority are treated like State organs, such that their acts are attributable to the State if the individual or organisation is exercising governmental authority.

23 Draft Articles on State Responsibility, Commentary accompanying Article 4, para. 13.

24 Draft Articles on State Responsibility, Article 8.

25 ICJ Nicaragua Judgment, para. 115.

26 Tadić Appeals Chamber Judgment, paras. 131, 145.

27 ICJ Genocide Judgment, paras. 403–5.

28 Tadić Appeals Chamber Judgment, para. 145.

those acts after their commission.[29] Political statements that are broadly supportive of the activities of the group or individuals, but do not go beyond that, will not generally suffice for attribution purposes.

5 Consider a situation in which citizens from State A cross the border into State B, use a tracked construction vehicle to smash through the perimeter fence of State B's nuclear command and control facility and start to demolish one of the buildings at that facility. If the intruding civilians were acting on their own initiative – say, because they wanted simply to demonstrate against State B's possession of nuclear weapons – their actions could not, without more, be attributed to State A and State B would have jurisdiction to deal with the criminal offences they have committed. If, however, it became clear that the intruding civilians had received specific instructions from State A authorities to damage the targeted facility and direction as to how this should be achieved, the acts of the civilians would be attributable to State A, giving State B the potential right to undertake countermeasures (on which, see paragraph 8 of this Commentary).

6 If assistance by a State does not amount to the instructions, direction or control specified in the preceding paragraph, while the conduct of the individual or group will likely not be attributable to the State, such acts may nevertheless be internationally wrongful.[30] However, Article 11 of the Draft Articles on State Responsibility provides: 'Conduct which is not attributable to a State under the preceding articles shall nevertheless be considered an act of that State under international law if and to the extent that the State acknowledges and adopts the conduct in question as its own.' There must have been both acknowledgement and adoption by the supporting State and this will require that the State goes beyond mere endorsement or tacit approval of the activities of the individual or group.[31] Consider again the situation described in the previous paragraph, but assume that no instructions or direction had been given by State A and that it exercised no control. At the time of the acts no attribution to State A would be possible. If, however, after the intrusion had taken place and after the damage had been caused to the building, State A's prime minister were publicly to say, 'We, the government were delighted to see the actions our citizens took last night. I urge the government of State B to refrain from any future nuclear activity; otherwise we, State A, will do nothing to prevent further activities by our citizens.' Such words would possibly be seen as amounting to acknowledgement and

29 Tadić Appeals Chamber Judgment, para. 132.
30 ICJ Nicaragua Judgment, para. 242.
31 Draft Articles on State Responsibility, Commentary accompanying Article 11.

adoption of the previous actions of the civilians, which could as a result be attributed retrospectively to State B. So, in situations where, at the time of the activity, the requirements of Article 8 of the Draft Articles on State Responsibility have not been met, attribution to a State of actions by an individual or a group may be based on the subsequent action of, or statements made by, the State.[32]

7 Acts that do not breach international law, such as espionage per se, are not addressed by this Rule. An internationally wrongful act or omission occurs only if what is done, or omitted, reflects all of the required elements of the corresponding legal breach. Consider a group of activists operating from the territory of State A and inflicting serious damage on a missile launching site in State B. Unless it had positive or constructive knowledge of the activists' activities (see Rule 5), State A cannot be held internationally responsible, because the conduct of private persons cannot be attributed to State A. Alternatively, consider a secret agent of State A retrieving crucial information from an NC3 system in State B. State B's agents, in trying to terminate the extraction of information, by mistake delete all data resident in the system, thus rendering it dysfunctional. State A has not caused those consequences, and the extraction of information is an act of non-prohibited espionage. Accordingly, State A cannot be held internationally responsible.

8 A State that suffers injury or damage as a result of an internationally wrongful act by another State may, subject to certain limitations,[33] undertake proportionate countermeasures against that State.[34] Countermeasures consist of necessary and proportionate action that the injured State takes against the State that has violated international law. The injured State's action would itself be unlawful but for the illegality of the prior activities of the State that has violated international law. The sole purpose of the countermeasures must be to induce the latter State to comply with international law or directly to secure that compliance. Once the violations of international law have come to an end, the injured State ought not to undertake or continue with countermeasures. While the injured State should, at least if feasible, first call upon the other State to cease its internationally wrongful activity, the effective preservation of its rights under international law may require the injured State to take more immediate action.[35]

32 Tehran Hostages Judgment, para. 74.
33 See Draft Articles on State Responsibility, Article 50.
34 Ibid., Articles 22, 49–53.
35 Consider ibid., Articles 52(1)(b), 52(2).

9 There is a body of opinion according to which, in exceptional circumstances, a State may resort to countermeasures that involve the use of force if the prior internationally wrongful act itself consists of a use of force that does not reach the threshold of an armed attack. This aspect is discussed in paragraph 1 of the Commentary accompanying Rule 7 below.

Countermeasures

Rule 7

If a State commits an internationally wrongful act against another State, the victim State may have the right to take countermeasures.

1 If a State is the victim of an internationally wrongful act committed by another State, the victim State has the right to take countermeasures. These are acts or omissions to act that would violate a legal obligation owed by the victim State to the State that committed the prior internationally wrongful act were they not being undertaken as countermeasures. The taking of countermeasures under such circumstances is permitted under international law. The Draft Articles on State Responsibility, in Article 50(1)(a), provide that '[c]ountermeasures shall not affect: (a) the obligation to refrain from the threat or use of force'. As will be discussed in the commentaries on Rules 8 and 11, not every use of force qualifies as an armed attack, which is understood as the gravest form of a use of force. Arguably, a use of force not reaching the threshold of an armed attack would entitle the victim State to respond by means of proportionate countermeasures of a military nature involving action that remains below the threshold of an armed attack.[36] However, such an interpretation is not generally adopted by States and it would be contrary to the object and purpose of *jus ad bellum*. Accordingly, countermeasures do not involve the use of force and must therefore be distinguished from self-defence action referred to in Rule 11. Countermeasures also must be distinguished from reprisals (on which, see Rule 76). Thirdly, countermeasures must be distinguished from retorsion, which consists of lawful but unfriendly acts.[37]

2 Countermeasures must have the purpose of inducing the State against which they are taken to come back into compliance with the international law obligations it owes to the victim State. Countermeasures may not affect fundamental human rights, nor may they violate a peremptory norm. They must also be proportionate to the damage done to the victim State.[38] The act or

36 See ICJ Oil Platforms Judgment, Dissenting Judgment of Judge Simma, paras. 13, 14.
37 Draft Articles on State Responsibility, chapeau to Chapter II of Part Three, para. 3.
38 Tallinn Manual 2.0, Rules 22, 23.

series of acts to which a countermeasure is responding must have been undertaken by, or at least must be attributable to, the State against which the countermeasure is directed.

3 Consider a situation in which armed force not rising to the level of an armed attack is used by State A against State B's nuclear weapons force command and control system, causing significant physical damage. State A has breached Article 2(4) of the UN Charter and this constitutes an internationally wrongful act to which State B may respond by taking lawful countermeasures. State B decides that the best way of inducing State A not to repeat its use of force is to confiscate certain financial assets that State A holds on deposit in State B's banking system. Such action would amount to a breach of the international financial arrangements under which the assets were deposited, but would be a lawful countermeasure in response to the use of force.

C

Resorting to the Use of Force in Nuclear Operations

This section is concerned with the law that regulates the resort to the use of force, often referred to as *jus ad bellum*. *Jus ad bellum*, largely based on the United Nations Charter, sets forth the general prohibition on the employment of force by States in the conduct of their international relations and contains the two recognised exceptions to that prohibition. *Jus ad bellum* is to be distinguished from *jus in bello* (i.e. the body of law which regulates the conduct of hostilities once an armed conflict is under way). The two bodies of law are distinct but are not entirely unrelated. Importantly, however, the principle of the equal application of *jus in bello* to the parties to an armed conflict means that, irrespective of which party may have perpetrated a breach of *jus ad bellum* and thus caused the armed conflict, the rights and obligations of *jus in bello* (as set forth in Sections E and G) and the law of neutrality (as explained in Section F) apply to both parties to the conflict equally.[1]

All States are party to the United Nations Charter and therefore its provisions bind all States as a matter of treaty law. The question of whether the contents of the UN Charter have customary law status is not entirely moot, as such status may, for example, have implications for the applicability to armed groups of some aspects of the law relating to armed attack. It is the opinion of the present authors that the provisions of the UN Charter that are referred to in this section do indeed have customary law status, with the consequence that actions of armed groups are capable of constituting armed attacks if the threshold applicable to armed attack is met.

The International Court of Justice (ICJ) has opined that Articles 2(4) and 51 of the UN Charter apply to 'any use of force, regardless of the weapons employed'.[2] It expressed this view when considering the legality of the threat or use of nuclear weapons. It is therefore considered to be uncontroversial that

[1] Preamble to API, para. 5; UK Manual, paras. 3.12, 3.12.1; Canadian Manual, para. 204.

[2] ICJ Nuclear Opinion, para. 39.

the Rules set forth in this Section apply to the threat or use of nuclear weapons. For a discussion of the ICJ's Advisory Opinion, see Section J.

Prohibition of the Threat or Use of Nuclear Force

Rule 8

All States must refrain in their international relations from the threat or use of nuclear force against the territorial integrity or political independence of any State, or in any other manner inconsistent with the purposes of the United Nations.

1 This Rule is based upon, and adopts the language of, Article 2(4) of the UN Charter. It is a rule of customary international law.[3] Acts or threats of nuclear force that 'are not directed against either the territorial integrity or political independence of a State may nevertheless violate the prohibition if they are inconsistent with the Purposes of the United Nations'.[4] The meanings of 'use of force' and 'threat of force' are addressed respectively in Rules 9 and 10.

2 The territorial integrity[5] of a State can sensibly be understood to refer to the practical ability of the attacked State, with its government and administration, both national and local, to continue to operate throughout its territory. A nuclear attack that has the effect of depriving the government of that State of the ability to exercise its sovereign rights and responsibilities throughout the territory of the State, for example, by denying safe access to a portion of the territory, will have been a use of force against the territorial integrity of the State.

3 Political independence refers to the right of the State to employ its own political processes and to make its own political decisions without external interference. It is the use of nuclear force, or a threat to use nuclear force, with the purpose thereby of forcing or influencing political processes or decision-making within the victim State that this part of the Rule prohibits.

4 The purposes of the United Nations are set forth in Article 1 of the UN Charter. They are:

1 To maintain international peace and security, and to that end: to take effective collective measures for the prevention and removal of threats to the peace, and for the suppression of acts of aggression or other breaches

[3] ICJ Nicaragua Judgment, paras. 188–90.
[4] Tallinn Manual 1.0, Commentary accompanying Rule 10, para. 2.
[5] 'Integrity', so far as relevant in the present context, is defined as 'the state of being whole; the condition of being unified or sound in construction'; see *Concise Oxford English Dictionary*, 11th ed. (Oxford University Press, 2006) 738.

of the peace, and to bring about by peaceful means, and in conformity with the principles of justice and international law, adjustment or settlement of international disputes or situations which might lead to a breach of the peace;

2 To develop friendly relations among nations based on respect for the principle of equal rights and self-determination of peoples, and to take other appropriate measures to strengthen universal peace;

3 To achieve international co-operation in solving international problems of an economic, social, cultural, or humanitarian character, and in promoting and encouraging respect for human rights and for fundamental freedoms for all without distinction as to race, sex, language, or religion; and

4 To be a centre for harmonizing the actions of nations in the attainment of these common ends.

A threat or use of force that is in any way inconsistent with these purposes breaches Article 2(4) of the UN Charter. It follows from the foregoing that the use of any force, including by means of nuclear weapons, is in violation of Article 2(4) and of the corresponding prohibition under customary law. The illegality of such use or threat thereof may, of course, be precluded by either self-defence or UNSC authorisation.

5 The Rule is concerned with the actions of States: it is States that are the object of the prohibition. Moreover, it is the armed forces of a State that will usually – perhaps almost invariably – be responsible for maintaining and operating nuclear weapons. It should be borne in mind, however, that, for these purposes, activities of a State's intelligence agency would be regarded as the actions of the State. Similarly, in the most unlikely event that a private contractor is responsible for maintaining and operating a State's nuclear weapon facilities, the actions of that private contractor may well be attributable to the State and may, thus, be regarded as the actions of the State. Attribution and state responsibility are addressed in Rule 6 and in the accompanying Commentary. Importantly, Article 2(4) of the UN Charter and its associated customary prohibition of the use of force do not apply to non-State actors unless, as mentioned earlier in this paragraph, their acts are attributable to a State. If a threat or use of nuclear force is undertaken by terrorists, by an organised armed group or even by individuals and is attributable to a State, it is the State that will have breached Article 2(4), not the group or the individuals.

6 If a threat or act falls below a threat or use of force for the purposes of this Rule, it may nevertheless constitute an unlawful intervention (on which, see the Commentary accompanying Rule 9).

Meaning of Use of Force

Rule 9

A nuclear operation amounts to a use of force when its scale and effects reach the threshold of a use of force.

1 It will be recalled that, for the purposes of the present book, a 'nuclear operation' includes all activities involving the use or threatened use of nuclear weapons, nuclear deterrent activities and all actions whose purpose is to target nuclear weapons and nuclear equipment as such, including their command, control and communications systems. As the present Rule makes clear, not all nuclear operations qualify as a use of force, but only those that fulfil the elements discussed in the following paragraphs.

2 The UN Charter does not specify which acts do or do not constitute a use of force. The ordinary meaning of the term force is 'physical coercion'. Accordingly, the use of means that are designed to cause, or in fact result in, damage, destruction, injury or death qualifies as a use of force. Such a broad interpretation would not, however, be based on a sufficiently broad consensus among States. In the light of the Charter's preamble – 'to save succeeding generations from the scourge of war' – it is safe to maintain that the use of methods and means of warfare will always have to be considered by reference to Article 2(4).

3 In determining which nuclear operations amount to a use of force, it is useful to note the statement by the ICJ in the *Nicaragua* case that 'scale and effects' must be considered when determining whether particular acts amount to an armed attack.[6] This would seem to be a helpful yardstick also for drawing the distinction between events that constitute a use of force and those that are something less. In other words, the scale and effects of an event can be used as the basis for distinguishing between uses of force and acts that should be regarded as *de minimis* and thus as not constituting a use of force. According to this approach, it is the nature and the degree of the consequences of a nuclear event, or of the expected consequences of a threatened nuclear event, that will determine whether it can properly be regarded as a use or threat of force. Moreover, it is widely accepted that mere economic or political pressure is not sufficient to constitute a use or threat of force.[7]

[6] ICJ Nicaragua Judgment, para. 195; Tallinn Manual 1.0, Commentary accompanying Rule 11, para. 1.

[7] This is so, even if the economic or political pressure prejudices the territorial independence or political integrity of the victim State. This is because political or economic pressure is not synonymous with the use or threat of force; see Tallinn Manual 1.0, Commentary accompanying Rule 11, para. 2.

4 A use or threat of nuclear force will usually be undertaken by the armed forces of a State. However, a nuclear-capable State might become involved in a non-international armed conflict by, for example, arming and training an organised armed group that is undertaking hostilities against the government of another State. The acts of arming and training the organised armed group might qualify as a use of force by the assisting State, particularly if they are accompanied by other significant assistance.[8] If, troublingly, nuclear material were to get into the hands of a non-State actor and if that non-State actor threatens to use it or actually uses it, that would not constitute a breach of Article 2(4), because that Article is limited to threats or acts by States. If, for example, an organised armed group were to lodge nuclear material or a nuclear weapon in a concealed location within a State and with that State's permission, the mere act by the State of giving that permission would not, without more, be generally regarded as sufficient for a subsequent threat or use of the nuclear material by the group to be regarded as a threat or use of force by the State. In the same example, if, however, the provision of such 'safe keeping' facilities were to be accompanied by other significant assistance from the State – such as the provision of a launch location and/or the supply of equipment required to launch such a weapon – the subsequent threat or use by the group would likely be regarded as a threat or use of force by that assisting State.[9]

5 As noted in the Commentary accompanying Rule 11 below, a nuclear event must rise to the level of an armed attack for the victim State to have the right to use force in self-defence. It is important to understand the relationship between actions that constitute a use of force and those that amount to an armed attack. The ICJ has described armed attacks as the most grave forms of the use of force.[10] So, any armed attack that is conducted by or attributable to a State will also constitute a use of force, but not all uses of force will amount to an armed attack. Accordingly, the authors reject the view, expressed by the United States, that any unlawful use of force is capable of being regarded as an armed attack triggering the right of the victim State to use force in self-defence. In the authors' view, only the most grave forms of use of force so qualify.[11]

6 It is generally agreed that '[a]cts that injure or kill persons or damage or destroy objects are unambiguously uses of force',[12] and one, if not all, of those

8 ICJ Nicaragua Judgment, para. 228.
9 Consider Tallinn Manual 2.0, Commentary accompanying Rule 69, para. 5.
10 ICJ Nicaragua Judgment, para. 191.
11 Consider US DoD Law of War Manual, para. 1.11.5.2; A. D. Sofaer, 'International Law and the Use of Force', 82 (1988) *Proceedings of the ASIL Annual Meeting* 420, 422.
12 Tallinn Manual 2.0, Commentary accompanying Rule 69, para. 8.

four occurrences – death, injury, damage or destruction – is the likely and perhaps inevitable consequence of a military operation involving the use of a nuclear weapon. Less straightforward is the situation in which either none of the four occurrences is caused or in which the casualties or damage are at the lower end of the spectrum. Consider, for example, a situation in which a State has taken action to try to render another State's nuclear command structure inoperable – say, by undertaking directed energy attacks against the computer equipment on which the nuclear command system relies. In the opinion of the present authors, there are two interlinked issues that arise when determining whether an event is a use of force contrary to Article 2(4). The first issue is whether the relevant event fulfils the legal criteria for establishing a use of force. The second issue is whether the victim State chooses in fact to characterise the event as a use of force – a decision that in turn will be influenced, but not necessarily determined, by what the victim State deduces would be the likely interpretation of the community of States.

7 Taking those issues together, it has been suggested that victim States will consider a number of factors when deciding whether to characterise an event as a use of force. The author of the original list[13] was identifying the factors States would have in mind when deciding whether to regard a specific cyber event as a use of force. He was at pains to make it clear that these factors do not represent legally prescribed criteria and the present authors think it instructive to consider how those factors can usefully be applied to nuclear operations. The present authors would therefore suggest that the 'Schmitt criteria' might be interpreted as follows:

Severity: Events that cause inconvenience, irritation or even anger, and little more, will not amount to a use of force. Events that cause physical harm will usually be capable of being a use of force, unless the harm is relatively minor. If important national systems are affected, but only to a minor degree, the importance of the systems will not cause the event to be a use of force. Accordingly, 'the scope, duration, and intensity of the consequences will have great bearing on the appraisal of their severity'.[14] So, to continue with the example of the attack on the nuclear weapon computerised control system, a military operation that has only a temporary disabling effect on such a system lasting a few seconds or a couple of minutes might not

[13] M. N. Schmitt, 'Computer Network Attack and the Use of Force in International Law: Thoughts on a Normative Framework', 37 (1999) *Columbia Journal of Transnational Law* 885, 914; Tallinn Manual 2.0, Commentary accompanying Rule 69, para. 9.

[14] Tallinn Manual 2.0, Commentary accompanying Rule 69, para. 9(a).

be regarded as a use of force, whereas one that takes the control system offline for a longer period is likely to be regarded as a use of force.

Immediacy: If a military operation has immediate adverse consequences, the victim State is poorly placed to prevent the ensuing harm and will thus be more likely to interpret the event as a use of force.

Directness: The more direct the causal link between the event and the harmful consequences, the more likely a State is to regard the event as a use of force. It is hard to think of a more direct link than that between the detonation of a nuclear device and the harm caused by the blast, the fragmentation and the contamination caused by the nuclear particles.

Invasiveness: This factor is concerned with the degree to which a particular operation invades a State's systems. The arrangements that a State develops for the command, control and communications associated with its nuclear forces are likely to comprise closed systems, unconnected to the Internet and with security measures, perhaps of an elaborate nature, designed to ensure that unwanted intrusion is prevented. So, for example, a military operation that intrudes into the nuclear weapon command system and that breaks a secure communications link, such as that between a superior commander and the commanders of nuclear-armed submarines, will certainly satisfy the invasiveness criterion. Equally, if a cyber or sabotage operation is targeting the private systems of a single State, the invasiveness criterion is likely to be satisfied. Note, however, that while espionage is highly invasive, it will not, without more, amount to a use of force and espionage does not breach the law of armed conflict.

Identifiable effects: If the effects of the nuclear operation can be objectively identified and even measured in some way, the operation itself is more likely to be seen as a use of force. Again, a nuclear explosion satisfies this criterion, in that the casualties can be counted, the area of land adversely affected can be measured and the structures that are damaged or destroyed can be listed. Equally, the impact of an operation to disable an enemy military command and communications system can be measured in terms of the duration of the disruption, the nature of the systems that are disabled, the functions that cannot be performed and so on.

Military character: The military nature of an activity will increase the likelihood of it being regarded by a victim State as a use of force. The use of a nuclear weapon, or a threat to use such a weapon, will be an event that is inevitably seen as military in nature, so this criterion will ordinarily be satisfied by either of those acts. Actions taken adversely to affect another State's nuclear command, control and/or communications may take a form that would not necessarily have military appearance. Thus, hacking operations undertaken from a non-military location, using civilian computing equipment, operated by civilians and undertaken through intermediary servers may not have the outward appearance of military activity. However, States are likely to view the target of such an operation as, per se, giving the operation military character and as thereby satisfying this criterion.

State involvement: There are two aspects to state involvement. First, the Article 2(4) prohibition specifically addresses States, so if a State is not in fact involved and is not seen to be involved, directly or indirectly, in the activity, then the activity cannot amount to a breach of Article 2(4). Second, the more visible the connection is between a State and the forceful activity being undertaken, or threatened, against another State, the more likely it is that third States will regard the activity as being a use of force.

Presumptive lawfulness: The provisions of the law of armed conflict generally prohibit acts or limit the circumstances in which they may lawfully be performed. It has therefore been suggested that acts which are not prohibited, either generally or in the relevant circumstances, are permitted.[15] This then leads to the somewhat circular argument that acts which are presumptively legal are less likely to be considered by States to be a use of force. If, during a period of peace, a State fires a nuclear weapon at another State, there is no presumptive lawfulness involved. The act is a manifestly unlawful use of force and will be seen as such by the global community at large. However, if a State is covertly gathering information about another State's NC3 systems, such activity is not prohibited by international law. During such an espionage operation, the secretive insertion of a kill switch or some other device to damage the intruded systems may well not be publicly visible, may therefore not cause States in general to appreciate the full nature of the action being taken and may accordingly be that much more difficult to characterise as a use of force.

8 Other factors will influence a State's publicly stated position on whether a use or threat of force has taken place. These will likely include: the

[15] Consider Tallinn Manual 1.0, Commentary accompanying Rule 11, para. 9(h).

political and diplomatic situation pertaining at the time; the strategic situation in which the victim State finds itself; any relevant rhetoric from the political and/or military leadership of the State believed to be responsible for the use or threat of force; any relevant events during the period preceding the act being assessed; and the kind of target against which force has been used. It is important to emphasise that the factors listed here and in the previous paragraph do not have legal force, that not all of them need to be present for an event to be classifiable as a use of force and that categorisation as a use of force is for the victim State to decide, basing its decision on a reasonable but necessarily subjective appreciation of what has happened.

9 It should be noted that not all uses of force are unlawful. Thus, if necessary and proportionate force is used in lawful self-defence (on which, see Rules 11, 12, 13 and 14) or if force is lawfully used pursuant to an authorisation by the United Nations Security Council (on which, see Rule 17 below), there will be no breach of the present Rule.

10 The implications of the distinction between a 'use of force' and an 'armed attack' must be fully understood. The former constitutes a breach by a State of an international law rule – namely, the prohibition in Article 2(4) of the UN Charter and in customary law. The perpetrating State has therefore committed an internationally wrongful act against the victim State, giving the victim State the right to take non-forceful countermeasures (see Rule 7 above). 'Armed attack', by contrast, is the state of affairs that must occur before a victim State has the legal right to use force by way of self-defence. A use of force contrary to Article 2(4) that does not also amount to an armed attack gives the victim State no right to use force in self-defence. Only if an armed attack occurs does the victim State have the legal right to act forcefully in self-defence (on armed attack and self-defence, see Rules 11, 12, 13, 14 and 15).

Meaning of Threat of Force

Rule 10

A nuclear operation amounts to an unlawful threat to use force when the threatened action, were it to be carried out, would be an unlawful use of force.

1 The prohibition of the threat or use of force is set forth in Rule 8.

2 It must be recalled that, for the purposes of this book, the term 'nuclear operation' includes all activities involving the use, or threatened use, of nuclear weapons, nuclear deterrent activities and all actions whose purpose

is to target nuclear weapons and nuclear equipment as such, including their command, control and communications systems. The notion of unlawful use of force is described in Rule 9 and the accompanying Commentary. If the force being threatened would be lawful – for example, because it would constitute necessary and proportionate force lawfully used in self-defence, or because it is authorised by the United Nations Security Council – the threat to use it will not be unlawful. In other words, for the threat to be unlawful, the force concerned must also be unlawful. The focus of the present Rule is on Article 2(4)'s prohibition of threats to use force, and most particularly on what constitutes a threat for these purposes.

3 The making of a threat involves the expression of an intention. Accordingly, the Tallinn Manual explains that the 'essence of a threat is that it is explicitly or impliedly communicative in nature'.[16] If a State merely acquires the capability to use nuclear force, this does not constitute an unlawful threat as no express or implied threat is being communicated. However, if, for example, the political leadership of the State were to publicly disclose that it has obtained the means to use a nuclear weapon and intends to use it against a named State unless that State takes specified action or desists from stated activities, that would constitute a threat to use unlawful force.

4 A more complex issue concerns the lawfulness of a nuclear deterrent policy. It makes sense at this point to note some of the remarks about deterrence made during the ICJ's deliberations on the lawfulness of the threat or use of nuclear weapons in the mid-1990s, although these are also discussed in Section J below. The ICJ observed:

> Some States put forward the argument that possession of nuclear weapons is itself an unlawful threat to use force. Possession of nuclear weapons may indeed justify an inference of preparedness to use them. In order to be effective, the policy of deterrence, by which those States possessing or under the umbrella of nuclear weapons seek to discourage military aggression by demonstrating that it will serve no purpose, necessitates that the intention to use nuclear weapons be credible. Whether this is a 'threat' contrary to Article 2, paragraph 4, depends on whether the particular use of force envisaged would be directed against the territorial integrity or political independence of a State, or against the Purposes of the United Nations or whether, in the event that it were intended as a means of defence, it would necessarily violate the principles of necessity and proportionality. In any of these circumstances the use of force, and the threat to use it, would be unlawful under the law of the Charter.[17]

[16] Tallinn Manual 2.0, Commentary accompanying Rule 70, para. 4.

[17] ICJ Nuclear Opinion, para. 48.

5 The Court declined to pronounce on the policy of deterrence but noted the fact that a number of States adhered to the practice during much of the Cold War and continued to do so.[18] As can be seen, the Court did not explicitly state whether the act of maintaining a policy of deterrence actually constitutes the communication, directly or indirectly, of a threat. One interpretation of the words used in paragraph 48 of the Advisory Opinion might suggest that members of the Court thought that a deterrence policy does indeed entail such an effective communication. An alternative interpretation would suggest that this was a subject on which the Court was deliberately declining to express a firm view.

6 In the view of the authors, a threat for present purposes necessarily must be directed towards another State or States. There must be a prospective victim of what would be an unlawful use of force. The mere taking of precautions in order to seek to promote a State's own security does not constitute the communication of a threat. Likewise, the development and maintenance of a nuclear capability as a deterrent against States in general does not amount to a threat for these purposes, because no threat is being communicated to any State in particular. It is only if a threat to use unlawful force is explicitly being communicated to a target State or States, or if the acts of the threatening State clearly show and thus communicate that it is intending to use unlawful force against a specific victim State or States, that an unlawful threat has been issued. It must, however, be made clear that, for a number of States, the mere possession of nuclear weapons by other States constitutes an implicit threat to use them in unspecified circumstances on unknown and unknowable occasions in the future. The position of such States is that the possession of nuclear weapons and the maintenance of a nuclear deterrent is therefore a breach of Article 2(4) of the UN Charter and, thus, is unlawful. The authors do not agree with that approach. In their view, an unlawful threat under Article 2(4) exists only where there is a communication by or on behalf of one State directed at another State or States that directly or indirectly threatens that State or those States with the use of unlawful force; a general policy of deterrence does not fulfil those criteria. Moreover, the approach taken by such States is not shared by those States that either maintain a nuclear deterrence policy or that have put themselves under the umbrella of nuclear weapon States. Accordingly, there is a lack of general consensus both on the interpretation of Article 2(4) and with regard to customary international law.

[18] ICJ Nuclear Opinion, para. 67. In para. 73 the Court described the practice of deterrence as 'still strong', and in para. 96 it commented that an appreciable section of the international community had been adhering to the policy for many years.

Specifically, in the opinion of the present authors, it cannot be said that there is a general practice of States accepted as law that equates deterrence with the communication of a threat.

7 A threat in breach of Rule 8 does not have to be accompanied by a coercive demand. Accordingly, if a State simply threatens to launch a nuclear weapon against another State without demanding specified action by the victim State as the price for not undertaking the attack, that would nevertheless be an unlawful threat contrary to Article 2(4). Likewise, a threat by one State to destroy a military facility where it believes another State holds part or all of its nuclear arsenal does not have to be accompanied by specific demands directed at the victim State for that threat also to constitute a breach of Article 2(4). A more difficult situation arises if the political leadership of a State threatens to undertake a nuclear attack when it is clear that it has no capability to do so. Expert opinion is divided on whether that would amount to a breach of the Rule. Much will inevitably depend on the precise words used and on the circumstances in which they are uttered.

Armed Attack and Self-Defence

Rule 11

A State has an inherent right of individual or collective self-defence if an armed attack occurs against it.

1 While the wording of the Rule follows closely that of Article 51 of the UN Charter, the right of a State to use force in self-defence is also a customary law right. The language of Article 51, and of the Rule, shows why it is important to clarify the characteristics of armed attacks.

2 To be an armed attack, the relevant military operation must cross an international border. So, the firing of a missile from a submarine located in international waters against a land-based target in a State and the flying of a combat aircraft from one State into the airspace of another State in order to drop a nuclear bomb in that State are both examples of a cross-border operation that will satisfy this criterion. Equally, if State A sends a special forces team from its own territory into State B in order to target and destroy an industrial installation used for the manufacture of ingredients for a nuclear device, this will also involve a sufficient cross-border element for present purposes. If the cross-border aspect is absent – in other words if, say, the attack on the industrial installation is planned and executed entirely from within the target State by an organised armed group at a time when no pre-existing armed

conflict is in progress – such an event cannot be classified as an armed attack. If the number and gravity of previous violent events are sufficient to show that a non-international armed conflict is taking place, the State's response will be governed by the law of non-international armed conflict. If the threshold of a non-international armed conflict has not been reached, human rights law and the domestic criminal and police law of the relevant State will determine the lawful responses of its law enforcement agencies.

3 The ICJ noted in its Nuclear Weapons Advisory Opinion that Article 51 does not specify the means whereby an attack must be undertaken in order for it to constitute an armed attack. The provision applies 'to any use of force, regardless of the weapons employed'.[19] This does not, however, mean that a weapon must be employed. It is the effects generated by the operation that are critically important here. If these are comparable to the effects normally associated with an armed attack, the mere fact that they were generated in a novel manner does not per se preclude the resulting operation from being treated as an armed attack. Consider, for example, a cyber operation that intrudes into the computer systems that control stored nuclear warheads. The intruder intentionally alters the storage arrangements so as to facilitate a large release of nuclear material. As a result, a number of staff members at the facility are killed, several warheads are extensively damaged and major environmental contamination is caused. The mere fact that a non-kinetic method is used to cause the casualties, the damage to the warheads and the environmental contamination does not prevent the cyber activity from amounting to an armed attack.

4 The authors take the view that not every use of force contrary to Article 2(4) of the UN Charter rises to the level of an armed attack.[20] It is the scale and effects of the operation that will mark the distinction here,[21] and these will be greater for armed attacks than for uses of force not amounting to an armed attack. The distinction is of utmost importance, as a victim State is permitted to use force in self-defence only in connection with an armed attack. When discussing 'scale and effects', the ICJ Nicaragua Judgment distinguished 'the most grave forms of the use of force (those constituting an armed attack) from other less grave forms'.[22] This causes one to wonder what grave scale and effects might look like. The ICJ did not give guidance on that issue, although expert opinion suggests that serious injury to, or death of, a number of persons

19 ICJ Nuclear Opinion, para. 39.
20 ICJ Nicaragua Judgment, para. 191.
21 ICJ Nicaragua Judgment, para. 195.
22 ICJ Nicaragua Judgment, para. 191.

or significant damage to, or destruction of, property would satisfy the requirement.[23]

5 While the threshold for armed attack is not defined in measurable terms, any use of a currently available nuclear weapon is highly likely to have sufficiently serious effects to constitute an armed attack. The possibility cannot, however, be entirely excluded that at some future time very limited-yield nuclear devices will be developed, the damaging and injurious effects of which might be significantly reduced. Moreover, operations against nuclear weapon capabilities may have effects at or around the threshold. It should therefore be borne in mind that if, for example, a State undertakes a series of attacks which, individually, would not meet the armed attack threshold, they might be considered cumulatively as having the required scale and effects.[24] For this approach to apply, however, the incidents in the series would need to be sufficiently related. Suppose, for example, that a State has on three recent occasions used proxy individuals in a neighbouring State to attack a railway line, causing a derailment with few casualties; set fire to a warehouse, causing the loss of some construction materials; and initiate a power surge, causing damage to numerous domestic appliances and some commercial equipment. None of these events would individually, or possibly cumulatively, constitute an armed attack. If, however, in a fourth incident, the same State disables part of the nuclear communications network, causing damage that requires the replacement of numerous components and the re-validation of the system, the victim State might be able to show that the cumulative scale and effects of the series of related incidents meet the armed attack threshold.[25]

6 A challenging question is which non-injurious, non-damaging cyber operations against nuclear command, control and communications systems can constitute an armed attack. It is evident from the discussion in Tallinn Manual 2.0 that expert opinion is likely to be divided. The present authors take the view that the nuclear command, control and communications systems of a State will be regarded as part of that State's critical national infrastructure. They further consider that any operation against such infrastructure that

[23] Tallinn Manual 2.0, Commentary accompanying Rule 71, para. 8. Note the later suggestion by the ICJ that an attack on a single military platform or installation might qualify as an armed attack; see ICJ Oil Platforms Judgment, paras. 57, 61.

[24] Consider, in this regard, International Law Commission, Responsibility of States for Internationally Wrongful Acts, Annex to UNGA Resolution 56/83, 12 December 2001, Article 15 (Breach consisting of a composite act).

[25] Note Tallinn Manual 2.0, Commentary accompanying Rule 71, para. 11.

does not involve physical destruction but renders the NC3 architecture, or important elements of it, inoperable would qualify as an armed attack.[26]

7 The question of intent may, at first glance, appear to cause difficulty. Often, the victim State will be unaware of any particular intention that the person undertaking the attack, or the State on behalf of which he or she was acting, may have had. Victim States will generally and properly assume that the violent consequences of a violent act like the detonation of a nuclear device were intended, and will proceed on that basis. If it is apparent that the nuclear event was not intended, the question of whether it nevertheless constitutes an armed attack is moot, because the use of force in self-defence is unlikely to meet the necessity requirement (see Rule 12 below).[27]

8 If the gravity of the use of force meets the armed attack threshold and the relevant operation was actually undertaken by persons who are organs of a State, the attack is attributable to that State and therefore qualifies as an armed attack by that State. The actions of a non-State actor, such as a private individual, a contractor's employee or members of an armed group, may also be attributed to a State and may thus become the acts of that State if the relevant persons were sent by or on behalf of the State to undertake such acts.[28] So, imagine that State A employs a private company to maintain computer systems in its defence ministry. If the State instructs a gifted hacker employed by that company to hack into State B's missile control computers, causing a missile that State B has test-fired to go off course and attack a civilian shopping centre with mass casualties, the attack would be attributable to State A and would have sufficiently grave consequences to constitute an armed attack.[29] If a nuclear attack causes effects in more than one State, the gravity of the effects in each State must be considered in order to determine whether an armed attack has occurred against that State.

9 International law is not yet settled on the question whether an attack that is undertaken by an armed group without any participation by a State can constitute an armed attack for the purposes of Article 51 and of the customary law right to use force in self-defence. Traditionalists take the view that the notion of armed attack applies only in the case of a State-on-State activity, with lawful responses to violent actions by non-State actors, even those with a cross-border element, being limited to law enforcement. A more progressive

26 Consider Tallinn Manual 2.0, Commentary accompanying Rule 71, para. 12.
27 Note ICJ Oil Platforms Judgment, para. 64.
28 ICJ Nicaragua Judgment, para. 195.
29 Tallinn Manual 2.0, Commentary accompanying Rule 71, para. 17.

interpretation would point to resolutions of the UN Security Council[30] and would note that Article 51 does not require the armed attack to be undertaken by a State. The 'if an armed attack occurs' language of Article 51, reflected in the present Rule, leaves open – perhaps deliberately – the question of the identity and status of the author of the armed attack. If, the progressives would say, the authors of Article 51 had wanted to narrow armed attacks down to actions of States, they could have done so explicitly in the same way as they did in Article 2(4). Traditionalists would complain that the progressive interpretation increases the scope for violent responses and thus is counter to the first, and arguably key, purpose of the United Nations – namely, to maintain international peace and security.

10 The present authors suggest that it would be illogical for the Security Council to characterise, as it has, terrorist acts by non-State actors as being capable of amounting to a threat to international peace[31] while at the same time denying victim States the right to defend themselves against such threats. Moreover, State practice seems to suggest that States consider themselves entitled to resort to extra-territorial self-defence against non-State actors that have committed armed attacks against them or their allies. In this context, it suffices to refer to the allied military activities against the so-called Islamic State in Syria in response to that group's armed attacks against Iraq. Finally, the reference in Article 51 of the UN Charter to the 'inherent' right of self-defence may be understood as an endorsement of the understanding of States before the adoption of the UN Charter. It may be recalled that the famous Caroline formula of 1842 was adopted with regard to British military operations against Canadian rebels who had taken refuge in the territory of the United States.

11 However, the sovereignty of the State from which the armed group operated must be properly respected. That State must be given a suitable opportunity to deal with the matter by taking steps to prevent any repetition. There is considerable controversy over what action the victim State can lawfully take if the State from which the armed group operated is either unable or unwilling to take effective preventive measures. Some governments and commentators argue that if the State 'hosting' the armed group is unable or unwilling to take effective preventive measures, the victim State has the right to use necessary and proportionate force in extra-territorial self-defence. They

30 Consider UNSC Resolution 1368 (2001), 12 September 2001; UNSC Resolution 1373 (2001), 28 September 2001; Statement by North Atlantic Council, 12 September 2001.

31 See UNSC Resolution 1368 (2001), 12 September 2001; UNSC Resolution 1373 (2001), 28 September 2001.

rely either on the due diligence obligation or on the lack of effective sovereignty of the 'hosting' State. Other governments and commentators insist that justifying self-defence action in such circumstances on the basis of unable/unwilling arguments unacceptably loosens the *jus ad bellum* constraints on the use of force. Accordingly, if an armed group located in State A were to use a nuclear device like a dirty bomb to create an explosion causing extensive destruction and damage and substantial numbers of casualties in State B, the effects would likely be sufficiently grave to meet the criteria for determining an armed attack. The important issue would then be the fact that it was an armed group based on the territory of State A that undertook the attack without the involvement of State A. The authorities of State A must be given a suitable opportunity to take required action to ensure that there is no repetition. If they are either unable or unwilling to do so, the controversy then arises. Some States, such as the United States, consider they have the legal right to use necessary and proportionate force in self-defence. Other States would dispute the legal right of State B to use force on the territory of State A in such circumstances.[32]

11 Further legal controversy attaches to the degree of organisation that is required for an armed group's violent activity to be characterisable as an armed attack. In the opinion of the present authors, the issue rather solves itself in the context of nuclear operations. For any kind of successful nuclear attack to be feasible, a very high level of group organisation is likely to be essential. Likewise, the capacity to mount an attack on a State's nuclear weapon facility will depend on operational co-ordination that, again, presupposes a very high level of organisation within the attacking group. In the less likely event that the attack is masterminded and executed by an individual acting alone, the authors believe that, in practice, a law enforcement response will be preferred in most circumstances.

12 The question that then arises is which violent acts outside the territory of a State nevertheless amount to an armed attack against that State. Attacks that target government employees and personnel and non-commercial facilities while they are located outside the territory of their State are capable of being armed attacks. Where other operations are concerned, the Tallinn Manual identifies relevant considerations as including: 'the extent of damage caused by the operation; whether the property involved is governmental or private in character; the status of the individuals who have been targeted; and whether the operations were politically motivated'.[33]

32 See also paras. 13 and 14 below.

33 Tallinn Manual 2.0, Commentary accompanying Rule 71, para. 22.

13 The exercise of the right to use force in self-defence is subject to considerations of necessity and proportionality, as reflected in Rule 12; it can include action in the territory of the State from which the attack originated, in international waters and airspace and in outer space; and it can be undertaken by kinetic or cyber means. A self-defence operation involving activity in a State to which the armed attack cannot be attributed can be undertaken if that State consents. If the State in which the defensive action is to take place does not consent, it has been suggested that self-defence action is nevertheless lawful if the principle of necessity is complied with; if the action to be taken is the only effective means of defence against the armed attack; and, subject to the points made in paragraph 10 above, if the territorial State is unable or unwilling to take effective action to repress the activity constituting the armed attack.[34]

14 Even if the progressive view is accepted, the victim State is usually obliged to take specified steps before taking action. These required steps are driven by the continuing obligation to respect the sovereignty of the territorial State so far as possible. The victim State must therefore instruct the territorial State to stop the acts constituting the armed attack and must give it time in which to do so. By issuing such an instruction and by giving time for compliance, it reduces the risk of erroneous action in self-defence. However, circumstances may arise in which it is unrealistic to expect the victim State to delay acting after issuing such a demand. Consider a situation in which State A has reliable information that an armed group within State B is about to fire a rocket containing a dirty bomb at one of State A's major cities. Intercepted messages show that the weapon will be fired within a very short time, with devastating consequences if the bomb were to hit the intended target. In such a situation, the victim State can act in self-defence without having to issue a prior demand.

15 Article 51 of the UN Charter provides that the victim State of an armed attack enjoys the right of self-defence set forth in that Article until such time as the Security Council has taken necessary measures. This may not be reflective of customary international law, because, so far, the UNSC has never passed a binding resolution terminating the exercise of the right of individual or collective self-defence. In this context, it is also worthy of note that the reporting obligation set forth in the second sentence of Article 51 of the UN Charter is also not customary in nature.[35]

[34] Tallinn Manual 2.0, Commentary accompanying Rule 71, para. 25.

[35] ICJ Nicaragua Judgment, para. 235.

Necessity and Proportionality

Rule 12

Force used by way of self-defence must be limited to what is necessary and proportionate.

1 The requirement that a State acting in self-defence may only use necessary and proportionate force is a rule of customary law.[36]

2 The first part of the Rule requires that the force that is used in self-defence be what is required 'to successfully repel an imminent armed attack or defeat one that is under way'.[37] Other, non-forceful measures may also be taken at the same time, but the necessity element in the Rule is satisfied if non-forceful measures alone will not suffice to deal with the situation. In other words, if it appears unlikely that non-forceful measures will be enough to stop an armed attack and prevent further armed attacks, the use of force in self-defence will be lawful. The judgment as to whether forceful action in self-defence is necessary is a subjective assessment by the victim State based on information that is reasonably available to it. This excludes an *ex post facto* evaluation. Of course, the victim State must act reasonably when deciding whether forceful action is needed. The decision will regularly be reasonable if the situation fulfils the criteria of the Caroline formula, according to which the exercise of self-defence by a resort to armed force is necessary if the situation is 'instant, overwhelming, leaving no choice of means, and no time for deliberation'.

3 Consider the example given in paragraph 14 of the Commentary accompanying Rule 11. If, as is likely to be the case, State A has no non-forceful way of preventing the firing of the rocket by the armed group in State B, the use of force by State A to stop the armed attack will meet the requirement of necessity. State A can make that judgment only on the basis of the information at its disposal. If it reasonably concludes that forceful action is needed and that no satisfactory non-forceful alternative is available, the necessity requirement is satisfied.

4 If the use of force is necessary in self-defence, the extent, duration and degree of the force actually used must not exceed what is needed to stop the armed attack or prevent the imminent armed attack. The amount of force that is required to achieve this will depend on the circumstances, and the degree of

[36] ICJ Nicaragua Judgment, 176, 194; ICJ Nuclear Opinion, para. 41; ICJ Oil Platforms Judgment, paras. 43, 73–4, 76. It should be borne in mind that this Rule is a rule of *jus ad bellum*. The principle of military necessity and the rule of proportionality that apply to military operations and to attacks during an armed conflict are separate notions and form part of a separate body of law, *jus in bello*.

[37] Tallinn Manual 2.0, Commentary accompanying Rule 72, para. 2.

force that is being applied in the actual or imminent armed attack will not dictate the degree of force that can lawfully be employed in self-defence. Equally, the kind of force that is used in self-defence may well be different to that being, or to be, employed in the armed attack.

5 It will be for the victim State to decide what kind and degree of forceful action in self-defence is needed. This will necessarily be a subjective assessment and must be based on the information reasonably available to that State. If information that was not available to the victim State at the time when it made its decision would have shown that the use of force in self-defence was no longer necessary or that the degree of force that the victim State decided to use was no longer needed for that purpose, this will not render the decision to use force, or that much force, unlawful.

Imminence and Immediacy

Rule 13

A State may use force in self-defence if an armed attack occurs or is imminent. The forceful action must comply with the requirement of immediacy.

1 The right to use force in self-defence if 'an armed attack occurs' is directly referred to in the language of Article 51. An armed attack can be regarded for these purposes as occurring if the effects are already being experienced. In the case of a nuclear strike, the effects are being experienced when an explosion is occurring and/or when blast, fragmentation, heat, radiation or any combination thereof are causing injury and/or damage. A nuclear-armed attack is also occurring, for example, at the time when the munition carrying the nuclear device has been launched, fired or dropped towards the target.

2 The question that then arises in connection with nuclear operations is whether a State is required to wait until a weapon that is likely to have devastating effects on the target State has either exploded or has been fired before it is permitted to take any forceful action in self-defence. Article 51 of the UN Charter, by limiting itself to 'if an armed attack occurs', carefully avoids the issue. It must, however, be remembered that the right to use force in self-defence is inherent and that, independently of Article 51, the right is a rule of customary international law. Curiously, support for a right to use force in anticipatory self-defence against an imminent armed attack is, inter alia, to be found in the notion of necessity discussed in the Commentary accompanying Rule 12. If, once an armed attack is imminent, waiting until it commences would frustrate the ability to take effective action to prevent the infliction of a devastating blow, an interpretation of the self-defence right that permits

forceful action only once the attack is under way would be inconsistent with an inherent right of States to use force to defend themselves. The present authors consider, therefore, that States have the inherent right to use necessary and proportionate force in self-defence, not only if an armed attack is under way but also if an armed attack is imminent. Further support for the right to use force where the armed attack is imminent is to be found in the well-known correspondence between Lord Ashburton and Daniel Webster arising from the Caroline incident.

3 There is a line of thought that considers that forceful action in self-defence is lawful only if the armed attack has actually been initiated.[38] In the nuclear context this would seem to imply that, for example, only when the missile carrying a nuclear warhead has been launched does the prospective victim State have the right to act in self-defence. With the development of technologies such as hypersonic missiles, States are likely to be given very little practical time in which to respond, and basic notions of national security are, it is thought, likely to drive most States into rejecting such a restrictive interpretation.

4 Academic discussion has debated the precise extent of permissible anticipatory self-defence. It has, for example, been suggested that the armed attack must be about to be launched for action in self-defence to be justified. The essential context for this discussion is the core purpose of the United Nations: maintenance of international peace and security. An excessively liberal interpretation of when force may be used in self-defence puts that very peace and security at risk if a greater set of circumstances is seen as justification for violent anticipatory action, while a more restrictive interpretation is going to be seen by many States as prejudicial to their individual security. A compromise interpretation that has been proposed would permit a State to take forceful action in self-defence if 'the attacker is clearly committed to launching an armed attack and the victim State will lose its opportunity to effectively defend itself unless it acts'.[39] This interpretation places less emphasis on the time dimension, in that the 'last window of opportunity' for a State to take effective action may be just as an attack is about to be launched, but may also be a considerable time before the commencement of the actual attack. It is thought that States will identify with this interpretation because it takes into account the variable circumstances in which self-defence decision-making

38 Consider Tallinn Manual 2.0, Commentary accompanying Rule 73, para. 3, citing I. Brownlie, *International Law and the Use of Force by States* (Oxford University Press, 1963) 275–8.

39 Tallinn Manual 2.0, Commentary accompanying Rule 73, para. 4.

must take place. It also recognises what the notion of self-defence is truly about – namely, the right of the victim or prospective victim to take necessary action to defend itself against grave attack. Requiring a State to wait until it is too late is actually depriving the State of that right and is therefore inconsistent with the inherent right of all States. Self-evidently, the longer the time interval before the armed attack is expected to occur, the more likely it is that the present time is not in fact the last window of opportunity. In this regard, the word 'last' deserves emphasis. The mere fact that 'a' window of opportunity to take effective action has arisen is not sufficient to render violent anticipatory action lawful. It must be the last opportunity in the subjective, but reasonable, opinion of the victim State.

5 Consider, for example, a situation in which the political leadership of State A has been threatening State B with nuclear attack. State B knows that the nuclear warheads are in long-term storage at a facility located deep underground. State B detects that the nuclear warheads are being moved from the long-term storage facility to another underground storage bunker located on a military base from which nuclear-capable missiles are launched. State A has announced that it will target State B with a nuclear missile attack at a time of its own choosing. If State B, acting in good faith, believes that the last opportunity it will have to take effective action in self-defence is by attacking the missiles while they are in transit from long-term storage to the military base, it would be justified, according to the last window of opportunity approach, in using necessary and proportionate force in self-defence at that moment. State B cannot sensibly be required to know exactly when State A plans to launch its nuclear attack, but its action in self-defence will be lawful only if it can be shown that State A does indeed have a firm intention to launch such an attack, or at least that it is reasonable for State B to conclude from the reasonably available information that State A so intends.

6 An important distinction must be drawn between activity that really forms part of the armed attack and activity that is not necessarily contributing to the conduct of the attack as such. So, the whole of the sequence of actions that must, in the ordinary course of events, be completed as part of the process leading to the firing of the missile forms part of the actual conduct of the armed attack. Once that sequence is commenced, the armed attack is under way. The loading of target data into the missile guidance system may be a preparatory act, but if it is done as part of the pre-firing procedure that action arguably also becomes part of the actual conduct of the armed attack. Other activities whose purpose is to maintain the readiness of the missile for future use constitute preparation, not the conduct of an attack. However, actions that represent the last window of opportunity for the target State to take effective

action in anticipatory self- defence may take place during the preparatory phase. Ultimately the lawfulness of the victim state's action in self-defence will depend on whether it was reasonable for it to use force to protect itself in the particular circumstances, whether it was necessary for force to be used and whether the amount of force used was that required to deal effectively with the situation.

7 In the example discussed in paragraph 5 but varying the facts somewhat, imagine that State A has developed a nuclear weapon capability and has published doctrine in which it asserts its willingness to use such weapons in circumstances where it has been the subject of a prior devastating armed attack. Tensions arise between State A and State B. State B would not be entitled to use force in self-defence on the mere ground that State A possesses nuclear weapons. The doctrinal statements by State A would also not justify the use of force by State B in self-defence, because they do not reveal any intent on the part of State A to use force, nuclear or otherwise, specifically against State B. Aggressive statements directed by State A against State B, but without evidence that State A is actually preparing to undertake an armed attack, also will not justify the use of force by State B. If, however, State A's statements and/or the actions it is seen to take manifest a clear intent to undertake against State B an attack that will rise to the level of an armed attack, State B would be legally permitted, in self-defence, to use force that is necessary and proportionate (see Rule 12) when the last realistic window of opportunity effectively to do so presents itself.

8 If the use of force in self-defence cannot be justified, but an internationally wrongful act has been committed by State A, State B may consider the use of countermeasures (Rule 7). It may also consider referring the matter to the UN Security Council (see Rule 16).

9 The requirement of immediacy, reflected in the second sentence of the Rule, addresses the interval that can properly elapse between the armed attack and the taking of action in self-defence. Depending on the precise nature and effect of the armed attack, a victim State may require a certain period of time to be in a position to take appropriate action in self-defence. The identity of an attacker that has used a nuclear weapon will usually be clear. However, time may be needed in order to decide which target(s) it would be proper to attack in self-defence, to make the necessary military deployment arrangements to be in a position to do so and, perhaps, to achieve the political consensus in the victim State in favour of defensive military action.

10 If an excessive period is allowed to elapse after the armed attack has taken place, the lawfulness of the self-defence action may be doubtful. Consider a situation in which a nuclear-capable State, State A, uses a conventional weapon to undertake an armed attack against a neighbouring State,

State B. State B is undecided as to whether it should use force in self-defence. A consensus cannot be achieved in its legislature and discussions take place between the governing party and the opposition. Eventually, after a number of weeks have elapsed, a consensus is achieved in favour of a limited strike in response. Appropriate instructions are given to the armed forces and the strike in response is undertaken a week after the political approval was given. Where the lawfulness of State B's strike in response is concerned, much will depend on what has been going on during that period of delay. If there have been no further uses of force by State A and if there is no indication of an intention on the part of State A to undertake further attacks, the immediacy requirement will likely not be satisfied, such that the use of force in response by State B will have been unlawful. If, however, during the period of delay there have been continuing threats or ongoing activities by State A, in either case showing that a further attack can be anticipated, the use of force in response would likely be regarded as lawful. Inevitably, however, much will depend on the particular circumstances and on the reasonableness of State B's conclusion that further attacks are likely to follow.

Collective Self-Defence

Rule 14

If a request for assistance is made by a State that is the victim of an armed attack, another State may exercise the inherent right of collective self-defence; forceful action taken in collective self-defence must be in accordance with any limitations imposed by the victim State.

1 This Rule is based on the wording of Article 51 of the UN Charter and reflects customary law. A State that has suffered an armed attack may request self-defence assistance from another State. Equally, if several States have been victims of an armed attack, they may act collectively in self-defence. However, a request for assistance must have been made by the State that is the victim of an armed attack to the assisting State before the latter is permitted to come to its aid by using force.[40] Both or all States that are involved in a collective self-defence operation must satisfy themselves individually that the right to use force in collective self-defence has arisen.

2 Not only must the assisting State(s) use force in self-defence only if requested by the victim State to do so, but the force that it uses must accord with any limitations imposed by the victim State. The victim State may, for

[40] ICJ Nicaragua Judgment, para. 199.

example, stipulate that certain kinds of weapon are not to be used, that certain kinds of target are not to be made the object of attack or that targets located beyond certain longitudes or latitudes are not to be made the object of attack. Such limitations must apply in addition to, and without prejudice to, the rules of targeting set forth in the law of armed conflict.

3 The collective self-defence arrangement may be reflected in a formal agreement that provides for future contingencies. The obvious example of such an agreement is Article 5 of the North Atlantic Treaty, which stipulates, in relation to State parties, that 'an armed attack against one or more of them in Europe or North America shall be considered an attack against them all and consequently they agree that, if such an armed attack occurs, each of them, in exercise of the right of individual or collective self-defence recognised by Article 51 of the Charter of the United Nations, will assist the Party or Parties so attacked'.[41] Accordingly, Article 5 gives standing consent to the use of force by any member State of NATO in collective self-defence of another member State that is the victim of an armed attack. Such standing consent may equally be reflected in an agreement between two States or in some other form of inter-State arrangement. Finally, a request may form part of an ad hoc agreement. What matters is not so much the formalities associated with the document as the fact of an agreement between the victim and assisting State(s). The action taken by the assisting State(s) must then be in accordance with the limitations, if any, prescribed in the agreement.

4 Rules 12 and 13 on necessity, proportionality, imminence and immediacy apply to collective self-defence, just as they apply to action taken in self-defence by the victim State.

Reporting Self-Defence Action to the UN Security Council

Rule 15

Measures taken by a State in the exercise of the right of self-defence provided for in Article 51 of the UN Charter must be immediately reported to the UN Security Council and do not affect the authority and responsibility of the Security Council under the UN Charter to take at any time such action as it deems necessary in order to maintain or restore international peace and security.

1 This Rule closely follows the language of the second part of Article 51 of the UN Charter. Although the Rule is not reflective of customary law,[42] the

[41] North Atlantic Treaty, 4 April 1949, 34 UNTS 243, Article 5.

[42] ICJ Nicaragua Judgment, para. 235.

obligation is binding on all States as a matter of treaty law, as all States are members of the United Nations.

2 The reporting obligation arises once self-defence measures are taken. There is no obligation to inform the Security Council in advance of the taking of self-defence action, but once self-defence action has been taken the Security Council must be informed straight away.

3 If a State were to employ forceful action in self-defence but then failed to report in accordance with the Rule, that would constitute a breach of Article 51 but would not render the action taken in self-defence unlawful, nor would the failure to submit the report deprive the victim State of the right to continue, in self-defence, with necessary and proportionate action that satisfies the imminence and immediacy requirements of Rules 12 and 13.

4 The facts that a State is acting in lawful self-defence and that a report under the present Rule has been sent to the Security Council does not affect the responsibility and authority of the Security Council to take the steps that it considers to be necessary in accordance with Chapter VII of the UN Charter (on which, see Rules 16 and 17).

UN Security Council Action

Rule 16

If the United Nations Security Council determines that action employing or in relation to nuclear weapons constitutes a threat to the peace, a breach of the peace or an act of aggression, it may decide what measures not involving the use of armed force are to be employed.

1 Article 39 of the UN Charter gives the Security Council the responsibility to decide if there has been a threat to the peace, a breach of the peace or an act of aggression.[43] Once the Security Council has decided that one of the three situations listed in Article 39 has arisen, Article 41 of the UN Charter provides that it 'may decide what measures not involving the use of armed force are to be employed to give effect to its decisions, and it may call upon the Members of the United Nations to apply such measures. These may include complete or partial interruption of economic relations and of rail, sea, air, postal, telegraphic, radio, and other means of communication, and the severance of diplomatic relations.'

43 The text of Article 39 is: 'The Security Council shall determine the existence of any threat to the peace, breach of the peace, or act of aggression and shall make recommendations, or decide what measures shall be taken in accordance with Articles 41 and 42, to maintain or restore international peace and security.'

2 Of considerable relevance to the topic of this book, the Security Council has identified the proliferation of weapons of mass destruction as a threat to the peace.[44] Equally, it may characterise a particular event or situation as a threat to the peace, a breach of the peace or an act of aggression. Consider a situation in which one State threatens another with nuclear attack or in which a State, confronted with a nuclear-armed State, threatens to take forceful action against its competitor's nuclear weapons facilities. Article 39 permits the Security Council, after considering the circumstances, to decide whether the situation comes within the Article and, if it does, to assess whether non-forceful action under Article 41 would be a suitable way of dealing with the matter. Moreover, the Security Council has the power to decide that certain generic kinds of nuclear weapon-related activity also come within Article 39. However, depending on the exact terms of such a proposed measure, it is perhaps likely that at least one of the five permanent members of the Security Council would veto such a decision.

3 The list of non-forceful measures given in Article 41 is non-exhaustive. Other categories of non-forceful action might be decided upon by the Security Council. The chosen measures will be those that, in the opinion of the Security Council, are most suitable for dealing effectively with the circumstances that gave rise to the Article 39 determination.

4 The decisions that the Security Council takes under Chapter VII must be implemented by all States,[45] but individual States have a discretion over how to go about implementing the Security Council's decision. Much will inevitably depend on the circumstances. Some measures may require the passing of legislation or the issuing of internal, national instructions or regulations. Other steps may necessitate the taking of practical action to stop particular activities referred to in the Security Council decision.

Forceful Action by the UN Security Council

Rule 17

If the Security Council has determined the existence of a threat to the peace, a breach of the peace or an act of aggression and if it considers that measures not involving the use of armed force would be inadequate or have proved to be inadequate, it may take such forceful action as is necessary to maintain or restore international peace and security.

1 This Rule is based on Article 42 of the UN Charter, which provides: 'Should the Security Council consider that measures provided for in Article 41 would

44 UNSC Resolution 1540 (2004), 28 April 2004.

45 UN Charter, Article 25.

be inadequate or have proved to be inadequate, it may take such action by air, sea, or land forces as may be necessary to maintain or restore international peace and security. Such action may include demonstrations, blockade, and other operations by air, sea, or land forces of Members of the United Nations.'

2 The required sequence of events is that, first, the Security Council must determine the existence of a threat to the peace, a breach of the peace or an act of aggression. If it does this, it must then decide whether non-forceful measures would be inadequate, or have proved to be inadequate, to deal with the relevant situation. This does not oblige the Security Council to necessarily try non-forceful measures. It is entitled to consider the situation it is dealing with and to conclude that non-forceful measures will not be an effective way of maintaining or restoring international peace and security. If it reaches that conclusion, the Security Council may authorise the use of force.

3 Consider a situation in which a State has declared that it has placed its nuclear weapon forces on a heightened level of readiness and has issued threatening, bellicose statements directed at a neighbouring State with which it has a dispute over the sovereignty of certain islands. The Security Council is likely to conclude that, when considered in the context of the bellicose statements, placing the nuclear weapon forces on heightened readiness constitutes a threat to the peace. Which measures are most likely to have the practical effect of maintaining international peace when a nuclear power is speaking and/or acting aggressively will be a matter for very careful deliberation. It is entirely possible that non-forceful measures will be preferred, for fear that any use of force will risk igniting a most dangerous set of circumstances. Equally, and depending on the facts, force may be the only option, although it is likely that the scope of the force that is being authorised will be carefully circumscribed.

4 When issuing a resolution under Article 42 of the Charter, the Security Council often authorises the taking of 'all necessary measures' to achieve the purposes stated in the resolution.[46] The language of the resolution will specify the purpose that 'all necessary measures' must be designed to achieve, but the term is generally understood as permitting the use of armed force in order to bring about the desired outcome. In the opinion of the present authors, a Security Council resolution containing this phrase will not be regarded by States as a sufficient authority for the use of a nuclear weapon by the armed forces implementing the resolution.[47] It is, however, imaginable that an armed

46 UNSC Resolution 1973 (2011), 17 March 2011.

47 This is on the assumption that the UNSC resolution does not contain a specific authorisation to use a nuclear weapon. Inclusion by the Security Council of a specific authorisation of that kind would seem to be most unlikely.

conflict that commences when force is used to implement such a resolution might subsequently give rise to a situation in which the use of a nuclear weapon is considered. In such a circumstance, the lawfulness of a threat or use of a nuclear weapon will be determined taking into account the factors discussed in Section J (discussion of ICJ Nuclear Opinion) and Section E (*jus in bello*).

5 Article 103 of the UN Charter provides: 'In the event of a conflict between the obligations of the Members of the United Nations under the present Charter and their obligations under any other international agreement, their obligations under the present Charter shall prevail.' This Article makes it clear that the Security Council is not required to take States' obligations under other legal arrangements into account when deciding on action under Article 42. However, States may disregard their obligations under other international agreements only if they actually conflict with their UN Charter obligations, and they may do so only for as long as such a conflict persists. The ability of the Security Council to ignore other international obligations of States is limited, however. For example, it may not deviate from *jus cogens* rules.[48]

Regional Organisations

Rule 18

If the United Nations Security Council mandates or authorises such action, international organisations, arrangements or agencies of a regional nature may conduct enforcement action in respect of nuclear weapons.

1 Article 53(1) of the UN Charter specifies that '[t]he Security Council shall, where appropriate, utilize … regional arrangements or agencies for enforcement action under its authority. But no enforcement action shall be taken under regional arrangements or by regional agencies without the authorization of the Security Council … .' The language of the Charter seems to encourage the Security Council to use regional arrangements or agencies for enforcement purposes, but suggests that prior authorisation of the Security Council is required before any enforcement action, whether under Rule 16 (Article 41) or Rule 17 (Article 42), can be taken by a regional arrangement or agency.

2 Little turns on the exact meaning of 'regional arrangements or agencies'. Under Article 48 of the Charter, 'action required to carry out the decisions of the Security Council for the maintenance of international peace and security

[48] Tallinn Manual 2.0, Commentary accompanying Rule 76, para. 9.

shall be taken by all the Members of the United Nations or by some of them, as the Security Council may determine.'[49] Article 48 continues: 'Such decisions shall be carried out by the Members of the United Nations directly and through their action in the appropriate international agencies of which they are members.'[50] It is therefore clear that the Security Council may authorise enforcement action by any group of States, whether previously formed into a formal arrangement or simply brought together by the circumstances that give rise to the enforcement action. In particular, and notwithstanding the reference to 'regional arrangements or agencies' in Chapter VIII of the Charter, there is no requirement for such a group to be linked with a geographical region.

3 'Enforcement action' in the present Rule means action under Article 41 or Article 42 of the UN Charter (see Rules 16 and 17 respectively). The word 'mandates' refers to a situation in which the Security Council has specifically mandated a regional arrangement or agency to undertake enforcement action. The word 'authorises' refers to a situation in which a regional arrangement or agency, or indeed individual States, perhaps acting as a coalition, take action under a more general authorisation issued by the Security Council.

49 UN Charter, Article 48(1).
50 Ibid., Article 48(2).

D

International and Non-International Armed Conflicts

International Armed Conflicts

Rule 19

An international armed conflict exists when hostilities, which may consist of or include nuclear hostilities, take place between two or more States.

1 Article 2 common to the four 1949 Geneva Conventions applies those Conventions to 'all cases of declared war or of any other armed conflict which may arise between two or more of the High Contracting Parties, even if the state of war is not recognized by one of them'. There must therefore be a State-versus-State situation for an international armed conflict to exist.

2 While there is no specific definition of armed conflict, it is clear that hostilities, comprising the collective application of means and methods of warfare, are required. The API Commentary expresses the view that '[a]ny difference arising between two States and leading to the intervention of armed forces is an armed conflict … '. The Commentary goes on to opine that 'it makes no difference how long the conflict lasts or how much slaughter takes place'.[1] This suggests that the threshold of violence that suffices for an international armed conflict to exist is fairly low, which is rather supported by the oft-quoted and authoritative statement by the ICTY Appeals Chamber in the *Tadić* case when ruling on the interlocutory appeal on jurisdiction: 'an armed conflict exists whenever there is a resort to armed force between States … '.[2]

3 According to the ICRC, however, '[i]t is important … to rule out the possibility of including in the scope of application of humanitarian law situations that are the result of a mistake or of individual *ultra vires* acts,

[1] API Commentary, para. 236.

[2] *Prosecutor* v. *Tadić*, International Criminal Tribunal for the Former Yugoslavia Case IT-94–1-A, Decision of 2 October 1995 on the Defence Motion for Interlocutory Appeal on Jurisdiction (Tadić Decision on Interlocutory Appeal on Jurisdiction), para. 70.

which – even if they might entail the international responsibility of the State to which the individual who committed the acts belongs – are not endorsed by the State concerned. Such acts would not amount to armed conflict.'[3] The present authors do not share that view. Firstly, wars or international armed conflicts of the past were possibly initiated by either a mistake or by ultra vires acts. Secondly, absence of State endorsement cannot be a criterion offering an operable basis on which to make such a distinction if the act in question was clearly committed by a State organ, such as the regular armed forces. Whose endorsement would be relevant? Thirdly, there would be an inherent contradiction in establishing a State's international responsibility for ultra vires acts by its organs while rejecting such acts for the purposes of conflict classification. In this context it must be remembered that a nuclear attack by a strategic submarine might be launched even though the political leadership has officially stated that it will refrain from the use of (nuclear) force.

4 A state of international armed conflict can exist irrespective of the view taken by an involved State. It is the factual circumstances that will determine whether the situation amounts to an international armed conflict and, thus, whether the rights and obligations set forth in the law of armed conflict will apply. That body of law will apply as soon as there has been a resort to armed force on a State-on-State basis. It therefore applies to the first use of force, whether this takes the form of an armed attack or a first use of force that has been authorised by the UN Security Council acting under Chapter VII. In this regard it must be borne in mind that *jus ad bellum* and *jus in bello* are distinct bodies of law. However, circumstances might arise in which a single act breaches both bodies of law. Consider, for example, a situation in which a State mounts an armed attack against its neighbour; the armed attack targets a civilian apartment block in the neighbouring State's territory and the apartment block is used exclusively for civilian purposes. That act will constitute both a breach of Article 2(4) of the UN Charter and an unlawful targeting of a civilian object.

5 A State-on-State situation will include circumstances in which an organised armed group that is subject to the 'overall control' of a State is involved in hostilities against another State.[4] While the control being exercised must go beyond 'the mere provision of financial assistance or military equipment or

3 ICRC Commentary on GCI (2016), para. 241.

4 Tadić Appeals Chamber Judgment, paras. 131, 145, 162. Consider also ICJ Genocide Judgment, para. 404; *Prosecutor* v. *Lubanga*, International Criminal Court, Case ICC-01/04-01/06, Trial Chamber I Judgment of 14 March 2012, para. 541.

training', the controlling authorities do not have to plan all the operations of the dependent units, choose their targets or give specific instructions as to the conduct of military operations. The required control exists when the relevant State '*has a role in organising, coordinating or planning the military actions* of the military group, in addition to financing, training and equipping or providing operational support to that group'.[5] Mere support by the State of a group that is engaged in a non-international armed conflict is insufficient to internationalise the armed conflict,[6] but it may constitute unlawful intervention in the internal affairs of the State where the non-international armed conflict is taking place.

5 Accordingly, if an organised armed group that is under the overall control of State A undertakes a series of cross-border attacks against commercial premises that are used for manufacturing key components of State B's inter-continental ballistic missile system, the resulting armed conflict will be international in nature because of the overall control being exercised by State A. It is not necessary for these purposes for State A to have specifically instructed the group to attack the particular target. The required degree of control will be present if State A gives general direction as to the kind of military campaign to be undertaken.[7]

6 Where the relevant actor is not an organised armed group but instead consists of individuals or loosely associated groups, the actions of the individuals or of the loosely associated group can be attributed to a State only if they are undertaken pursuant to specific instructions from, or under the effective control of, the State or the State subsequently acknowledges and adopts the action taken as its own.[8] So if, in the example given in the previous paragraph, the operation were to be undertaken by a group of individuals that is insufficiently organised to constitute an organised armed group, their actions could not be attributed to State A and would not render the conflict international in character.

7 While armed forces involvement is not essential to the characterisation of a situation as an international armed conflict, in the nuclear context relevant activities will often involve armed forces personnel and equipment. It should also be borne in mind that an armed conflict will exist if one State declares war against another State, irrespective of whether hostilities have yet taken place. Moreover, the law of international armed

5 Tadić, Appeals Chamber Judgment, para. 137 (emphasis in original).
6 Tadić, Appeals Chamber Judgment, para. 137.
7 Tallinn Manual 2.0, Commentary accompanying Rule 82, para. 4.
8 Consider Tadić Appeals Chamber Judgment, paras. 132, 137, 141, 145; ICJ Tehran Hostages Judgment, para. 74.

conflict will apply if a State or States are in belligerent occupation of another State's territory.[9]

Non-International Armed Conflicts

Rule 20

A non-international armed conflict occurs when protracted violence takes place in the territory of a State between its armed forces and organised armed groups or between such groups.

1 Article 3 common to the four Geneva Conventions of 1949 refers to 'the case of armed conflict not of an international character occurring in the territory of one of the High Contracting Parties' and provides for some basic protection that reflects customary law.[10] So the law of non-international armed conflict applies where governmental armed forces are fighting against non-governmental organised armed groups or where such organised armed groups are fighting among themselves, in both cases in the territory of a State. The hostilities must attain a minimum level of intensity and the parties to the conflict must be sufficiently organised.

2 In the opinion of the present authors, Article 3's wording 'in the territory of one of the High Contracting Parties' is effectively referring to *any* State. The mere fact that, for example, nuclear operations are conducted by an organised armed group from outside the borders of the State in question does not cause the armed conflict to be international in nature.[11] It is the non-international nature of the conflict that is the important factor, and the law of non-international armed conflict will apply to all action between the parties to the conflict that relates thereto, irrespective of whether that action occurs inside or outside the territory of the State in question.[12]

3 Certain circumstances do not meet the intensity requirement that has to be satisfied for a non-international armed conflict to exist. Thus, 'situations of internal disturbances and tensions, such as riots, isolated and sporadic acts of violence, and other acts of a similar nature' do not meet the intensity

[9] If a naval or aerial blockade is established, this is likely to bring about an international armed conflict; see ICRC Commentary on Geneva Convention I (2016), para. 223.

[10] The same threshold is referred to in the Rome Statute, Article 8(2)(c). Note also UK Manual, para. 3.3; US DoD Law of War Manual, para. 17.1.1; AMW Manual, Commentary accompanying Rule 1(f); NIAC Manual, para. 1.1.1.

[11] AMW Manual, Commentary accompanying Rule 2(a).

[12] Tallinn Manual 2.0, Commentary accompanying Rule 83, para. 4.

requirement and are not non-international armed conflicts (NIACs).[13] It was the *Tadić* judgment that drew attention to the requirement of protracted armed violence between organised armed groups within a State.[14] There are therefore two essential elements that must pertain for a state of non-international armed conflict to exist: hostilities of sufficient intensity and the participation of an organised armed group.

4 In determining whether the intensity requirement is satisfied, the jurisprudence of the International Criminal Tribunal for the Former Yugoslavia suggests that the relevant factors will include the gravity and frequency of attacks, the time span and territorial extent of the hostilities, the degree to which the respective parties control territory, the mobilisation of volunteers, the distribution of weapons among the parties to the conflict and the extent to which the hostilities give rise to displacement of members of the population.

5 An armed group is organised if there is an established command structure and if it is able to conduct sustained military operations.[15] While the degree of organisation usually seen in a conventional unit of the armed forces is not required and while the organisation requirement is not precisely defined in international law, the general view seems to be that loosely associated groups of individuals that lack any form of leadership or command structure will generally not satisfy the 'organisation' criterion.

6 Ultimately, it will be a question of fact whether the intensity of the hostilities is sufficient and whether the armed group is sufficiently organised. Those issues will be determined by an objective assessment of the relevant information, irrespective of the interpretations of the parties involved.[16]

7 APII applies to armed conflicts not covered by Article 1 of API 'which take place in the territory of a High Contracting Party between its armed forces and dissident armed forces or other organized armed groups which, under responsible command, exercise such control over a part of its territory as to

[13] APII, Article 1(2). See also Rome Statute, Article 8(2)(f); UK Manual, para. 15.2.1; US DoD Law of War Manual, para. 17.1.1; Canadian Manual, para. 1709; AMW Manual, Commentary accompanying Rule 2(a).

[14] Tadić Decision on Interlocutory Appeal on Jurisdiction, para. 70.

[15] *Prosecutor* v. *Limaj et al.*, International Criminal Tribunal for the Former Yugoslavia, Case IT-03-66, Judgment of 30 November 2005, para. 129.

[16] *Prosecutor* v. *Akayesu*, International Criminal Tribunal for Rwanda, Case ICTR-96-4-T, Judgment of 2 September 1988, para. 603; ICRC Commentary on Geneva Convention I (2016), paras. 861–9.

enable them to carry out sustained and concerted military operations and to implement this Protocol'.[17] So, while Article 3 and the customary law of non-international armed conflict apply to all NIACs, APII applies only to the particular kind of NIAC defined in Article 1(1) of the treaty, and the treaty will apply only if the State in question is a party thereto.

17 APII, Article 1(1).

E

The Conduct of Nuclear Hostilities

Persons Who Participate

Rule 21

The law of armed conflict does not prohibit any category of person from participating in hostilities, including nuclear hostilities. The legal consequences of such participation will depend on the nature of the armed conflict and on the status of the individual concerned.

1 The customary law of armed conflict (LOAC) does not prohibit any class of individuals from taking a direct part in hostilities in an international or non-international armed conflict. While Article 43(2) of API classifies members of the armed forces of a party to an international armed conflict, other than medical and religious personnel, as combatants and provides that combatants have the right to participate directly in the hostilities, there is no inference that persons who are not combatants are prohibited from taking part.[1]

2 Combatants, however, are immune from prosecution for their acts of war that comply with LOAC. Combatant status does not apply to non-international armed conflicts. Combatants, and certain other classes of individual, are entitled to prisoner-of-war status if captured by the enemy during an international armed conflict. Moreover, combatants are liable to be made the object of attack throughout the entire duration of an armed conflict, while persons other than combatants who take a direct part in hostilities are liable to be made the object of attack only during periods of such direct participation. Where relevant, these matters will be discussed further in connection with the following Rules in this Section.

[1] Moreover, a person who does not satisfy the requirements for combatant status but who nevertheless takes a direct part in hostilities does not, without more, commit a war crime.

Combatants

Rule 22

During an international armed conflict, members of the armed forces of a party to the conflict other than medical and religious personnel are combatants; that is to say, they have the right to take a direct part in the hostilities, including in nuclear operations.

1 For States that are not parties to API, customary law entitlement to combatant status is specified in Article 1 of the Hague Regulations.[2] Article 4A(1) and (2) of Geneva Convention III applies similar standards when determining entitlement to prisoner-of-war status for combatants. Combatancy and prisoner-of-war status apply only during international armed conflicts. There is no corresponding status during non-international armed conflicts.

2 Combatants who have taken part in hostilities, including nuclear operations, are entitled to prisoner-of-war status from the moment they fall into the hands of an adverse party to the conflict.[3] Their entitlement to combatant immunity[4] means that they may not be prosecuted for their hostile activities that comply with LOAC. Accordingly, if a combatant participates in the use of a nuclear weapon, he or she will be liable to prosecution before an international or domestic court only if the use of the nuclear weapon constituted a war crime, a crime against humanity or genocide.

3 For States that are not parties to API, members of the armed forces of a State that is a party to an armed conflict, including members of militias and volunteer corps that are part of such armed forces, are combatants. In addition, members of other militias or other volunteer corps and members of organised resistance movements that belong to a party to the

[2] Article 1 states:

> The laws, rights, and duties of war apply not only to armies, but also to militia and volunteer corps fulfilling the following conditions:
>
> 1. To be commanded by a person responsible for his subordinates;
> 2. To have a fixed distinctive emblem recognizable at a distance;
> 3. To carry arms openly; and
> 4. To conduct their operations in accordance with the laws and customs of war.
>
> In countries where militia or volunteer corps constitute the army, or form part of it, they are included under the denomination "army".

[3] GCIII, Article 4A.

[4] Combatant immunity derives from customary law and thus applies to all States; see API, Article 43(2).

international armed conflict also have combatant status if they fulfil four conditions, namely:

they must be commanded by a person responsible for his or her subordinates;
they must wear a fixed distinctive sign or uniform recognisable at a distance;
they must carry their arms openly; and
they must conduct their operations in accordance with LOAC.[5]

The members of irregular forces that meet these conditions qualify as combatants, enjoy combatant immunity, have the right to participate in lawful nuclear operations during an international armed conflict and have the right to prisoner-of-war status if they are captured during such a conflict. Members of armed forces of States that are party to an international armed conflict are assumed to meet the four stated criteria and thus to have combatant status. Members of such forces that are assimilated to the armed forces have combatant status at customary law only if the armed group meets the four criteria.

4 Members of armed groups assimilated to the armed forces of a party to an international armed conflict satisfy the requirement of 'belonging to' a party to the conflict if a 'de facto' relationship exists between the organised group and the party to the conflict. No overt or public declaration of the relationship is necessary. It suffices if a tacit agreement or conduct makes it clear for which party the members of the group are fighting.[6] Consider a situation in which a State uses the services of a group of private persons to undertake particular tasks connected with the use of nuclear weapons, for example, because members of the group have skills that are required in connection with the employment of the nuclear weapons. By virtue of a State's use of those services, the group is regarded as belonging to the State, so the members of the group will have combatant status if the group fulfils the other requirements set out earlier. Hence, 'belonging to a Party to the conflict' is an essential requirement; if it is not met, the group cannot have combatant status.

5 There is an essential link between the group being commanded by a person responsible for his or her subordinates and the 'organised' character of the group. This is normally not an issue in relation to either State armed forces or firmly established armed groups. The 'fixed distinctive sign' requirement is normally met by the wearing of a uniform. While Article 44(3) API

5 Hague Regulations, Article 1.

6 ICRC, *Interpretive Guidance on the Notion of Direct Participation in Hostilities under International Humanitarian Law*, ed. N. Melzer (May 2009) (ICRC Interpretive Guidance), 23.

provides an exception to the rule for the 174 States that are parties to that treaty, that exception does not reflect customary law and therefore does not bind States that are not parties. However, it can be argued that in situations where combatants are located within a military object that in turn is required to bear military and nationality markings, such as a military aircraft or warship, there is no specific requirement for personnel on board to wear uniform or a fixed distinctive sign.[7]

6 The 'carrying arms openly' aspect refers to the obligation to carry personal weapons openly and does not relate to the carriage of nuclear weapons. The obligation of compliance with LOAC applies to the group as a whole. The fact that individual members of the group occasionally fail to comply does not deprive the group as a whole of combatant status, provided that the group as a whole generally complies. Those individuals who fail to comply will be liable to trial for any war crimes they have committed.

7 Paramilitary and law enforcement agencies may be incorporated by a State into its armed forces.[8] Other parties to the international armed conflict must be notified if this is done, but if the incorporating State fails to notify other States, that does not mean that the members of the relevant agencies remain civilians.[9] Once incorporation has taken place, the members of the relevant agencies have the right to take a direct part in hostilities, while retaining the right to perform their normal paramilitary or law enforcement duties, but are liable to be made the object of enemy attack so long as the armed conflict continues.[10] If there is no such incorporation, the members of the agency have no right to participate in the hostilities.

8 Members of armed groups that do not fulfil the requirements set forth in the preceding paragraphs of this Commentary do not qualify for combatant status under customary law. If they nevertheless take a direct part in the hostilities, they will have no combatant immunity; they will be liable to be prosecuted for all their hostile acts, including those which comply with LOAC; and, if captured, they will have no right to prisoner of war status. If, however, such persons come within Article 4A(4) or (5) of Geneva Convention III, they will retain prisoner-of -war status, but will be liable to be tried for the offences they have committed.

9 The notion of combatancy does not apply in non-international armed conflicts. In most circumstances, applicable domestic law and international

7 Consider AMW Manual, Commentary accompanying Rule 117. The danger in not wearing uniform is that if such persons become separated from the aircraft or ship and are thereafter captured, they are at risk of being treated as spies.

8 API, Article 43(3).

9 AMW Manual, Commentary accompanying Rule 10.

10 Unless they are rendered *hors de combat*, on which see Commentary to Rule 27 below.

human rights law will apply and the former will determine whether prosecution is legally possible and appropriate.

10 For States that are parties to API, Article 43(1) defines the armed forces of a party to an international armed conflict as consisting of 'all organized armed forces, groups and units which are under a command responsible to that Party for the conduct of its subordinates, even if that Party is represented by a government or an authority not recognized by an adverse Party'. It adds that '[s]uch armed forces shall be subject to an internal disciplinary system which, *inter alia*, shall enforce compliance with' LOAC. Article 43(2) then designates such members of the armed forces, other than medical personnel and chaplains, as combatants, with the consequence that 'they have the right to participate directly in hostilities'. Incorporation of paramilitary or law enforcement agencies into the armed forces is then provided for in Article 43(3).

11 Article 44(1) stipulates that any combatant who falls into the power of the enemy 'shall be a prisoner of war' and, in order to promote civilian protection, Article 44(3) sets forth the obligation of combatants to distinguish themselves from the civilian population while engaged in an attack or in a military operation preparatory to an attack.[11] This will usually involve wearing uniform or a fixed, recognisable emblem and will also usually involve carrying their weapons openly. However, Article 44 makes special provision in respect of difficult situations of combat, which were originally intended to apply in certain guerrilla warfare situations. If, in the relevant situations, an armed combatant cannot distinguish him- or herself, combatant status is retained if the combatant carries arms openly 'a) during each military engagement, and b) during such time as he is visible to the adversary while he is engaged in a military deployment preceding the launching of an attack in which he is to participate'.[12] This circumstance is unlikely to arise in connection with the actual use of a nuclear weapon. However, consider a situation in which special forces personnel from State A have been instructed to attack the nuclear missile launching facility operated by State B during an ongoing armed conflict between the two States. State B has extensive security arrangements in place to protect the relevant facility. State A's special forces do not wear uniform or any identifying emblem at any time during the operation. Were they to do so, the base security personnel would shoot them on sight. While they are concealed in the thick forest surrounding the facility, their personal weapons remain concealed. However, as they break cover, they carry their

[11] API, Article 44(3), first sentence.

[12] API, Article 44(3), second sentence.

weapons openly as they approach and scale the perimeter fences and then approach the part of the facility that is the target of the operation. By carrying their arms openly from the point when they would be visible to the adversary and throughout the military engagement, they have distinguished themselves for the purposes of the rule in the second sentence of Article 44(3).

12 Medical and religious personnel are non-combatants.[13] They must be respected and protected,[14] and must not be made the object of attack unless, and for such time as, they are used to commit, outside their humanitarian function, acts that are harmful to the enemy.[15]

Naval and Air Warfare

Rule 23

In naval and aerial warfare, the exercise of belligerent rights, including nuclear operations, is limited to warships and military aircraft as defined in international law. This Rule does not apply in situations of non-international armed conflict extending to international airspace or to sea areas beyond the outer limit of the territorial sea.

1 During an international armed conflict, naval operations will regularly occur in sea areas beyond the outer limits of the territorial sea of the parties to the conflict (i.e. in high sea areas which continue to be used by the ships of other States). Therefore, and because of the prohibition of privateering in the 1856 Paris Declaration, the right to exercise belligerent rights is strictly limited to warships.[16]

2 'Warship' means 'a ship belonging to the armed forces of a State bearing the external marks distinguishing such ships of its nationality, under the command of an officer duly commissioned by the government of that State and whose name appears in the appropriate service list or its equivalent, and manned by a crew which is under regular military discipline'.[17] Warships include surface and subsurface platforms. Accordingly, a submarine that fulfils these criteria is entitled to launch lawful attacks, including lawful nuclear attacks. At the same time, warships are military objectives by nature.

13 API, Article 43(2).
14 GCI, Article 24; GCII, Article 36.
15 AMW Manual, Rule 74(a).
16 US DoD Law of War Manual, para. 13.3.3; German Manual, para. 1019; San Remo Manual, Explanation accompanying Rule 13, para. 13.21.
17 UNCLOS, Article 29; San Remo Manual, para. 13(g).

3 Ships not fulfilling the above criteria do not qualify as warships and are not entitled to exercise belligerent rights. Ships belonging to the armed forces of a State but under the control of a civilian master are auxiliary vessels and as such are prohibited to exercise belligerent rights.[18] The same holds true for any other vessels, such as police or merchant vessels. It is a matter of ongoing debate whether unmanned maritime systems/vehicles which naturally lack a crew under regular military discipline are to be considered, or assimilated to, warships if they belong to the armed forces of a State, are marked as such and are under the control of a duly commissioned officer. The present authors are of the view that the presence of a crew is not absolutely required and that, therefore, unmanned maritime systems/vehicles may qualify as warships and be used for all operations at sea, including nuclear operations. It may be added that a (nuclear) torpedo is a platform that is not usually recoverable, is not therefore a warship and is therefore classed as a means of warfare.

4 Air operations during an international armed conflict will usually occur in, or extend to, international airspace that continues to be used by the aircraft of other States. Accordingly, the same considerations regarding ships apply to aircraft. According to customary law, the exercise of belligerent rights, including the launch of a nuclear missile, is strictly limited to military aircraft.[19]

5 'Military aircraft' means 'any aircraft (i) operated by the armed forces of a State; (ii) bearing the external markings of that State; (iii) commanded by a member of the armed forces; and (iv) controlled, manned or preprogrammed by a crew subject to regular armed forces discipline'.[20] Accordingly, there is no requirement for the aircraft to have human operators on board, so unmanned aerial vehicles (UAVs) qualify as military aircraft if the elements of the definition are fulfilled, and they are therefore entitled to launch lawful attacks, including nuclear attacks. As in the case of warships, a distinction must be made between usually recoverable platforms, on the one hand, and means of warfare, such as (nuclear) missiles, on the other.

6 The limitation of the exercise of belligerent rights to warships and military aircraft, as defined, does not apply in situations of non-international armed conflict.[21]

18 US DOD Law of War Manual, para. 13.3.3; German Manual, para. 1020.

19 US DoD Law of War Manual, para. 14.3.3.1; German Manual, para. 1103; AMW Manual, para. 17.

20 AMW Manual, para. 1(x).

21 US DoD Law of War Manual, para. 13.3.3.1; AMW Manual, Commentary accompanying Rule 17, para. 7.

Mercenaries

Rule 24

A mercenary who is involved in nuclear operations does not enjoy combatant immunity and, in the event of capture by the adverse party in an international armed conflict, is not entitled to prisoner-of-war status.

1 For LOAC purposes, a mercenary is defined in Article 47 of API. At customary law mercenaries are not entitled to combatant privileges,[22] but combatancy does not apply to non-international armed conflicts.

2 Article 47(2) of API defines a mercenary as a person who fulfils six cumulative conditions, namely:

(a) is specially recruited at home or abroad in order to fight in an armed conflict;
(b) does, in fact, take a direct part in the hostilities;
(c) is motivated to take part in the hostilities essentially by the desire for private gain and, in fact, is promised, by or on behalf of a Party to the conflict, material compensation substantially in excess of that promised or paid to combatants of similar ranks and functions in the armed forces of that Party;
(d) is neither a national of a Party to the conflict nor a resident of territory controlled by a Party to the conflict;
(e) is not a member of the armed forces of a Party to the conflict; and
(f) has not been sent by a State which is not a party to the conflict on official duty as a member of its armed forces.

3 If any one of the stated criteria does not apply, the individual is not a mercenary. However, if a person is, for example, recruited by a party to an armed conflict to discharge a particular technical role that is directly related to the use of a nuclear weapon and if that person, say, is paid significantly more than members of the party's own armed forces who are similarly employed, the individual in question is at risk of mercenary classification if the remaining conditions listed above are met. Compare this with the situation where there is no similarly employed member of the State's own armed forces, for example, because the State's own armed forces lack personnel with the relevant skills and/or experience. In such circumstances, the mere facts that the individual is motivated by gain, has been specially recruited in connection with an armed conflict and fulfils the other listed criteria do not cause the individual to be

[22] UK Manual, paras. 4.10–4.10.4; Canadian Manual, para. 319; German Manual, para. 303; ICRC Customary Law Study, Rule 108. See, however, US DoD Manual, para. 4.21, according to which a mercenary cannot be denied combatant status in all circumstances.

classed as a mercenary, because there is no person with a similar function in the State's own armed forces.

Civilians

Rule 25

Civilians comprise all persons who are neither combatants nor non-combatants, or who are not members of a State or non-State organised armed group. Civilians are not prohibited from taking a direct part in nuclear operations that amount to hostilities but may be made the object of attack for such time as they do so.

1 Article 51 API defines 'civilians' in negative terms as meaning all persons who are neither combatants nor non-combatants (i.e. who are neither medical nor religious personnel).[23] The term 'combatants' includes members of a *levée en masse*.[24] As the notion of civilians spontaneously taking up arms to resist an invading force would appear to have little or no relevance to nuclear weapon operations, it is not discussed further here, other than to note that, when assessing the compliance of a planned attack with the proportionality rule (see Rule 38), the participants in any *levée en masse* that may be taking place in the target area will not count as civilians during such time as the *levée en masse* is in progress.

2 The definition of civilians set forth in paragraph 1 is consistent with the provisions of Geneva Conventions III and IV. It follows that when nuclear targeting decisions are made in connection with an international armed conflict, civilians consist of all persons who are not members of the armed forces or of groups assimilated to the armed forces and who are not members of a *levée en masse*.

3 The treaty law of non-international armed conflict does not provide a negative definition of 'civilian'. However, it follows from the constitutive elements of the concept of non-international armed conflict that members of governmental or non-State organised armed groups taking part in such conflicts must be distinguished from civilians. According to the ICRC, however, those members of a non-State organised armed group who are not performing a continuous combat function qualify as civilians.[25] The present authors are

23 See Commentary accompanying Rule 22 above.

24 A *levée en masse* refers to a situation in which '[t]he inhabitants of a territory which has not been occupied, … on the approach of the enemy, spontaneously take up arms to resist the invading troops without having had time to organize themselves in accordance with Article 1'. They are regarded as 'belligerents if they carry their arms openly and if they respect the laws and customs of war'. Hague Regulations, Article 2.

25 ICRC Interpretive Guidance, 27ff.

willing to agree with such a distinction, if it is limited to a non-State organised group that has political and military wings. Then, only the members of the military wing may be considered non-civilians, whereas those belonging to the political wing qualify as civilians. The criterion does not apply to the members of the military wing, however.

4 LOAC does not prohibit civilians from taking a direct part in nuclear hostilities connected with an international or non-international armed conflict. The legal consequences of such direct participation are that the civilians concerned lose their protection from being made the object of attack for the duration of their direct participation and, if captured, are liable to be prosecuted for whatever violent acts they may have committed or participated in. Such participation does not cause the relevant civilians to lose their civilian status, however.

5 The effect of the points made in paragraph 3 above is that if, say, a civilian is employed in deciding which location should be made the object of a nuclear attack, that civilian can be targeted during the period of that activity, and if that civilian were to be captured by the adverse party, he or she could be prosecuted and punished for his or her role in the nuclear operations.

6 For purposes of completeness, although the use of nuclear weapons in connection with a non-international armed conflict would seem highly unlikely, the absence of combatant status in such conflicts means that civilians are regarded as being all persons who are not fighters. Fighters consist of members of a State's armed forces, members of dissident armed forces and members of other organised armed groups.

7 Civilians other than those who are directly participating in hostilities must not be made the object of attack. Moreover, they are protected by the rules on indiscriminate attack, the proportionality rule and the rules on precautions in attack and precautions against the effects of attacks.

Doubt as to the Status of Persons

Rule 26

In case of doubt as to whether a person is a civilian, that person shall be considered to be a civilian.

1 This is a customary rule,[26] based on the second sentence of Article 50(1) API. It is binding on all States and applies in both international and non-international armed conflicts. However, in the opinion of the authors,

[26] Consider AMW Manual, Commentary accompanying Rule 12a; ICRC Customary Law Study, Commentary accompanying Rule 6; UK Manual, para. 5.3.1; Canadian Manual, para. 429.

the Rule 47 obligation on States in control of territory to take precautions against the effects of attacks is a factor that attackers are entitled to take into account when deciding whether there is in fact doubt such as to involve the application of the present Rule.

2 The degree of doubt that must arise for this Rule to apply is not clear. While the UK interpretation is that substantial doubt must still remain after assessing the information from all sources that is reasonably available at the relevant time,[27] reasonable doubt has been cited as the threshold in the context of a war crimes prosecution.[28] In the opinion of the present authors, the doubt must be such as would cause a reasonable decision-maker to call off the planned nuclear attack or attack on a nuclear facility. Relevant factors would seem to include the nature, location and military importance of the target; the overall military situation; the size and characteristics of the weapon to be used; the numbers of persons expected to be affected and the degree of doubt as to the status of those persons; and whether there is an alternative target upon which an attack would be likely to accomplish the desired military purpose.

3 The Rule applies when there is doubt as to whether the persons are combatants or civilians. It has no application to a situation where doubt exists as to whether civilians are taking a direct part in hostilities. In the latter case, there is no presumption at law. The decision-maker must consider all of the information that is reasonably available at the relevant time and must reach a decision that is reasonable in all the circumstances.

4 In a non-international armed conflict, if there is significant doubt as to whether a person is a fighter or a peaceable civilian who is protected from attack, application of the principle of distinction requires that he or she is presumed to be a protected civilian.

Persons Who May Be Made the Object of Nuclear Attack

Rule 27

Members of the armed forces, members of organised armed groups, civilians taking a direct part in hostilities and, during an international armed conflict, participants in a levée en masse *may be made the object of an attack, including a nuclear attack.*

1 This Rule is based on the customary practice of States. LOAC is generally expressed as prohibitions. The fact that treaty law contains no express

[27] Statements made by the United Kingdom on ratification of API on 28 January 1998, para. (h); UK Manual, para. 5.3.4.

[28] Galić Trial Chamber Judgment, para. 55.

permissions of the kind reflected in this Rule does not detract from the general practice of States, recognised as law, that certain categories of person, as listed in the Rule, may be made the object of attack during an armed conflict.[29] It is their status as members of the armed forces or organised armed groups that renders attacks on them lawful, whereas, in the case of civilians who directly participate in the hostilities, it is their conduct that has a like effect. However, the use of a nuclear weapon to undertake such an attack would raise the grave concerns to which reference is made in Section A. The terms in which the present Rule and Commentary are expressed should not be misinterpreted as detracting in any way from those concerns.

2 For the purposes of this Rule, 'members of the armed forces' comprise the persons referred to in paragraphs 3 and 10 of the Commentary to Rule 22. However, medical and religious personnel and persons who are recognised, or in the circumstances should be recognised, as being *hors de combat* must not be made the object of attack.[30]

> A person is *hors de combat* if:
>
> (a) he is in the power of an adverse party;
> (b) he clearly expresses an intention to surrender; or
> (c) he has been rendered unconscious or is otherwise incapacitated by wounds or sickness, and therefore is incapable of defending himself;
>
> provided that in any of these cases he abstains from any hostile act and does not attempt to escape.[31]

The authors consider that this definition now reflects customary law. Accordingly, it would be unlawful, for example, to make a large group of combatants who have fallen into the hands of an adverse party to the conflict the object of any attack, nuclear or conventional.

3 The members of organised armed groups referred to in the Rule are those with a combat function or who are members of the military wing of a non-State organised armed group. Persons who are members of such groups but whose functions do not involve combat – say, because they are exclusively concerned with diplomatic, administrative or social activities on behalf of the

29 The Tallinn Manual reaches a similar conclusion based on negative implication from other Rules. The present authors consider that while the inferences from the negatively expressed LOAC rules can properly be drawn, there is actually a positive permission to attack the listed categories of person based on customary law.

30 GCI, Articles 24, 25; API, Article 41; US DoD Law of War Manual, para. 5.10, UK Manual, para. 5.6; Canadian Manual, para. 309; German Manual, para. 601; AMW Manual, Rule 15 (b); NIAC Manual, paras. 2.3.2, 3.2; ICRC Customary Law Study, Rule 87.

31 API, Article 41(2).

group – should be accorded civilian status and are therefore protected from attack so long as they continue to have no combat function. If, therefore, an organised armed group comprises political as well as military elements, it is only the military elements that may be made the object of attack, including nuclear attack.

4 The situation of civilians who participate directly in hostilities is dealt with under Rule 28. In principle, civilian employees of contractors to the armed forces enjoy protection as civilians, unless and for such time as they directly participate in the hostilities. There is a controversy over whether a company that contracts with a party to the conflict to undertake particular kinds of military operation consequently qualifies as an organised armed group. The authors take the view that those members of the company that are involved in activities that amount to direct participation in hostilities may be made the object of attack throughout the period of such activity, and that facilities that are used for such purposes are likely to be military objectives in accordance with Rule 34. Whether a contractual relationship is sufficient in itself for a company to be regarded as an armed group belonging to a party to the conflict is legally uncertain and is likely to be of limited practical relevance in nuclear targeting. However, civilian persons – whether civil servants of the State or employees of a company – who are involved in the conduct of nuclear operations will be targetable by the adverse party on the basis of that participation for as long as the participation continues.

5 While it seems unlikely that a *levée en masse* would be the object of a nuclear attack, it should nevertheless be noted that participants in a *levée en masse* may be made the object of attack, as they have the status of combatants for the duration of the *levée*.

Protection of Civilians

Rule 28

Civilians are protected unless and for such time as they take a direct part in hostilities.

1 This Rule is based on Article 51(3) of API and on Article 13(3) of APII; it applies as a rule of customary law to international and non-international armed conflicts.[32] The Rule applies only to civilians. It does not apply to members of the armed forces or members of a *levée en masse*, nor to members

[32] US DoD Law of War Manual, para. 5.9; UK Manual, paras. 5.3.2, 5.8; Canadian Manual, paras. 318, 1720; German Manual, para. 517; AMW Manual, chapeau to Section F; NIAC Manual, paras. 1.1.3, 2.1.1.2; ICRC Customary Law Study, Rule 6.

of organised armed groups who have a combat function. Members of an armed group that does not qualify as an 'organised' armed group and members of an organised armed group that have no combat function (e.g. because they are exclusively employed on diplomatic and other non-military duties on behalf of the group) will both be classed as civilians.

2 The Rule refers to protection in general, because civilians who take a direct part in hostilities not only lose their protection from being made the object of attack but also cease to be considered as civilians when the discrimination principle and proportionality rules are being considered in respect of a planned attack. Moreover, precautions in attack are not required in respect of directly participating civilians.

3 There is controversy as to the exact meaning of 'direct part in hostilities'. API and APII give no guidance as to how the expression should be interpreted, and while the ICRC has published 'Interpretive Guidance' on the subject, that publication has been the subject of criticism by States and commentators. For present purposes, it suffices to say that, to qualify as direct participation in hostilities, the activity must have the intended or actual effect of adversely affecting the enemy's military activities or capabilities or of positively affecting the conduct of hostilities by a party to the conflict other than the enemy. So, in times of armed conflict, fulfilling a role that contributes directly to nuclear targeting and installing software designed to render a State's own nuclear command and control systems immune from cyber-attack will both amount to direct participation in hostilities. However, there must be a direct causal link between the civilian's activity and either the infliction of harm on the enemy or enhancing the ability of the civilian's own party to conduct hostilities. So, a civilian who has a merely peripheral role in nuclear weapon use (e.g. a role that is limited to servicing the command and control computers associated with a nuclear-armed missile system) is unlikely to be regarded as directly participating in the nuclear hostilities. By contrast, and again by way of examples, a civilian who prepares and loads targeting data for such a system, who controls the launch of such missiles or who commands such operations will be regarded as directly participating in such hostilities because of the direct causal link between the civilian's acts and the harm caused to the adverse party when the weapon impacts on the target. Finally, there must be a direct link between the civilian's action and the nuclear hostilities.[33] This will often be evident from the nature of the target that the nuclear weapon is intended to engage.

[33] Consider ICRC Interpretive Guidance, 41–58; AMW Manual, Commentary accompanying Rule 29.

4 Activities that are widely accepted as amounting to direct participation in nuclear operations include acts that make nuclear attacks possible, such as designing a nuclear weapon specifically to be used against a known, previously identified target. Obtaining and collating intelligence information on which to base nuclear targeting decisions will be direct participation, whereas mere maintenance of equipment associated with nuclear operations is unlikely to amount to direct participation. There are no precise demarcation lines in this part of the law. Each situation must be considered by reference to all of the relevant aspects of the activity, but, in general, States would be well advised to avoid employing civilians in roles that are directly associated with the conduct of nuclear attacks.

5 A civilian who takes a direct part in nuclear hostilities may be made the object of attack throughout the duration of such direct participation. If the civilian participates directly in only an isolated act – which is unlikely to be the case in relation to nuclear operations – he or she will be targetable while actually performing the act, preparing to perform it, travelling to the place where it is to be performed and returning from that place to his or her normal civilian location. If the civilian's activity involves a sequence of acts, the authors consider that the civilian will be regarded as directly participating for the entire time span of the sequence of acts. So, for example, a civilian who is responsible for inserting target data into a nuclear armed rocket system and who inserts such data on a regular basis over a period of several months will be targetable throughout that period of several months on a twenty-four-hours-a-day, seven-days-a-week basis. It should, however, be noted that some commentators take the view that the 'for such time as' language in the Rule means that a civilian loses and regains protected status, respectively, at the beginning and end of each specific act of direct participation, thus creating what has been described as a 'revolving door' of protection. Those commentators would argue that, in the previous example, the civilian who undertakes nuclear weapon activities during the daytime would lose protection when leaving home to travel to the nuclear weapon facility and would regain protected status each evening upon arriving home. The authors reject this 'revolving door' of protection notion as impractical and, therefore, as not reflecting the law.

6 If there is doubt as to whether a civilian is taking a direct part in hostilities, the obligation for the attacker is to consider all reasonably available information before making a decision on attack. He or she may decide in favour of making an attack only if a reasonable decision-maker, possessing that information, would so decide. If it is not reasonable to decide in favour of an attack in the relevant circumstances, the attack, whether nuclear or conventional, should not proceed.

Nuclear Targeting: Applying the Principle of Distinction

Definition of Nuclear Attack

Rule 29

A nuclear attack is a nuclear operation that constitutes an act of violence against the adverse party, whether in offence or defence.

1 This definition applies in both international and non-international armed conflicts and is based on Article 49(1) of API, which is considered to reflect customary law.

2 'Attack' is an important concept, as many rules of the law of targeting specifically apply to attacks. However, some rules of targeting law apply to the broader notion of military operations. Military operations, in this context, comprise military activities that do not involve the use of violence but that adversely affect the enemy. Non-violent operations that are also non-harmful, such as espionage or psychological operations, qualify neither as attacks nor as military operations.

3 'Acts of violence' are not limited to acts that release kinetic force.[34] Chemical, biological and radiological attacks tend to have no kinetic impact on their targets, yet it is generally accepted that the rules on attack apply to them.[35] A nuclear attack occurs if a nuclear weapon or other nuclear capability is used to cause injury or death to persons, or damage or destruction to objects. A nuclear attack also occurs if an act of violence, whether nuclear or conventional, has as its object a nuclear weapon or capability. The notion would therefore, for example, include a nuclear operation in which a nuclear explosion generates an electro-magnetic pulse in order to disable the enemy's command, control, communications and intelligence infrastructure. The principles and rules of the law of targeting will apply to any nuclear attack. Minimal damage or destruction will not be sufficient to characterise an event as an attack. However, death, injury, damage or destruction may be directly caused by the use of a nuclear capability or may be the indirect consequence of such use. Equally, death, injury, damage or destruction may be the consequence of an act of conventional violence directed at a nuclear weapon or capability. In either case, the death, injury, damage or destruction will cause the military operation to be classed as an attack, because the said effects are reasonably foreseeable.

34 Tallinn Manual 2.0, Commentary to Rule 92, para. 3.

35 Tallinn Manual 2.0, Commentary to Rule 92, para. 3; *Prosecutor* v. *Tadić*, International Criminal Tribunal for the Former Yugoslavia Case IT-94-1-A, Decision of 2 October 1995 on the Defence Motion for Interlocutory Appeal on Jurisdiction, paras. 120, 124.

4 To constitute an attack, the violence must be directed against the adverse party. This notion extends to uses of nuclear or conventional force that are directed against lawful targets and to acts of nuclear violence that have as their object of attack civilians, civilian objects or other protected persons or objects belonging to the adverse party to the conflict. It also extends to attacks which, for whatever reason, cause little or no damage or injury to the objects or persons that were the object of the attack, but which occasion incidental damage or injury to other objects or persons. Equally, it also applies to attacks which are directed at protected persons or objects in the mistaken belief that they are lawful targets. The lawfulness of the act of violence is not a prerequisite for its classification as an attack.[36] For these purposes, 'injury', as that word is used in the present Commentary, includes mental suffering that rises to the level of an injury but does not extend to anxiety, irritation or other similar nervous reactions. Of particular potential relevance in the context of military nuclear operations is the fact that acts or threats of violence whose primary purpose is to spread terror among the civilian population are explicitly prohibited.[37] For the rule to be broken, three elements must be present. First, there must be either an act of violence, such as nuclear violence, or a threat thereof. Second, the primary purpose of the act or threat must be the causing of terror among civilians. Third, that purpose must relate to the civilian population in general (as opposed to a collection of individuals, for example). So, if a party to the conflict threatens to use a nuclear weapon against a populated area, and the chief purpose of issuing the threat is to cause terror to the population there, as it very likely would, then the rule in Article 51(2) will have been broken.[38]

5 A nuclear operation constitutes an act of violence if it would have caused death, injury, damage or destruction to the adverse party were it not for defensive measures that prevented the damaging and/or injurious effects.

The Principle of Distinction

Rule 30

The principle of distinction applies to military nuclear operations.

1 The principle of distinction has its roots in the preamble to the St Petersburg Declaration,[39] which asserts that 'the only legitimate object which States

[36] Tallinn Manual 2.0, Commentary to Rule 92, para. 7.

[37] API, Article 51(2).

[38] Indeed, making such a threat would also likely be considered to conflict with the principle of distinction, as reflected in API, Article 48, and with the obligation to take constant care, as reflected in Article 57(1), and thus to breach a customary law rule binding on all States.

[39] St Petersburg Declaration, 1868.

should endeavour to accomplish during war is to weaken the military forces of the enemy'.[40] In the judgment rendered by the International Court of Justice when it considered the lawfulness of the threat or use of nuclear weapons, the Court described the principle of distinction as one of two 'cardinal' LOAC principles.[41]

2 The modern and customary formulation of the principle is reflected in Article 48 of API, which provides: 'In order to ensure respect for and protection of the civilian population and civilian objects, the Parties to the conflict shall at all times distinguish between the civilian population and combatants and between civilian objects and military objectives and accordingly shall direct their operations only against military objectives.'[42] Arguably, many of the specific rules on attacks set forth in Articles 51–58 of API, the majority of which reflect customary law, are reflections and/or applications of this principle.[43] The principle applies to nuclear operations undertaken in connection with international and non-international armed conflicts. It relates to the conduct of military operations which, it will be recalled, is a notion that is broader than attacks and comprises military operations that adversely affect the enemy.

3 How the principle applies in non-international armed conflicts is less straightforward. The obligation to distinguish between, on the one hand, members of the armed forces, members of dissident armed forces, members of organised armed groups and civilians who are directly participating in hostilities, collectively best referred to as 'fighters', and, on the other hand, peaceable civilians is clear. Less clear is whether there is a corresponding duty to distinguish between military objectives and civilian objects. Neither Article 3 common to the Geneva Conventions nor Article 13 of APII explicitly provides for protection of civilian objects during non-international armed conflicts. However, it is widely accepted that customary law does indeed provide such protection.[44]

40 Ibid., preambular para. 2.

41 ICJ Nuclear Opinion, para. 78. In the following paragraph of its judgment, the ICJ described the principle as 'intransgressible'.

42 See also US DoD Law of War Manual, para. 5.3.2 and n. 16; UK Manual, paras. 2.5–2.5.3; Canadian Manual, para. 423; AMW Manual, Rule 10; NIAC Manual, para. 1.2.2; ICRC Customary Law Study, Rules 1, 7; San Remo Manual, para. 39; Rome Statute, Article 8(2)(b)(i)–(ii) and (e)(i)–(ii).

43 Note, for example, the reference to the very word 'distinction' in the definition of indiscriminate attacks in API, Article 51(4).

44 DoD Law of War Manual, para. 17.7. See also UK Manual, paras. 15.16, 15.16.1; ICRC Customary Law Study, Rule 10 and associated Commentary; NIAC Manual, para. 1.2.2, Tallinn Manual 2.0, Commentary accompanying Rule 93, para. 3.

4 Not all operations directed against civilians are unlawful. Activities by the armed forces that do not cause harm (e.g. propaganda, psychological and certain cyber operations) are not prohibited by the principle of distinction. The present authors would not agree with the suggestion in the Tallinn Manual that '[o]nly when a cyber operation against civilians or civilian objects (or other protected persons and objects) rises to the level of an attack is it prohibited by the principle of distinction and those rules of the law of armed conflict that derive from the principle'.[45] The present authors consider that the principle of distinction applies not only in the case of attacks but also in respect of military operations.[46] Accordingly, if a military nuclear operation is intended, or may be expected, to have an adverse effect on the enemy that does not amount to death, injury, damage or destruction, the principle of distinction will apply.

5 The effect of the principle of distinction is that a nuclear operation that is intended, or may be expected, to have an adverse effect on the enemy will be unlawful if the object of the operation consists of civilians or civilian objects. Moreover, a nuclear attack will be unlawful if it is indiscriminate. For these purposes, a nuclear attack would be indiscriminate if it is not directed at a specific military objective. A nuclear attack would therefore be unlawful if the expected loss of civilian life and/or the damage to civilian objects would be excessive in relation to the military advantage anticipated from the attack. So, while a nuclear attack that targets a densely populated area may seem likely to stave off strategic defeat or to bring the war to an early end, such an attack will breach the principle of distinction and those involved in prosecuting it will be liable for prosecution as war criminals (on which, see Section H).

Prohibition of Attacking Civilians

Rule 31

The civilian population and individual civilians must not be made the object of nuclear attack.

1 This Rule applies to persons the principle of distinction set forth in the previous Rule. It is based on customary law, as reflected in Article 51(2) of API and Article 13(2) of APII, and therefore binds all States in relation to

45 Tallinn Manual 2.0, Commentary accompanying Rule 93, para. 5.

46 Consider API, Articles 48, 51(1), 57(1).

both international and non-international armed conflicts.[47] Civilians are defined in Rule 25 and the civilian population refers to all persons classed as civilians. The presence within the civilian population of persons who do not come within the definition of civilians or of civilians who are taking a direct part in hostilities does not deprive the civilian population of its civilian character.[48] The term 'nuclear attack' has the meaning given in Rule 29.

2 The object of a nuclear attack is, for the purposes of the present Rule, the person or, more likely, persons that the attack is intended to target. A civilian loses protection under this Rule if and for such time as he or she participates directly in hostilities.

3 If a nuclear attack is directed at both persons and objects, they will collectively constitute the object of the nuclear attack. So, for example, if a nuclear strike is intended to destroy a military facility, such as a military air base, but the nuclear fallout is also intended to kill or injure a civilian community living in the vicinity of the air base, then both the air base and the civilian community would be regarded as the 'object' of the nuclear strike, because the intended impact of the attack on each of them will amount to death, injury, damage or destruction and thus, in each case, will satisfy the requirements of an attack. If, however, a nuclear attack is directed at a military objective, such as a military air base, but also causes unintended, incidental injuries or deaths among the local civilian population, the affected civilians cannot be regarded as having been an 'object' of the attack, and the harm the civilians can be expected to suffer should be considered when the proportionality assessment discussed in Rule 38 is made.

Terror Attacks

Rule 32

An act or threat of nuclear violence the primary purpose of which is to spread terror among the civilian population is prohibited.

1 This Rule is based on the second sentence of Article 51(2) of API and the second sentence of Article 13(2) of APII. Accordingly, the Rule applies in international and non-international armed conflicts.

47 US DoD Law of War Manual, paras. 5.3, 17.7; UK Manual, paras. 2.5.2, 5.3; Canadian Manual, paras. 312, 423; German Manual, paras. 404, 502; AMW Manual, Rule 11; NIAC Manual, para. 2.1.1.1; ICRC Customary Law Study, Rule 1; Rome Statute, Article 8(2)(b)(i) and (ii), 8(2)(e)(i) and (ii).

48 API, Article 50(2) and (3).

2 The reference to an 'act or threat of nuclear violence' makes clear that the Rule applies to attacks and to threatened attacks with the stated primary purpose. The Rule therefore does not apply to acts or threatened acts that do not or would not constitute attacks[49] (e.g. military activities that have an adverse effect on the enemy but do not involve the use or threat of violence). It is useful to consider two examples. First, a news report suggesting that the adverse party to the conflict is planning to undertake a nuclear attack would not breach this Rule, because the activity constitutes neither an act nor a threat of violence but, rather, a report, whether true or false. Second, a nuclear attack whose main purpose is to destroy a large military facility but which has the secondary effect of causing widespread panic among the civilian population will also not breach the Rule, this time because the panic or terror is not the primary purpose of the act of violence. Accordingly, it is the primary or main purpose of the act or threat of violence that is key in this Rule.

3 The intent must be to cause terror to a significant segment of the population. A primary purpose to cause terror to a group of individuals will not constitute a breach of this Rule. However, an act of violence directed against a single individual or a small group of individuals, but with the main purpose of causing terror to the population at large, will cause the Rule to be broken. It should also be noted that it is the civilian population as defined in paragraph 1 of the Commentary on Rule 31 that is protected by this Rule. The Rule will not be breached if the main purpose of the act or threat is to cause terror among enemy combatants.[50]

4 A threat that breaches the Rule may be communicated by numerous means, including broadcasts or social media, email or more traditional written, telegraphic, telephonic or other means. There must, however, be the explicit communication of a threat. This is to be distinguished from deterrence policies, for example, where the possession and further development of nuclear weapon capabilities are designed to deter an adversary or potential adversary from undertaking hostile activity. Viewed from a legal perspective, deterrence consists of the visible maintenance of a state of military preparedness with the purpose of dissuading adversaries or potential adversaries from undertaking certain unwelcome action. The deterrence may or may not be directed at a specific State but – importantly, for present purposes – it does not take the form of a specific threat to use stated force against a named target on

[49] Consider API Commentary, para. 1940; Tallinn Manual 2.0, Commentary to Rule 98, para. 2.
[50] Tallinn Manual 2.0, Commentary accompanying Rule 98, para. 5.

a particular occasion. No explicit threat is involved, so policies of nuclear deterrence that accord with this broad description do not breach this Rule.

5 Article 33 of Geneva Convention IV prohibits 'measures of intimidation or of terrorism' directed against persons protected by that Convention.[51] The prime terrorising purpose reflected in the Rule does not apply to Article 33 GCIV. Moreover Article 33 is not limited to acts or threats of violence. The present authors take the position that there are two distinct rules at play here. When interpreting Article 33, it must be remembered that the provision is limited in its application to situations governed by GCIV, whereas the broader Rule to which the present Commentary relates is more generally applicable to the protection of civilian populations.

Prohibition of Attacking Civilian Objects

Rule 33

Civilian objects shall not be made the object of attacks, including nuclear attacks. Civilian objects are all objects which are not military objectives.

1 The St Petersburg Declaration provided that 'the only legitimate objective which States should endeavour to accomplish during war is to weaken the military forces of the enemy'.[52] The more modern formulation in Article 52(1) of API is reflected in the present Rule. The Rule has customary law status and applies in both international and non-international armed conflicts. The Rule extends to nuclear attacks as defined in Rule 29.

2 Civilian objects are defined in negative terms as being all objects which are not military objectives. Accordingly, all objects are either military objectives or civilian objects. There is no third category of object.

3 The directing of an attack against a civilian object is sufficient to breach this Rule, irrespective of whether the attack caused damage.

4 The first sentence of the Rule, which prohibits making a civilian object an object of attack, should be distinguished from the prohibition of indiscriminate attacks reflected in Rule 37. A breach of the present Rule arises when the attacker is aiming at a civilian object, whereas an indiscriminate attack occurs when an attack is not, or cannot be, directed towards a specific target.

[51] Namely, those who, during a conflict or occupation, find themselves in the hands of a party to the conflict or occupying power of which they are not nationals, unless the State of which they are nationals has normal diplomatic representation in the State in whose hands they find themselves. GCIV, Article 4(1) and (2).

[52] St Petersburg Declaration, preamble.

Definition of Military Objectives

Rule 34

In so far as objects are concerned, military objectives are those objects which, by their nature, location, purpose or use, make an effective contribution to military action and whose total or partial destruction, capture or neutralisation, in the circumstances ruling at the time, offers a definite military advantage.

1 The Draft Hague Rules of Aerial Warfare defined 'military objective' as 'an object of which the destruction or injury would constitute a distinct military advantage to the belligerent'.[53] The more modern conventional law formulation in Article 52(2) of API adopts the language that is reflected in the present Rule. The same language has been widely used by States in military manuals[54] and reflects customary law applicable to international and non-international armed conflicts. The legal term 'military objective' has the precise meaning given in the Rule and is used throughout this book only in that sense. Where looser, operational concepts of military objectives are referred to, they will be described using suitable, but different, language.

2 The Rule relates only to objects. The legal status of persons during armed conflict is a separate matter that is dealt with in Rules 21, 22, 24, 25, 26, 27, 28 and 31. An object is something that is 'visible and tangible'.[55] It does not therefore include more nebulous notions such as morale, confidence, political opinions or productivity.

3 An object may be qualified as a military objective, and thus as a lawful target for an attack, on the basis of any one of the four criteria given in the Rule. The 'nature' criterion refers to the inherent character of an object. It refers, for example, to objects that are fundamentally military and that are designed to contribute to military action.[56] So, a nuclear weapon launch/delivery platform – warships, including submarines, (strategic) bombers and cruise missiles – as well as the nuclear weapons themselves would be obvious examples of objects that are military objectives by nature. Likewise, nuclear weapon command, control and communications facilities will also be military objectives by nature. Similar considerations apply when selecting targets for

53 Draft Hague Rules of Aerial Warfare, 1923, Article 24(1).

54 US DoD Law of War Manual, para. 5.7.3; UK Manual, para. 5.4.1; Canadian Manual, para. 406; German Manual, para. 442; AMW Manual, Rule 1(y); NIAC Manual, para. 1.1.4; ICRC Customary Law Study, Rule 8; San Remo Manual, Rule 40. See also Protocol II to CCW, Article 2(4); Protocol III to CCW, Article 1(3).

55 API Commentary, paras. 2007, 2008.

56 API Commentary, para. 2020; see also Tallinn Manual 2.0, Commentary to Rule 100, para. 8.

nuclear attack. Accordingly, military depots and facilities, including military airfields, naval ports, military redeployment sites and military bases are among the many examples of military objectives by nature. 'The fact that civilians (whether government employees or contractors) may be operating these [facilities] is irrelevant to the question of whether they qualify as military objectives.'[57]

4 The 'location' criterion refers to a place – usually a geographical feature – that is of military importance.[58] An elevated piece of ground overlooking a plain or a mountain pass might be examples of locations that, in the context of the military operations taking place at the time or that are contemplated, constitute military objectives. The 'purpose' criterion refers to the intended future use of the object, whereas 'use' is concerned with the current use that is being applied to the object. So if, for example, the top of a civilian office block is being used by the enemy as an observation post from which to call in artillery fire, the current use of what otherwise would be a civilian object will render the office block a military objective. Likewise, if there is reliable information that the enemy intends to use a department store to accommodate troops and weapons, the department store will become a military objective now by virtue of that intended future use. Accordingly, civilian infrastructures (e.g. rail and other communications networks, radio and television stations, civilian airfields and ports) may well become military objectives either by virtue of their current use or their intended future use ('purpose'). Factories that produce equipment, clothing, weapons, ammunition and other supplies for military use will be military objectives by virtue of 'use'. While any provision of supplies for military purposes will, technically, render the supplying factory a military objective, whether such a facility should be attacked will depend, for example, on whether the military advantage anticipated to be gained from the attack outweighs the expected civilian injuries and damage (on which, see Rule 38).

5 If an object is a military objective by use and all military use ceases, the object reverts to being a civilian object, with the consequence that the protection of the object from nuclear attack resumes. However, if the enemy intends to use the object again for military purposes, it will remain a military objective by virtue of that intended future use ('purpose'). The mere fact that an object was once used for military purposes does not necessarily, without more, mean that the enemy intends to use it again for such purposes. It may be

57 Tallinn Manual 2.0, Commentary to Rule 100, para. 8.

58 API Commentary, para. 2021.

difficult to determine the enemy's intentions as to the future use of an object. The doubt rule, as reflected in Rule 36, applies only in cases of doubt as to an object's current use. While no presumption in relation to intended future use applies, the attacker must act reasonably. If a reasonable decision-maker would find that the information reasonably available to the attacker is sufficient to support a conclusion that the civilian object is going to be used for military purposes, it will be appropriate for the attacker also to reach that conclusion.

6 The Rule requires that the object in question makes an effective contribution to military action. This means that the object must in some way directly support or contribute to the military activities of the enemy. If, however, a facility is only offering indirect support, this will not be sufficient for these purposes. Consider, for example, a television station that schedules programmes that are patriotic or that contain propaganda material. This alone will not cause the television station to become a military objective, with the result that it will remain a civilian object that is protected from attack.

7 Objects that satisfy the 'nature' criterion will be military objectives, save unusual circumstances, because they will be making an effective contribution to military action. In exceptional circumstances, such as when an object that had a military nature in some past era has become a cultural object, the object will be a civilian object, because, notwithstanding its nature, it no longer makes an effective contribution to military action and therefore does not fulfil the definition in the Rule. Only if an object makes an effective contribution to military action by virtue of its nature, location, purpose or use will its destruction, capture or neutralisation offer a definite military advantage. While the Rule sets forth a twin-pronged test, in practice an object that makes an effective contribution to military action will also be an object whose destruction, capture or neutralisation, in whole or in part, will offer a definite military advantage.

8 It should be noted that the United States holds that 'war-sustaining' objects can be military objectives. As the US DoD Law of War Manual explains:

> Military action has a broad meaning and is understood to mean the general prosecution of the war. It is not necessary that the object provide immediate tactical or operational gains or that the object make an effective contribution to a specific military operation. Rather, the object's effective contribution to the war-fighting or war-sustaining capability of an opposing force is sufficient. Although terms such as 'war-fighting', 'war-supporting' and 'war-sustaining'

> are not explicitly reflected in the treaty definitions of military objective, the United States has interpreted the military objective definition to include these concepts.[59]

This approach would qualify as military objectives staple resources or products on which the enemy's economy is based and on which the enemy therefore relies to fund the war effort. A similar line of reasoning would also treat cash that is available for the payment of fighters or enemy combatants or that would be used to acquire weapons, ammunition or military equipment for enemy use as a military objective and thus as the lawful object of attack, including nuclear attack. At its broadest, this war-sustaining concept would render a military objective, and thus a lawful object of attack, any object that gives any support, however minimal, to the continuance of the war. The present authors consider that this goes too far, as the connection between the war-sustaining object and military action is insufficiently direct and almost any enemy object can be expected to give a degree of support of some kind, however minimal, to the enemy's war effort. In the view of the present authors, objects become military objectives when they have a direct war-fighting or direct hostilities-supporting role. In the latter case, a facility is hostilities-supporting if, for example, it produces objects or materials that are used by the armed forces, such as ammunition, military equipment or weapons. The distinction here is between a facility that makes, delivers or prepares objects that are to be used in the conduct of warfare and a facility that generates the financial, fiscal or economic capacity to carry on the armed conflict. The former element involves a direct link between the target and the military capability, whereas with the latter the link between the object and war fighting is indirect. The distinction explained in the current paragraph may appear to be a fine one but is nonetheless important, because it is the foundation of the protective effect of the cardinal and intransgressible principle of distinction.

9 The Rule makes it clear that the advantage must be military in nature. If attacking the object will produce only economic, political or psychological advantage, this will not be sufficient to cause the object to become a military objective.[60] It follows from this that an object the nuclear attack of which is only intended to make a political point to the adverse party's leadership or population will not satisfy the Rule and will not therefore be a military objective. The 'effective contribution' and 'advantage' aspects of the Rule are most important, and each must be military in nature.

59 US DoD Law of War Manual, para. 5.7.6.2 (citations omitted).

60 Tallinn Manual 2.0, Commentary accompanying Rule 100, para. 21.

10 This Rule is only concerned with whether the object in question can lawfully be made the object of an attack. Once that has been established, the Rules on indiscriminate attacks, proportionality and precautions, set forth respectively in Rules 37, 38, and 39–46, apply to any decision actually to undertake the attack.

11 Necessarily, the decision as to whether an object is a military objective is made before the attack occurs. The decision is based on the information that is reasonably available when the decision is being made and will be informed by the decision-maker's assessment of that information. The lawfulness of the attack can be properly assessed only by reference to the information then available. If enemy action causes the nuclear weapon, or the weapon that is being used to attack a nuclear weapon-related facility, to perform in a manner other than that intended when the attack was launched, this will not, of itself, call into question the lawfulness of the decision to undertake the attack.

Dual-Use Objects

Rule 35

An object that is used for civilian and military purposes is a military objective.

1 This Rule makes it clear that an object which fulfils the requirements of the previous Rule is a military objective even if it is also used for civilian purposes. The civilian use does not exclude its classification as a military objective, although principles and rules as to indiscriminate attack, proportionality and precautions in attack will have to be complied with, as is the case with all attacks.

2 The proportionality rule may have particular relevance when dual-use objects are to be attacked. While the object in question will qualify as a military objective, any expected harm to civilian objects or any expected injury and/or death among civilians (collectively referred to as collateral damage) must be taken into consideration when the proportionality rule is being applied. Difficult and controversial legal issues arise if the object of an attack constitutes part of a composite structure. Consider, for example, a situation in which part of an apartment block or an individual structure within a cluster of buildings constitutes the object whose destruction or neutralisation will offer a definite military advantage. While the entire building will constitute a military objective, those involved in the conduct of the attack must take all feasible precautions to avoid, and in any event to minimise, death and injury to civilians and damage to civilian objects in the vicinity

of the building. Thus, while the whole of the apartment block and the complete cluster of buildings would be regarded as the military objective, the indiscriminate attack, proportionality and precautions rules will apply and must be complied with scrupulously. It follows from this that the use of nuclear weapons against composite targets of the sort discussed in the present paragraph is in most circumstances likely to be unlawful, and this would be especially so if a more discriminating weapon is available that would achieve the intended military purpose.

Doubt as to the Status of Objects

Rule 36

If, after a careful assessment has been made, there remains substantial doubt about whether an object that is normally dedicated to civilian purposes is being used to make an effective contribution to military action, it must be assumed that it is not being so used.

1 This Rule applies in both international and non-international armed conflicts. The presumption probably binds only States that are parties to API. Article 52(3) of API provides that '[i]n case of doubt whether an object which is normally dedicated to civilian purposes … is being used to make an effective contribution to military action, it shall be presumed not to be so used'.[61] The API provision and the Rule create a presumption that applies only where doubt as to use exists and only to the decision on whether an object is a military objective and, thus, whether it can lawfully be made the object of attack. The Rule does not apply where doubt arises in relation to the nature, location or purpose criteria in Rule 34.

2 The formulation of the present Rule does not follow the API language exactly. States that are parties to API will be bound to apply Article 52(3) of the treaty as written. However, for States that are not parties to the treaty and for those that are parties but made interpretive statements to this effect, the Rule applies only if the doubt is substantial and if it persists after all reasonably available information has been considered. The language of the Rule therefore seeks to reflect the treaty language, adjusted so as to take account of certain statements made on ratification of API.

3 So, if doubt arises as to whether an object is being used for military purposes and therefore can be made the object of nuclear attack, the Rule requires that a careful assessment be made and stipulates that, if doubt still

[61] Consider also Amended Protocol II to CCW, Article 3(8)(a).

exists after that careful assessment, the object must not be made the object of attack, including nuclear attack. Given the potentially very serious consequences to be expected from a nuclear attack, it is sensible to conclude that this Rule should be applied most stringently to any attack involving nuclear capabilities. If, furthermore, the doubt is about whether, for example, a building is being used to accommodate a nuclear weapon, the collateral consequences that would be expected to arise from the attack may well also be very severe, such that a similarly high degree of caution will be required.

4. The Rule is a development of the widely accepted requirement that those who plan, decide upon or execute an attack must do everything that is practically possible to verify that the object of the attack is neither a civilian object nor subject to special protection, but is a military objective.

5 The Rule applies only if the object is normally dedicated to civilian purposes. If the object is also used for military purposes on anything more than rare, spasmodic occasions, it cannot be regarded as normally dedicated to civilian purposes. The careful assessment referred to in the Rule must be sufficiently thorough for it to be reasonable to conclude that the object is indeed being used for military purposes. That conclusion can properly be reached only by considering all of the information that is reasonably available; by assessing how reliable that information appears to be; by reflecting on how up to date the information is; by considering whether there is evidence of deception; and by seeking to ensure that all of the available information is interpreted correctly, both individually and collectively.

6 This decision does not require certainty. The proper test is whether, given what is known at the relevant time, a reasonable commander would conclude that the enemy is using the object in question to make an effective contribution to military action (e.g. by using the target object for military purposes). If a reasonable attacker would not hesitate before undertaking the attack, neither should the decision-maker.[62]

7 The Rule applies to decisions that are made in advance of an attack. Information that comes to light after the attack is not relevant to the application of this Rule if it was not available to those who planned, approved or executed the attack. It follows that an attacker complies with this Rule by taking all practically possible steps to determine the uses to which the object is being put and by determining that those uses include activity that makes an effective contribution to military action. For these purposes, the information which is reasonably available to the decision-maker will depend on the information gathering and processing systems that support the decision-maker

62 AMW Manual, Commentary accompanying Rule 12(b).

or that support the functions he or she performs. Some States and some armed forces may have more access to timely and reliable information than others, and, to a degree, the particular decision that is made must be judged by reference to the information actually available to the specific decision-maker at the relevant time.

However, lack of access to information does not give a party to the conflict licence to 'fire blind'; the prohibition of indiscriminate attacks will continue to apply (on which, see Rule 37 below).

8 If the particular military use ceases, the object will revert to being a civilian object, unless it is being used in another way for military purposes or has become a military objective on some other ground, such as nature, location or purpose. Furthermore, States in control of territory have the duty to take feasible precautions against the effects of attacks, and this duty includes the application of distinctive marks to 'objects dedicated to religion, art, science or charitable purposes, historic monuments, hospitals, and places where the sick and wounded are collected'.[63]

Indiscriminate Attacks

Rule 37

Nuclear attacks that are not directed at a specific military objective and that, as a result, are of a nature to strike military objectives, civilians and civilian objects without distinction are prohibited.

1 Some of the ideas reflected in this Rule were first articulated in the Lieber Code, Articles 22 and 23. The modern formulation of the Rule is Article 51(4)(a) of API. The Rule applies in both international and non-international armed conflicts, reflects customary law and therefore binds all States in relation to their use of all weapons, including nuclear weapons.[64]

2 This Rule prohibits nuclear attacks that, for whatever reason, are not directed at a specific lawful target. Common sense suggests that this may be because the weapon is incapable of being directed at a lawful target,[65] or because the weapon's effects cannot be reasonably limited to the vicinity of a lawful target,[66] or because the attacker simply fails to direct the weapon at

63 Hague Regulations, Article 27.

64 Consider Amended Protocol II to CCW, Article 3(8); US DoD Law of War Manual, para. 6.18; UK Manual, paras. 5.23–5.23.2; Canadian Manual, paras. 416, 613; German Manual, para. 404; AMW Manual, Rule 13; ICRC Customary Law Study, Rules 11, 12 and Commentary accompanying Rule 11; NIAC Manual, Rule 2.1.1.3; San Remo Manual, Rule 42b.

65 This proposition is based on API, Article 51(4)(b), and is a rule that reflects customary law.

66 This proposition is based on API, Article 51(4)(c), and is a rule that reflects customary law.

a lawful target. If the attacker simply fails to direct a weapon, whether nuclear or conventional, at a lawful target and an indiscriminate attack results, there is general agreement that this will render the attack unlawful on that ground. The law is not so clear, however, where the application of Article 51(4)(b) and 51(4)(c) to nuclear weapons is concerned. When ratifying API, numerous NATO States made statements to the effect that the new rules introduced by the treaty would not apply in relation to nuclear weapons.[67] While, as shown in paragraph 1 above, the prohibition of indiscriminate attacks was not a new rule introduced by the treaty, the extensions of that rule in sub-paragraphs (b) and (c) were, arguably, new and would not, therefore, apply to nuclear weapons for States that made the relevant statements. Arguably, therefore, while Articles 51(4)(b) and 51(4)(c) are customary law in their application to non-nuclear weapons, they do not have that status in relation to nuclear weapons. That said, these provisions do apply as a matter of treaty law to States that are parties to API and that made no statement on ratification of the sort referred to earlier in this paragraph.

3 Notwithstanding the legal complications set forth in the previous paragraph, indiscriminate attacks using nuclear weapons are prohibited, and the present authors take the view that, if the circumstances referred to in Article 51(4)(b) or 51(4)(c) caused the attack to be indiscriminate, this will not prevent the resulting attack from being unlawful. So, if the attacker fires a nuclear weapon without taking suitable steps to direct it towards a specific lawful target, the indiscriminate attacks rule will have been broken. Sometimes, a weapon that is in principle capable of discriminating use might be used in circumstances which render its use indiscriminate. So, for example, if a nuclear weapon is equipped with laser guidance technology, that will often enable the weapon to be directed towards a specific target with considerable precision. It is well known that obscurants such as cloud, smoke, sandstorms, and the like will tend to impede the operation of the laser guidance technology and may render an attack indiscriminate. If the attacker, knowing that such conditions prevail in the target area, nevertheless proceeds with a nuclear attack with indiscriminate effects, the resulting attack will breach the Rule. Similarly, if the nuclear fallout or contamination caused by the attack cannot be controlled, and if it is known before the attack takes place that weather conditions in the target area can be expected to cause the nuclear fallout to spread so as to affect populated areas to such a degree as to render the attack

[67] An example is the statement made by the UK on ratification of API on 28 January 1998; see Commentary accompanying Rule 64 below, para. 3.

indiscriminate, then the attack will breach the Rule and, thus, will be unlawful.

4 Indiscriminate attacks that breach the present Rule must be distinguished from attacks that are directed at protected persons or objects and that therefore, for example, breach Rule 54. It will be the individual circumstances of the particular attack that will determine whether it was indiscriminate. These circumstances will include the characteristics of the weapon that is used and of its guidance system; the nature and location of the target; the prevailing and forecast weather conditions; the nuclear command, control and communications arrangements; circumstances applying to the persons planning, commanding and undertaking the attack; and other relevant factors.

5 The mere fact that an indiscriminate attack is intercepted before a weapon, including a nuclear weapon, reaches its target does not affect the illegality of the attack.[68]

6 States that ratified API without making the 'nuclear statement' referred to in paragraph 2 are bound by a provision in Article 51(5)(a) that is stated there to be an example of an indiscriminate attack. The effect, for those States, of the provision's application to nuclear weapons is to prohibit nuclear attacks that treat as a single military objective a number of clearly separated and distinct military objectives that are located within a similar concentration of civilians or civilian objects. So, Article 51(5)(a) is concerned with a situation in which military objectives and civilian objects and/or civilians are co-mingled in such a way that it is nevertheless feasible to attack the military objectives individually. Accordingly, the API provision will apply where, for example, individual military objectives such as barracks, depots or ammunition factories are in different locations within a populated town and could be targeted individually. In such circumstances, States that are bound by Article 51(5)(a) in its application to nuclear weapons would be prohibited from using a nuclear weapon to target the town as a whole and would be required to treat the military objectives individually. What is separate and distinct for these purposes will depend on the circumstances. If available weapons would be capable of engaging the targets individually, then the targets can safely be regarded as separate and distinct for the purposes of the API provision. However, if any State – including States that made the nuclear statement upon ratifying API and those that are not parties to the treaty – were to use a nuclear weapon to attack the town in the stated

[68] However, depending on the circumstances, it may be difficult to detect whether an attack that is intercepted at altitude would have had indiscriminate effects if completed.

example, the attack would almost certainly be indiscriminate and thus unlawful if, as is assumed, it has the effect of striking civilian objects and military objectives without distinction.

7 Where nuclear weapons are concerned, it must be noted that the rule introduced in Article 51(5)(a) of API applies only to States that are parties to the treaty and that have not made statements excluding the application of the new rules introduced by API. It should also be stressed, however, that States that are not parties to API or that made the nuclear statement remain bound by the general prohibition of indiscriminate attacks set forth in the present Rule. If, through the kind of nuclear attack contemplated in Article 51(5)(a), an indiscriminate attack results, the present authors consider that the attack will be unlawful on that ground, notwithstanding the legal complications discussed here and in the previous paragraph.

8 For those States that are bound by the provision referred to in paragraph 6 in respect of nuclear weapons use, that provision applies independently of the proportionality rule (Rule 38). This means that a State that is a party to API and that did not make a nuclear statement must consider three legal rules in relation to indiscriminate nuclear attacks. The first rule is that discussed in paragraph 6. The second rule is the proportionality rule (Rule 38). The third rule is the general prohibition of indiscriminate attacks, given that attacks not covered by the first two provisions may nevertheless be indiscriminate.

Proportionality

Rule 38

An attack, including a nuclear attack, that may be expected to cause incidental loss of civilian life, injury to civilians or damage to civilian objects, or a combination of those things, that would be excessive in relation to the anticipated concrete and direct military advantage is prohibited.

1 The basis for this Rule is Article 51(5)(b) of API. While the API provision is known as the proportionality rule, it will be noted that excessiveness is the key notion. The Rule applies in both international and non-international armed conflicts and, as a rule of customary law, binds all States.[69] While the API

[69] Second Protocol to the Hague Convention of 1954 for the Protection of Cultural Property in the Event of Armed Conflict, The Hague, 26 March 1999, Article 7; Amended Protocol II to CCW, Article 3(3); US DoD Law of War Manual, para. 6.18; UK Manual, paras. 5.23.2, 15.15.1; Canadian Manual, GL-5; AMW Manual, Rule 14 and accompanying Commentary; NIAC Manual, para. 2.1.1.4; ICRC Customary Law Study, Rule 14; API Commentary, para. 4772.

provision is set forth in Article 51(5)(b) merely as an example of the kind of attack that is prohibited by virtue of being indiscriminate, in Article 57 of the treaty it is the proportionality rule that must be one of the key focuses of the precautions that attackers must take. The precautionary rules are set forth in Rules 39–46 below.

2 The focus of the present Rule is situations in which attacks cause incidental harm to civilians and/or civilian objects. The intended object of attack will have been a lawful target (i.e. a military objective, combatants or directly participating civilians), but attacking that target also involves the danger that civilians and/or civilian objects will suffer injury or damage, collectively referred to in the remaining paragraphs of this Commentary as 'collateral damage'. The mere likelihood that collateral damage will arise as a result of an attack on a lawful target does not, per se, render the attack unlawful. It is only when the expected collateral damage is excessive when compared with the anticipated military advantage that this Rule would be broken were the attack to take place.[70]

3 It is the collateral damage reasonably expected by the attacker that must be considered. However, certain effects of attacks affecting civilians fall below notions of collateral damage and therefore do not have to be considered for these purposes by the attacker. These effects include fear, inconvenience, irritation, worry and stress. Such effects do not amount to injury; it is for this reason that they fall outside the matters that need to be considered when the proportionality rule is being applied.

4 Collateral damage can include the effects that are the direct consequence of an attack, including a nuclear attack, as well as those that are somewhat indirect. The important factors are whether the particular collateral damage is expected to occur and whether it will be caused by the attack. If the indirect effects should be expected by the persons planning, approving or executing the attack, they should be included in the collateral damage when a decision is being made as to whether the prospective attack breaches the Rule. Consider, for example, a planned conventional strike against a nuclear weapon storage facility. When applying the present Rule, planners, commanders and those undertaking the attack must consider all the expected consequences of the attack, including the civilians that will be killed or injured and the civilian objects that will be destroyed or damaged as a result of the blast and fragmentation released by the explosion. They must also consider the collateral damage that is expected to be caused by the release and subsequent spread of nuclear contamination as a result of the attack. The vital element here is the

70 Note the definition of the corresponding war crime in Rome Statute, Article 8(2)(b)(iv).

requirement carefully to assess what collateral damage, whether direct or indirect, should be expected.

5 The notion of excessiveness that is central to the rule is not defined. It 'is not a matter of counting civilian casualties and comparing them to the number of enemy combatants that have been put out of action'.[71] Indeed, there is no commonly accepted scale for the measurement of military advantage. It is a somewhat subjective notion, best viewed through the eyes of the person who is making the targeting decision. Equally, measuring expected civilian casualties and damage to civilian objects is no straightforward matter. Even if scales could be devised for military advantage and for collateral damage, those scales would not have similar units of measurement, which further complicates the application of the Rule. What is required is that the decision-maker must consider carefully what the military benefit is that is anticipated from the proposed attack and must assess the degree of death or injury to civilians and damage to civilian objects that can be expected to arise from the attack. Acting in good faith, the attacker must then decide whether a reasonable decision-maker, knowing what he or she knows, would proceed with the attack. If, after suitably careful thought, the decision-maker determines that the answer is in the affirmative, he or she should proceed with the attack. In the context of nuclear operations, it may well be the case that the military advantage that is anticipated as accruing from such an attack will be very large. The notion of 'proportionality' implicitly recognises that even if the incidental collateral damage that is expected is considerable, it may not necessarily be excessive in relation to the size of the anticipated military advantage. It is important to remember that the proportionality rule is only breached if the expected collateral damage is excessive in relation to the concrete and direct military advantage that is anticipated as accruing from the attack. Accordingly, if a reasonably well-informed person in the circumstances of the actual decision-maker, making reasonable use of the information available to him or her, could have expected excessive civilian casualties or damage to result from the attack, whether nuclear or conventional, but nevertheless proceeds with the attack, that may well amount to a war crime.[72] It is widely accepted that considerable/extensive expected collateral damage could prove not to be excessive if the anticipated military advantage is sufficiently great. Likewise, even rather small collateral damage may be excessive in relation to a modest degree of military advantage.[73]

71 AMW Manual, Commentary accompanying Rule 14.
72 Consider Galić Trial Chamber Judgment, para. 58.
73 Tallinn Manual 2.0, Commentary accompanying Rule 113, para. 8.

6 The words 'concrete and direct' show that speculation and guesswork have no place in the proportionality assessment. The anticipated military advantage must be real, and the decision-maker must be able to articulate what it consists of. Some authorities suggest that the military advantage must also, in many cases, be quantifiable.[74] The present authors agree with the AMW Manual that, while this will often be the case, it will not necessarily be so; what matters is that it be identifiable and capable of articulation. The Commentary to API states that 'the expression "concrete and direct" was intended to show that the advantage concerned should be substantial and relatively close, and that advantages which are hardly perceptible and those which would only appear in the long term should be disregarded'.[75] The treaty language does not specify whether the time period within which the advantage must be realised must or can be short, medium or long. However, the greater the time gap, the more likely it is that the advantage is either speculative or indirect, and thus should be excluded from consideration. The present authors reject arguments to the effect that the use of nuclear weapons to bring a conflict to an early end is justifiable on that ground alone, notwithstanding that, by reference to the principle of distinction and its subsidiary rules, the nuclear operation in question would be regarded as unlawful.

7 The concrete and direct military advantage to be considered when applying the proportionality test is generally accepted as being what is expected to stem from the attack considered as a whole and not from isolated or particular parts of it.[76] It is imaginable that in the future very limited yield nuclear weapons could be used as part of a broader attack (e.g. involving a major advance, an amphibious landing or some attack of similar breadth and magnitude). The proportionality test should be considered by reference to the broader attack as a whole, not by reference only to the part of it that involved the use of the limited yield nuclear weapon. It seems unlikely that nuclear weapons of any size will be used to divert attention from the focus of a major attack. If, say, a conventional weapon were to be used to divert the enemy's attention in that way, it will be the military advantage to be derived from the

74 UK Manual, para. 5.33.3; Canadian Manual, para. 415; AMW Manual, Commentary accompanying Rule 14, para. 9.

75 API Commentary, para. 2209.

76 See UK statement on ratification of API on 29 January 1998, para (i); similar statements made by Australia, Germany, Italy and the Netherlands; UK Manual, para. 5.33.5; Canadian Manual, para. 415; German Manual, para. 444; ICRC Customary Law Study, Commentary accompanying Rule 14; NIAC Manual, Commentary accompanying para. 2.1.1.4. Note also the use of the word 'overall' in Rome Statute, Article 8(2)(b)(iv).

overall major attack that should be considered when applying the proportionality rule.

8 The words 'expected' and 'anticipated' make it clear that this Rule is concerned with decisions that are made before the attack takes place. This reinforces the point, made earlier, that those who plan, approve or execute such attacks must make decisions that are reasonable by reference to all apparently reliable and reasonably available information.[77] So, when any attack including a prospective nuclear attack is being considered, absolute certainty as to the prospective military advantage is not required, but a mere possibility of a military advantage will be insufficient even to be considered in the proportionality evaluation. While in conventional attacks the terms 'expected' and 'anticipated' give a reasonable scope for the exercise of individual judgment,[78] something close to certainty as to the military advantage will, in practice, be required in the case of a nuclear attack.

9 The relationship between this Rule and the Rules on precautions in attack is important. The focus of the present Rule is to prohibit attacks that breach it. The precautions Rules, by contrast, prescribe steps that attackers and those in control of territory liable to be attacked must take in order to seek to ensure that the principle of distinction, the prohibition of indiscriminate attacks and the rules on special and specific protection from attack are complied with.

Nuclear Targeting: Precautions

How exactly the rules on precautions in attack apply in relation to nuclear attacks is a matter of no small controversy. There are those who argue that the constant care principle is the only rule to apply in such circumstances. Others suggest that most of the precautions set forth in Article 57 of API apply when nuclear weapons are to be used. By way of an additional complication, States that are parties to API but that made nuclear statements when ratifying that treaty such as the statement referred to in footnote 67 above might argue that the rules in Article 57(2) and (3) of API constitute sophisticated developments

77 Galić Trial Chamber Judgment, paras. 58–60; *United States of America* v. *William List et al. (The Hostages Trial)*, United States Military Tribunal in Nuremberg, Case 47 (8 July 1947–19 February 1948) *Law Reports of Trials of War Criminals*, vol. VIII (1949) 34, 69; AMW Manual, Commentary to Rule 14; UK Manual, para. 5.20.4; Canadian Manual, para. 418; NIAC Manual, Commentary accompanying para. 2.1.1.4. Note also statement (c) made by the United Kingdom on ratification of API on 28 January 1998; some other States made statements in similar but not necessarily identical form.

78 API Commentary, para. 2210.

of the obligation to take precautions in attack and that, as such, they constitute new rules introduced by API to which the nuclear statement applies. This would mean that, for such States, Article 57(2) and (3) would not apply to the use of nuclear weapons – though, arguably, would continue to apply to conventional attacks against nuclear weapon facilities.

The present authors take the position that, for all States, the constant care principle applies both to nuclear attacks and to conventional attacks on nuclear weapons. They also consider that, to the extent that the additional Article 57 rules articulate precautions that a nuclear attacker must of necessity take if constant care is in practice to be complied with, those additional rules therefore apply to all States if nuclear weapons are to be used or are to be made the object of an attack. This is the position that is reflected in the following Rules.

Constant Care

Rule 39

During nuclear operations constant care shall be taken to spare the civilian population, individual civilians and civilian objects.

1 The Rule is based on Article 57(1) of API. It reflects a principle of customary law that applies in both international and non-international armed conflicts. The Rule applies to nuclear operations. While in most – probably all – circumstances the use of a nuclear weapon will amount to a devastating attack, Article 57(1) refers to 'operations'; it is thought right to reflect that notion, wider as it is than attacks, in the Rule.

2 The Rule requires those undertaking nuclear operations to consider the injurious and/or damaging effects of such operations on civilians and civilian objects.[79] The Rule should be interpreted as supplementing the distinction principle set forth in Rule 30, the indiscriminate attacks rule set forth in Rule 37 and the proportionality rule set forth in Rule 38. The obligation is for all those involved in the conduct of nuclear operations to take constant care commensurate with their respective roles and their involvement in the operation. 'The degree and nature of the responsibility of each individual depends, *inter alia*, on the nature and extent of that individual's role, on the rank of the individual, on the operational relationships between the persons involved, and on the information available to the particular individual at a specific time.'[80]

[79] API Commentary, para. 2191.
[80] Oslo Manual, Commentary accompanying Rule 44, para. 3.

The constant care duty is therefore subject to this practicability caveat, which may be particularly relevant in the case of a commander of a naval submarine or indeed the pilot of a nuclear-armed aircraft, who may be in no position to undertake the precautionary measures prescribed by Article 57 of API and who may accordingly be relying on the precautionary steps taken by others in the operational planning process. Nevertheless, all persons involved in nuclear operations are legally required at all times to be cognisant of the effects of their operations on the civilian population, individual civilians and on civilian objects. They must, to the extent that they are able, always seek to avoid any such effects that are unnecessary and adverse.[81]

3 The word 'constant' indicates that there is no time during the preparation and conduct of nuclear operations when care can be dispensed with. The duty to take care applies throughout such operations and all those involved must discharge it.[82] There is no time during the planning and execution processes when those involved are permitted to ignore the effects of their nuclear operations on the civilian population and/or on civilian objects.[83] The practical compliance with this Rule will inevitably presuppose the application of the further precautionary measures referred to in Rules 40–46.

Verification of Target Status

Rule 40

Those who plan or decide upon a nuclear attack shall do everything feasible to verify that the objective to be attacked is neither civilians nor civilian objects and is not subject to special protection.

1 This Rule is based on Article 57(2)(a)(i) of API. It applies in both international and non-international armed conflict and has customary law status. While Article 57(2)(a)(i) is arguably a new rule introduced by API, and therefore is a rule to which the nuclear statements made by NATO States when ratifying the treaty would apply, the Rule also describes action that an attacker must of necessity undertake if the constant care principle set forth in Rule 39 is to be complied with. The present authors are therefore satisfied that this Rule applies to all States in respect of attacks using nuclear weapons. Unlike Rule 39, which applies to nuclear operations, this Rule applies to nuclear attacks as defined in Rule 29.

81 Consider UK Manual, para. 5.32.1.
82 Tallinn Manual 2.0, Commentary accompanying Rule 114, para. 5.
83 AMW Manual, Commentary accompanying Rule 30.

2 It is important to be clear as to the persons towards whom this Rule is directed. The planning process will necessarily include decision-making about certain features of the intended attack. The notion of 'those who plan' may therefore include more individuals than may be initially apparent. Planners will comprise all persons who are involved in the targeting process up to the point when the final decision to attack is made, including those who make decisions as to the preferred exact target point; as to the preferred yield of the device that is to be used; as to compliance with distinction, discrimination and proportionality; as to the chosen manner of delivery (where there is a choice); as to the route to be followed; as to how precautions in attack will be implemented; as to battle damage evaluation; and as to numerous other matters. Essentially, they will be all the persons charged with drawing up the operational orders and instructions that will govern the conduct of the attack.

3 'Those who decide upon a nuclear attack' will be the persons whose task it is to decide that the attack shall be undertaken. In the case of nuclear attack, such decisions will generally be taken at the highest level of government and will be transmitted to the armed forces for execution. Senior armed forces commanders may be privy to the probably strategic basis for the decision to undertake a nuclear attack and may also become aware of information that suggests that the object of the attack is no longer a lawful target. In such circumstances, while the senior commander may not have decided upon the nuclear attack, he or she must take appropriate steps, such as drawing the further information to the attention of the original decision-maker in a timely way.

4 A person who executes a nuclear attack (e.g. the commander of a nuclear-armed submarine or the pilot of a bomber aircraft) may have no capability to determine the nature of the target that is to be engaged and may, equally, have no practical possibility of determining whether distinction, discrimination, proportionality and precautions principles and rules have been complied with. Ignorant as that commander or pilot may well be as to the nature and circumstances of the target, the extent of his or her role will be to fire the missile containing the nuclear weapon against predetermined co-ordinates, the geographical significance of which may be unknown to him or her. The chances are that the submarine commander or the pilot will not have available to him or her the information on which the planning of the attack and the high-level decision to execute it were based. Moreover, if, as is likely, a nuclear attack would involve the employment of stand-off capabilities, the submarine commander or bomber pilot is likely to be in no position to conduct real-time observation

of the target area with a view to confirming or negating the information that led to the conclusion that the object or persons in question constitute a lawful target. It follows from this that the question for the submarine commander or bomber pilot is whether he or she has any information leading him or her to conclude that the decision to direct the nuclear attack at the chosen target on the specified occasion is apparently wrong. If the submarine commander or bomber pilot has little or no information available to him or her as to the status of the target or of the target area, he or she will have no basis for questioning the superior instruction to undertake the nuclear attack. The responsibility for that decision and for the ensuing attack will rest with the authority that authorised the attack.[84]

5 The word 'feasible' has been widely interpreted as an obligation to do that which is practicable or practically possible, taking into account all circumstances ruling at the time, including humanitarian and military considerations.[85] Feasible action to verify the status of the target as a lawful target will necessarily involve the obtaining and consideration of all reasonably available information about the target. If information is available, it must be assessed to determine its reliability and it must then be considered in conjunction with the other apparently reliable and available information. The purpose of the process is to determine whether the available information, considered as a whole, confirms that the object of the attack consists of a military objective, combatants or directly participating civilians. If it is practicable to obtain a particular item of apparently relevant information, it must be obtained and considered. If it is not practicable to obtain that item, the obligation does not apply.

6 As to the standard applicable in naval and air warfare, see Rule 42.

7 If, on the basis of the reasonably available information, it is not possible to determine whether the object of the suggested attack is or is not a lawful target, the suggested attack cannot proceed. If the reasonably available information clearly shows, however, that some smaller object or group of persons is a lawful target, the Rule will have been satisfied in respect of that smaller target, but a more limited, conventional attack will almost certainly be called for because of the reduced scope of the persons or object(s) that can lawfully be made the object of the attack.

84 AMW Manual, Commentary accompanying Rule 32a, para. 4.

85 See statement (b) made by the United Kingdom on ratification of API on 28 January 1998; UK Manual, para. 5.32; Canadian Manual, A-4; AMW Manual, Rule 1q; ICRC Customary Law Study, Commentary accompanying Rule 15.

Choice of Means or Methods

Rule 41

Those who plan or decide upon an attack, including a nuclear attack, shall take all feasible precautions in the choice of means and methods of attack with a view to avoiding, and in any event to minimising, incidental loss of civilian life, injury to civilians and damage to civilian objects.

1 This Rule is based on Article 57(2)(a)(ii) of API. It reflects action by an attacker that is in practice required if the principles of distinction and discrimination are properly to be complied with and is an essential manifestation of the constant care rule set forth in Rule 39. It cannot be consistent with the generally accepted obligation to take constant care to spare the civilian population and civilian objects for parties to an armed conflict to undertake a particular nuclear attack knowing that, by choosing an alternative weapon or method of undertaking the attack, the military purpose could be achieved with reduced collateral damage.

2 The Rule reflects customary international law and applies in both international and non-international armed conflicts. As to the meaning of 'those who plan', see paragraph 2 of the Commentary on Rule 40. As to the meaning of 'those who decide upon a nuclear attack', see paragraph 3 of the Commentary accompanying Rule 40. As to 'feasible' see paragraph 5 of the Commentary accompanying Rule 40. As to the meaning of 'means' and 'methods', see Rule 69.

3 It is important to understand the relationship between the present Rule and the proportionality rule, set forth at Rule 38 above and operationally applied in Rule 43 below. Even if a method of attack has been chosen that complies with the proportionality rule, the present Rule requires that an alternative method be chosen if it will further reduce collateral damage. All available options for achieving the desired military advantage must be considered. So, imagine a situation in which an attack on a military port facility using a nuclear weapon is being contemplated. In the hypothetical example, the port facility that is the focus of the intended attack could be eliminated equally efficiently and reliably by means of an air attack using a number of 2,000 lb laser-guided bombs. The nuclear option would risk the release of nuclear particles that could be expected to cause large numbers of casualties among the civilian population living near the port. The obligation to exercise constant care to spare the civilian population requires that the attack option be chosen that minimises loss of civilian life and injury to civilians. However, and importantly, this Rule does not require an attacker to select an alternative method of attack that yields less military advantage.

4 The Rule addresses the avoidance or minimisation of civilian injury, death and/or damage which is incidental to the securing of the anticipated military advantage. Accordingly, civilian injury, death or damage that would be the direct or indirect consequence of an attack must be avoided or minimised to the extent it is practically possible to do so.[86] This means that weapons must be chosen and ways of using them must be selected with a view to avoiding where possible, and at any event to minimising, collateral damage.

Specifics of Naval and Air Operations

Rule 42

In the conduct of naval and air operations, the parties to the conflict shall take all reasonable precautions to avoid losses of civilian lives and damage to civilian objects.

1 This Rule is based on Article 57(4) of API, which, according to Article 49(3) of API, applies only to 'air or sea warfare which may affect the civilian population, individual civilians or civilian objects on land'. In the conduct of naval and air operations directed against targets on land, the obligations under Rules 39–46 continue to apply.

2 Arguably, neither the standard of 'feasibility' nor the standard of 'reasonableness' applies to naval and air operations that are not directed against targets on land and that are not able to affect protected persons and objects on land. In other words, the Rules on precautions in the present Section would be inapplicable to sea-to-sea, air-to air, air-to-sea and sea-to-air operations that are not expected to affect individuals or objects on land. Consider a nuclear or conventional attack against a nuclear-propelled aircraft carrier in the high seas. At least the States that are parties to API and have not made a nuclear statement will therefore have to decide which precautionary standard they are to apply.

3 However, in the view of the present authors, the possible interpretations of the relevant provisions in API are without prejudice to the corresponding obligations under customary international law. Arguably, there is no substantial difference between 'feasible' and 'reasonable' precautions,[87] so the same precautionary standards apply to any sea and air operations, including nuclear operations.[88]

86 See US DoD Law of War Manual, para. 5.11.

87 US DoD Law of War Manual, para. 5.3.3.1.

88 San Remo Manual, para. 46; AMW Manual, para. 32 (both recognising the standard of 'feasible').

4 The Rule is of considerable relevance for naval and air operations in the high seas or in international airspace involving the use of nuclear weapons against enemy targets or consisting of conventional attacks against nuclear-propelled or nuclear-carrying enemy platforms. In both situations, the parties to the conflict are obliged to take all reasonable precautions to avoid harmful effects on innocent shipping and, to the extent it is protected under customary international law, on the marine environment.

Precautions in Implementing the Proportionality Rule

Rule 43

Those who plan or decide upon attacks, including nuclear attacks, shall refrain from deciding to launch any attack that may be expected to cause incidental loss of civilian life, injury to civilians or damage to civilian objects, or a combination thereof, which would be excessive in relation to the concrete and direct military advantage anticipated.

1 This Rule is based on Article 57(2)(a)(iii) of API. It reflects action by an attacker that is in practice required if the principles of distinction and discrimination are to be complied with properly and is an essential manifestation of the constant care rule set forth in Rule 39. It cannot be consistent with the generally accepted obligation to take constant care to spare the civilian[89] population, civilians and civilian objects for parties to an armed conflict to simply proceed with an attack knowing that it can be expected to cause collateral damage that outstrips the military advantage that the attack, whether nuclear or conventional, is anticipated to yield. The Rule reflects customary law and applies in both international and non-international armed conflicts.

2 The proportionality rule is reflected in Rule 38 above. The present Rule reflects the obligation of planners and decision-makers to apply the proportionality rule when deciding whether a conventional or nuclear attack shall be undertaken.

3 A person who executes a nuclear attack (e.g. the commander of a nuclear-armed submarine or the pilot of a bomber aircraft) may have no capability to determine the status of the target or of the target area nor whether distinction, discrimination, proportionality and precautions principles and rules have been complied with. Ignorant as that commander or pilot may well be as to what is going on in the target area, the extent of his or her role will be to fire the

89 Canadian Manual, para. 417; German Manual, para. 457; AMW Manual, Rule 32c and chapeau to Section G; ICRC Customary Law Study, Rule 18.

missile containing the nuclear weapon against predetermined co-ordinates without knowing what is in fact going on in that location. The chances are that the submarine commander or the bomber pilot will not have available to him or her the information on which the planning of the attack and the high-level decision to execute it were based.

Moreover, if, as is likely, a nuclear attack would involve the employment of stand-off capabilities, the submarine commander or bomber pilot is likely to be in no position to conduct real-time observation of the target area with a view to confirming or negating the information that led to the conclusion that the nuclear attack would comply with the proportionality rule. It follows from this that the question for the submarine commander or bomber pilot is whether he or she has any information leading him or her to conclude that the decision to undertake that nuclear attack is clearly wrong. If the submarine commander or bomber pilot has little or no information available to him or her as to the status of the target or of the target area, he or she will have no basis for questioning the superior instruction to undertake the nuclear attack. The responsibility for that decision and for the attack will rest with the authority that authorised the attack.[90]

Choice of Targets of Nuclear Attack

Rule 44

This Rule applies only to States that are parties to API. When a choice is possible between several military objectives for obtaining a similar military advantage, the objective to be selected for a nuclear attack shall be that the attack on which may be expected to cause the least danger to civilian lives and to civilian objects.

1 The Rule is based on Article 57(3) of API. The authors note that the United States considers this Rule not to have customary law status[91] and they share that view in its potential application to nuclear attacks. Indeed, it is questionable whether this Rule is a necessary element of the constant care principle. Arguably, it is a new rule that was introduced by API, so, for the States which, when ratifying the treaty, made statements excluding the application of such new rules to nuclear weapons, this Rule will indeed not apply in relation to nuclear attacks. The Rule will, however, apply to all States that are parties to

[90] AMW Manual, Commentary accompanying Rule 32a, para. 4.
[91] US DoD Law of War Manual, para. 5.11.5.

API and that did not make such a statement excluding or materially limiting the application of Article 57(3).

2 The Rule does not limit its application to planners or decision-makers. It must therefore be complied with by all those who are involved in selecting targets for nuclear attack, in approving such targets and in actually conducting nuclear attacks.[92] The notion of danger to civilian lives and objects suggests that civilians must be at risk of injury or death and/or that civilian objects must be at risk of destruction or damage. Any of these four dangers will be sufficient for the Rule to apply.

3 The Rule applies only if a choice is possible – that is, if attacking the alternative military objective(s) is militarily feasible and offers a reasonable expectation of success. Moreover, the alternative target(s) must offer a similar military advantage. When the required comparison is made, the alternative attacks must be considered as a whole, not isolated elements of them. It is in practice unlikely that alternative targets will be available the nuclear attack of which may be expected to offer similar military utility. The more likely situation will be a choice between a large-scale nuclear attack of a military facility such as a base and, as the alternative, a smaller-scale, conventional attack against a significantly more limited target. If the military purpose can be successfully achieved by means of a smaller-scale attack that poses less danger to civilians and civilian objects, this is the option that should be adopted.[93]

Cancellation or Suspension of Nuclear Attacks

Rule 45

An attack, including a nuclear attack, shall be cancelled or suspended if it becomes apparent that the objective of the attack is not a military one or is subject to special protection or that the attack may be expected to cause incidental loss of civilian life, injury to civilians or damage to civilian objects, or a combination thereof, which would be excessive in relation to the concrete and direct military advantage anticipated.

1 This Rule reflects Article 57(2)(b) of API. It is a necessary manifestation of the constant care principle reflected in Rule 39 and therefore applies as a rule of customary law to the conduct of nuclear attacks. To proceed with a nuclear attack when it has become apparent that the object of the attack is no longer

92 Tallinn Manual 2.0, Commentary accompanying Rule 118, para. 3.

93 Consider AMW Manual, Commentary accompanying Rule 33, paras. 3–6; Tallinn Manual 2.0, Commentary accompanying Rule 118, paras. 5–7.

a lawful target or that the attack will cause excessive collateral damage by reference to the anticipated military advantage would be clearly inconsistent with the obligation to take constant care to spare civilians and civilian objects. The Rule is customary in nature and applies in international and non-international armed conflicts.

2 It should be noted that this Rule is not subject to the feasibility criterion. The obligation to cancel or suspend is therefore an absolute requirement if the circumstances set forth in the Rule apply. A previous determination may have been made that, for example, an object is a military objective and that attacking it would comply with the proportionality rule. If, however, further information becomes available showing that, for example, the object is no longer being used for military purposes or that civilians are now located closer to the object and in larger numbers, the Rule requires the attacker either to cancel the attack or at least to suspend it until the additional information can be considered to decide whether the object remains a military objective and whether, under the changed circumstances, the attack still complies with the proportionality rule.

3 Consider, for example, a compound that is known to contain some nuclear material and which a party to the armed conflict has decided to attack. The collateral damage estimate and the targeting decision are made on a Monday, with a view to the attack actually taking place forty-eight hours later on the Wednesday. During the intervening period, on the Tuesday morning, a group of civilian internally displaced persons is seen to have taken up residence near the perimeter fence of the military facility. The decision to attack should at least be suspended for long enough to determine what the revised estimate as to civilian casualties amounts to and to assess whether the expected increased injuries and deaths among the civilians would be excessive in relation to the military advantage that a successful attack of the object can be anticipated to yield. It may be possible to make that revised assessment rapidly, but the assessment must be a proper one, based on an appropriate consideration of all available information, including that which has become available recently.

4 The circumstances, and the capabilities of the particular weapon system, will determine whether at any particular moment it is practically possible to cancel or suspend an attack. If the missile has not yet been launched and if there is continuous communication between the authority that directed the launch and the platform tasked with carrying it out, the communication rescinding that order should be sent as urgently as possible, with a requirement that the recipient acknowledge receipt of the rescinding instruction immediately. A considerably more difficult situation arises if there is no such

continuous communication. While very great caution is always required before any instruction to launch a nuclear weapon is sent, if there is no continuous communication with the launch platform, that caution should be extreme.

5 If the missile has already been launched and if the attack cannot be aborted, it follows that cancellation or suspension will not be possible following launch and that the Rule will therefore cease to apply after launch has taken place. If, however, during the period after launch and before detonation the weapon support systems can enable the diversion of the missile from the target and the disarming of the missile, such action should be taken if it becomes clear that either of the circumstances mentioned in the Rule applies. While there is no rule of law requiring that such missiles be controlled by an operator and that they be capable of diversion and/or disarming, such a capability would seem to the authors to be highly desirable, as it would enable a potentially disastrous attack to be avoided or at least to be mitigated. Consider, for example, a situation in which an operator of a nuclear-armed missile notices that the munition is flying towards the wrong co-ordinates. Without a mission abort mechanism, the operator would be unable to prevent the wrongful attack of, say, a civilian object. If the weapon were to have such a capability and depending on the exact nature of that capability, the person at the controls would be able to divert the missile from its erroneous target and/or at least to disarm the missile. While the constant care principle probably does not actually require the fitting of such a monitoring and aborting/diverting facility, it would certainly be desirable for such a capability to be fitted.

Warnings

Rule 46

Effective advance warning shall be given of an attack, including a nuclear attack, that may affect the civilian population, unless circumstances do not permit.

1 This Rule is based on Article 26 of the Hague Regulations and Article 57(2)(c) of API. It reflects customary international law and applies in international armed conflicts.[94] The position is less clear in relation to non-international armed conflicts. With regard to cultural property, see Rule 62 below. The Rule

94 US DoD Law of War Manual, para. 5.11.1; UK Manual, para. 5.32.8; Canadian Manual, para. 420; German Manual, paras. 447, 453, 457; AMW Manual, Rule 37 and accompanying Commentary; ICRC Customary Law Study, Rule 20.

applies only if the civilian population is exposed to the risk of death or injury, as will often be the case with a nuclear attack and with a conventional attack on a nuclear weapon capability. It does not apply if – perhaps unusually – the danger is limited to damage to or destruction of civilian objects. It is generally accepted that the Rule is not engaged if the effect on the civilian population will consist of mere inconvenience, annoyance, fear or stress.[95]

2 To be effective, the person or persons to be warned must receive the warning in time to be able to act accordingly.[96] If the warning is to be effective, it must be understood by the persons to whom it is directed. If it consists of text, this must be in a language that the recipients understand. Alternatively, it may consist of clear, intelligible drawings, or may take the form of audible communications. It may be communicated via leaflets dropped from an aircraft; messages broadcast via broadcasting stations used by the relevant population; emails, social media or other means; or indeed any combination of these methods. There is no obligation to use the most effective or individual method of communication that may be available. Ultimately, the warning will be effective – and, thus, comply with the Rule – if it generally comes to the attention of the population intended to receive it and if they understand the action they should take.

3 Certain operational contexts may preclude the giving of warnings. Thus, if giving a warning will prejudice an attack, the circumstances do not permit the giving of a warning and no warning is required.[97] Depending on the location and other circumstances surrounding the attack, a strategic nuclear attack is likely to affect the civilian population in the sense of the present Rule and is unlikely to be prejudiced by the giving of a warning. Accordingly, in such circumstances a warning will usually be required. If, however, surprise is an essential aspect of, say, a successful conventional attack on a facility where nuclear weapons are being held (because the giving of a warning would enable the enemy to take defensive measures that would frustrate or preclude the attack), this would exclude the application of the Rule. Such defensive measures might include the use of combat aircraft, ground-based air defence, the employment of cyber techniques or, indeed, other measures such as the concealment of the weapons that are to be targeted. Equally, if the giving of a warning would prompt the enemy to pre-empt the situation by undertaking a similar attack itself, or if force protection considerations demand that no

95 AMW Manual, Commentary accompanying Rule 37.

96 UK Manual, para. 5.32.8.

97 US DoD Manual, para. 5.11.1.3; UK Manual, para. 5.32.8; Canadian Manual, para. 420; AMW Manual, Commentary accompanying Rule 37; API Commentary, para. 2223.

warning be given, these may also justify a decision not to give a warning. It should, however, be emphasised that such factors will not necessarily preclude the giving of a warning, and if a warning will not adversely affect the attack arrangements, a warning should be given.

4 An aspect that should be taken into account when deciding whether to issue a warning is that the warning may be rather general in nature, referring to attacks against a type of target but not specifying the date, time or precise nature of the particular attack.

5 Alternatively, the giving of a warning may support the strategic purpose that prompts consideration of a nuclear attack. The warning may combine compliance with the present Rule with an attempt to persuade the enemy leadership to take a preferred course of action, such as attending peace talks. There is, however, an important difference in purpose between threatening a nuclear attack and giving a warning for the purposes of the present Rule. Such a threat is essentially coercive in nature, whereas the purpose of the warning under the present Rule is essentially protective. Both, however, will send a powerful message to the adversary.

6 A warning under the present Rule may be issued as a ruse (i.e. with the purpose of misleading the adverse party).[98] Such action would not be unlawful,[99] but may be militarily counterproductive if the coercive effect of future threats is thereby eroded.

Precautions against the Effects of Attacks

Rule 47

The Parties to the conflict shall, to the maximum extent feasible, take necessary precautions to protect the civilian population, individual civilians and civilian objects under their control against the dangers resulting from nuclear attacks.

1 The basis for this Rule is Article 58(c) of API, but it also derives some support from Article 27(2) of the Hague Regulations.[100] While Article 58(c) refers to protection from military operations, the historical provisions – to the extent that they are relevant – suggest that the customary provision applies to

98 Tallinn Manual 2.0, Commentary accompanying Rule 121, para. 10. See also Rule 49 below.

99 API, Article 37(2).

100 Consider also Draft Hague Rules of Aerial Warfare, Articles 25(2), 26(4). These early provisions do not entirely reflect the contents of the present Rule, but indicate early thinking of that kind.

protection against the effects of attacks.[101] The Rule has customary international law status and applies during international armed conflicts. During non-international armed conflicts, the obligation of the government forces to take such precautions will derive from the sovereign duty of the State to take appropriate steps to ensure the security of the population.

2 As the text of the present Rule makes clear, its focus is on the duty of a party to the conflict that controls territory to take precautions to protect the population and civilian objects in that territory. These precautions are sometimes referred to as 'passive' or 'defender's' precautions. Both labels are misleading. The required precautions may well involve positive action, not just passivity; and a party that is in control of territory may have secured that control in the course of an invasion or military advance which is anything but defensive in nature. It is better to regard the precautions required by the present Rule as those which are needed to seek to ensure, as far as possible, the safety of the population and of civilian objects from the dangers associated with attacks, including nuclear attacks. It will be for each party to the conflict to determine which precautions are necessary for this purpose.

Consideration will need to be given, inter alia, to the following:

removing the civilian population, individual civilians and civilian objects from the vicinity of military objectives;[102]
avoiding locating military objectives near populated areas;[103]
constructing suitable shelters for the civilian population to protect them against attacks, including nuclear attacks;
issuing guidance to the civilian population on what to do in the event of nuclear attack;
developing a warning system to warn of impending nuclear attack;
promulgating the details and significance of the various warning signals;
stockpiling food and water for use by the civilian population in the event of nuclear attack;
issuing of protective clothing, masks and other equipment necessary to protect against the effects of nuclear attack;
ensuring that medical facilities are available to deal with the likely numbers of patients affected by nuclear contamination;

101 Note that the title of Article 58 refers to 'Precautions against the effects of attacks'.
102 AMW Manual, Rule 43; ICRC Customary Law Study, Rule 24; Tallinn Manual 2.0, Commentary accompanying Rule 121, para. 10.
103 AMW Manual, Rule 42; ICRC Customary Law Study, Rule 23; Tallinn Manual 2.0, Commentary accompanying Rule 121, para. 11.

establishing, maintaining and equipping an appropriately trained civil defence force; and

establishing, maintaining and equipping efficient civilian emergency services.

These are, of course, only examples of the kinds of precautionary measure that a party to the armed conflict that is in control of territory will have to consider. Some such measures may require action before the commencement of hostilities. Other such measures may more sensibly be taken a little later. Not every armed conflict involving a nuclear power will give rise to the use of nuclear weapons. Indeed – fortunately – history suggests that most will not. What is required by this Rule is that the governmental authorities of a party to the conflict assess the precautionary action that is required to ensure the security and safety of the civilian population and then take that required action.

3 This Rule does not re-state explicitly Article 58(a) and (b) of API, because removing the civilian population from the vicinity of military objectives and avoiding locating military objectives near populated areas are, as the previous paragraph of this Commentary has demonstrated, subsumed within the overall obligation set forth in the Rule. Nevertheless, in fulfilling its duties under this Rule, a State in control of territory must take necessary and feasible action to keep the civilian population and military objectives apart from one another.

4 The Rule limits the action required through its use of the words 'to the maximum extent feasible'. The word 'feasible' is widely understood as referring to action that is practicable or practically possible taking into account all circumstances ruling at the time, including humanitarian and military considerations.[104] The requirement is therefore to take all practically possible protective precautions, but there is no requirement to do that which is impractical.[105] It will be recalled that any military use of an object that otherwise fulfils civilian purposes has the effect of rendering that object a military objective. It will often be impractical either to move such objects away from centres of population or to move the civilian population. However, if moving the object and moving the population are both impractical, other measures will still be required with a view to affording the civilian population as much protection as possible.

5 Whether a party to the conflict is in control of territory will be a question of fact. Territory under its control will include its national territory that it continues to control and any parts of the adverse party's territory that it has

[104] See statement (b) made by the United Kingdom on ratification of API on 28 January 1998.

[105] Consider API Commentary, para. 2245.

invaded or over which it is otherwise exercising control. Territory the control of which is disputed (e.g. because ongoing hostilities are such that no party is in effective control) is not included within this Rule.

6 The dangers to which this Rule refers will comprise the risk that civilians will be killed or injured, that they will suffer sickness and that civilian objects will be damaged or destroyed. They will not include the risk of inconvenience or irritation, so a party to the conflict is not obliged to take precautions against such non-injurious consequences. While the Rule does not, arguably, require precautions to be taken where the anticipated consequences are limited to major disruption, in practice it seems likely that the consequences of a nuclear attack would in fact include injury or death of civilians and damage or destruction of civilian objects and major disruption. It would be sensible for parties to an armed conflict to include within the precautions they take under this Rule action aimed at mitigating such disruptive effects, although the Rule arguably does not explicitly require this.

7 The failure of a party to the conflict that is in control of territory to take necessary precautions in accordance with this Rule does not, per se, prohibit the other party to the conflict from conducting an attack, including a nuclear attack.[106] Equally, the failure of the party in control of territory to take necessary precautions in accordance with this Rule does not excuse the other party to the conflict from the obligation to take all required precautions when undertaking attacks. That attacking party remains bound by the principles and rules on distinction, discrimination, proportionality and precautions. However, and depending on the particular circumstances of a specific attack, the failure of the party in control of territory to take necessary precautions in accordance with the present Rule may render the precautions taken by an attacker less effective – a factor that should be borne in mind when the attacker's conduct and its effects are being considered.

Methods of Nuclear Warfare

LOAC prohibits certain methods of warfare and imposes constraints on the employment of others. In the following Rules these prohibitions and restrictions will be stated and explained. The meaning of methods of nuclear warfare is given in Rule 69.

[106] ICRC Customary Law Study, Commentary accompanying Rule 22.

Perfidy

Rule 48

In the conduct of nuclear operations, it is prohibited to kill or injure an adversary by resort to perfidy. Acts inviting the confidence of an adversary to lead him or her to believe that he or she is entitled to receive, or is obliged to accord, protection under the law of armed conflict with intent to betray that confidence constitute perfidy.

1 For the purposes of this book, perfidious killing or wounding and treacherous killing or wounding can be regarded as synonymous. Article 23(b) of the Hague Regulations provides that 'it is especially forbidden ... (b) to kill or wound treacherously individuals belonging to the hostile nation or army'. Article 37(1) of API defines perfidy as '[a]cts inviting the confidence of an adversary to lead him to believe that he is entitled to, or is obliged to accord, protection under the rules of international law applicable in armed conflict, with intent to betray that confidence'. Killing or injuring a member of the adverse party to the conflict by resorting to perfidy is prohibited by customary law in both international and non-international armed conflicts.[107]

2 States that are parties to API are also prohibited by Article 37(1) of API from capturing an adversary by resort to perfidy. However, in the opinion of the present authors, this aspect of the treaty rule does not reflect customary law.[108] The perfidy rule does not include causing damage or destruction by resort to perfidy.[109] Similarly, a mere act of perfidy without adverse consequences for the enemy is not prohibited. It is the causing of death or injury (or capture) by this method that is prohibited.

3 The Rule is broken if the persons who are deceived are not the same persons as those who are killed or injured as a result of the deception, so long as those who are killed or injured were the intended casualties. However, there must be a direct causal link between the act of perfidy and the resulting death or injury. While it has been argued that an attempt to cause death or injury by resort to perfidy is also prohibited under this Rule,[110] the authors consider that Article 23(b) of the Hague Regulations and Article 37(1) of API both clearly

107 Hague Regulations, Article 23(b); US DoD Law of War Manual, para. 5.21; UK Manual, paras. 5.,9 15.12; Canadian Manual, paras 603, 706, 857; German Manual, para. 472; AMW Manual, Commentary accompanying Rule 111(a); NIAC Manual, para. 2.3.6; ICRC Customary Law Study, Rule 65; Rome Statute, Article 8(2)(b)(xi) and 8(2)(e)(ix).

108 AMW Manual, Commentary accompanying Rule 111(a).

109 AMW Manual, Commentary accompanying Rule 111(a).

110 API Commentary, para. 1493. However, misuse of certain signs, indicia, uniforms, etc. is prohibited under LOAC, as reflected in the Rules below.

require death or injury to have resulted from the perfidious act for the treaty rules to be broken.

3 The perfidious element consists in inviting the adversary's confidence that he or she is either entitled to receive protection under LOAC or obliged to give that protection to the party to the conflict that is practising the deception. Article 37(1) lists as examples of perfidy: feigning an intent to negotiate under a flag of truce or of a surrender; feigning an incapacitation by wounds or sickness; feigning civilian, non-combatant status; and feigning protected status by the use of signs, emblems or uniforms of the United Nations or of neutral or other States that are not parties to the conflict.

4 Consider, for example, a nuclear attack mission in which an aircraft bearing civilian markings and giving all the appearances of having civilian status is specially adapted to enable it to undertake a nuclear attack. Imagine that the attacking aircraft follows a routing routinely used by civilian commercial aircraft and that the adverse party's air traffic control authorities, believing the aircraft to be flying for normal civilian, commercial purposes and thus to be protected from attack, permits it to enter and fly through its national airspace in the usual way. The deaths and injuries resulting from the use of the nuclear weapon will have been caused by the perfidious act of feigning civilian status in order that the enemy considers itself obliged to grant the attacking aircraft protection, but with the intention of betraying the enemy's confidence. Accordingly, the present Rule will have been broken.

5 If a similar deception were to be employed, this time to enable a party to the conflict to attack its enemy's nuclear weapons, and if military personnel and/or civilians of the adverse party are killed or injured as a result of the attack, the Rule will again have been broken in the opinion of the present authors. However, consider the situation where, in the course of a mission to discuss a ceasefire, parlementaires take advantage of their presence in enemy-held territory to take action to disable or disrupt a critical part of the enemy's nuclear command and control system. If the effects of such an operation are limited to disabling or disrupting the system and if no death or injury of individuals belonging to the adverse party results, the present Rule will not have been broken.[111] If a member of the armed forces fails to identify himself or herself as a combatant, this alone does not constitute perfidy. Likewise, if

[111] The parlementaires will, however, have breached their status. Note also that a distinction must be drawn between perfidy and espionage. However, if a spying mission causes death or injury to an individual of the adverse party, this may also breach the present Rule if pretence as to protected status is involved.

a military aircraft does not exhibit its military and national markings, that is not, per se, a perfidious act. It is the actual feigning of some other status protected under LOAC, with the intention thereby to deceive, that distinguishes perfidy. Likewise, using stealth technology in order to conceal the presence of an attack platform, such as a combat aircraft, is not perfidious. The deception that is being perpetrated concerns not protected status but rather the presence of the aircraft.

6 Lawful deception operations are addressed under Rule 49.

Ruses

Rule 49

Ruses of war are not prohibited by the law of armed conflict.

1 This Rule is based on Article 24 of the Hague Regulations and Article 37(2) of API. It reflects customary law and applies in both international and non-international armed conflicts.[112]

2 Ruses are 'acts which are intended to mislead an adversary or to induce him to act recklessly but which infringe no rule of international law applicable in armed conflict and which are not perfidious because they do not invite the confidence of an adversary with respect to protection under the law'.[113]

3 Examples of lawful ruses include:

- using enemy codes, signals or passwords;
- communicating false intelligence information with the intention that the enemy intercepts it and acts on it;
- transmitting false orders purporting to have been issued by enemy commanders;
- transmitting false information leading the adverse party to believe that nuclear weapons are being held in a false location;
- sending communications that give a false impression as to the sending State's nuclear preparedness or intentions;
- camouflaging installations at nuclear bases, camouflaging nuclear weapon delivery platforms or camouflaging other relevant systems;
- constructing decoy facilities to divert enemy attacks; and
- undertaking mock operations.

[112] US DoD Law of War Manual, para. 5.25; UK Manual, paras. 5.17 and 15.12; German Manual, para. 471; AMW Manual, Commentary accompanying Rule 113; NIAC Manual, Commentary accompanying para. 2.3.6; ICRC Customary Law Study, Rule 57.

[113] API, Article 37(2).

4 Accordingly, giving the enemy a false impression as to what is happening so as to secure a military advantage is what lies at the core of lawful ruses. It must, however, be emphasised that, to be a lawful ruse, the deception must not involve any misrepresentation as to protected status under LOAC and the deception must itself not be unlawful (i.e. it must not breach any other LOAC rule).[114] So, for example, if enemy codes and signals are used to confuse the enemy air defence forces and thus enable a nuclear attack to be undertaken unhindered, the misuse of the enemy codes and signals would be regarded as a lawful ruse of war. Likewise, consider the position where a State generates fake communications which appear to consist of instructions from the chief of its defence staff to the operational commander of its nuclear forces. The fake communications appear to instruct the subordinate commander to prepare to attack a specified target on a designated date and at a designated time by using a particular platform – say, a submarine – but the party to the conflict issuing the fake communications has no intention of undertaking such an attack, or of attacking the specified target. Such a ruse would not be unlawful, so long as the issue of protection under LOAC is not involved.

Improper Use of Protective Indicators

Rule 50

It is prohibited to make improper use of the protective emblems, signs or signals that are provided for in the law of armed conflict.

1 This is a rule of customary law that applies to international and non-international armed conflicts.[115]

2 The protective emblems, insignia, etc. that are covered by this Rule include the Red Cross, Red Crescent and Red Crystal;[116] the distinctive sign for civil defence;[117] the distinctive emblem for cultural property;[118]

[114] See AMW Manual, Commentary accompanying Rule 116(a).

[115] Hague Regulations, Article 23(f); API, Article 38(1); APII, Article 12; APIII, Article 6(1); US DoD Law of War Manual, paras. 5.23, 5.24; UK Manual, para. 5.10; Canadian Manual, paras. 604, 605; German Manual, paras. 641, 932; AMW Manual, Rule 112(a) and (b); NIAC Manual, para. 2.3.4; ICRC Customary Law Study, Rules 58, 59, 61; Rome Statute, Article 8(2)(b)(vii).

[116] GCI, Articles 38–44; GCII, Articles 41–5; APIII, Article 2(1); US DoD Law of War Manual, para. 5.24.2.

[117] API, Article 66; UK Manual, para. 5.10 n. 41.

[118] Convention on the Protection of Cultural Property in the Event of Armed Conflict, The Hague, 14 May 1954 (Hague Cultural Property Convention), Articles 16, 17; US DoD Law of War Manual, para. 5.24.6; AMW Manual, Commentary accompanying Rule 112(a).

the flag of truce;[119] and electronic protective marks referred to in Annex 1 to API.[120] The basis for these prohibitions lies in the likelihood that misuse of the indicators will make it more difficult for the persons or objects they are intended to protect to be identified, will cause the adverse party to doubt the credibility of such protective signs and thereby will expose protected persons and objects to greater danger. However, the improper use does not have to occasion death or injury for the Rule to be broken. Equally, if the misuse of the emblem, indices, etc. is used to cause damage but no death or injury results, the Rule will have been breached by virtue of the misuse, irrespective of the lack of resulting casualties.

3 LOAC includes additional indicators, such as the special sign indicating works and installations containing dangerous forces, as provided for in Article 56(7) of API and Article 16 of Annex I to the treaty. While the protection afforded to such objects by API does not have customary law status, the special sign is nevertheless provided for in LOAC and its improper use would constitute a breach of the present Rule.

4 A use is improper if its function is not to identify the location, object or personnel that serve the protected purpose. The Rule is specific in referring to the false use of the protective emblems, signs or signals. While other action to feign protected status, but that does not involve the use of protective emblems, signs or signals, may breach other LOAC rules, it will not breach the present Rule.

5 Accordingly, if the protective emblem provided for in Article 56(7) of API – namely, a group of three bright orange circles placed on the same axis – were to be displayed on an installation where nuclear weapons are being stored, the present Rule would be breached. Equally, if a nuclear strike aircraft were to display Red Cross emblems, the Rule would also be breached. A third example would be to act on the knowledge that the enemy is planning a nuclear strike against a military installation by displaying the civil defence distinctive sign on it in an attempt to prevent the attack. In all of these circumstances, the Rule is broken by the misuse of the emblem, irrespective of the motive.

119 Hague Regulations, Article 23(f); API, Article 38(1); US DoD Law of War Manual, para. 5.24.7; AMW Manual, Commentary accompanying Rule 112; ICRC Customary Law Study, Rule 58.

120 API, Annex 1, Article 9.

Unauthorised Use of United Nations Emblem

Rule 51

It is prohibited to make use of the distinctive emblem of the United Nations except as authorised by that organisation.

1 A rule of customary law prohibits the unauthorised use of the United Nations emblem in both international and non-international armed conflicts.[121]

2 If the UN emblem has been used and that use has not been authorised by the UN, the Rule will have been broken. However, the UN may have become a party to an armed conflict, or UN personnel or units may be taking a direct part in the hostilities. In such circumstances, the UN emblem loses its protective character and UN objects, facilities and equipment and UN personnel become lawful targets for as long as the UN remains a party to the conflict or the UN personnel continue to take a direct part in the hostilities. However, if a situation mentioned in this paragraph occurs, UN personnel who are not performing military functions will retain protected civilian status and the UN facilities and equipment that are not used for military purposes will retain protection as civilian objects. Neither may be made the object of attack.

3 So, if, for example, the UN emblem is applied to a structure without the permission of the UN, the Rule is breached, irrespective of the military or other purpose that the party to the conflict is seeking to achieve through that misuse.

Improper Use of Enemy Indicators

Rule 52

It is prohibited to make use of the flags, military emblems, insignia or uniforms of the enemy while visible to the enemy during an attack, including a nuclear attack.

1 The use of flags, military emblems, insignia[122] or uniforms of an adverse party to the conflict is forbidden in the course of attacks.[123] The Rule has customary law status and applies in both international and non-international armed

[121] API, Article 38(2); UK Manual, para. 5.10.c; Canadian Manual, para. 605(c); AMW Manual, Rule 112(e); NIAC Manual, Commentary accompanying para. 2.3.4; ICRC Customary Law Study, Rule 60; Rome Statute, Article 8(2)(b)(vii).

[122] 'Insignia' means 'distinguishing badge or emblem of military rank, office or membership' (*Concise Oxford English Dictionary*, 11th ed. (2006), 735).

[123] Hague Regulations, Article 23(f); API, Article 39(2).

conflicts.[124] The authors share the position taken in the Tallinn Manual that the Article 39(2) extension of the prohibition beyond use during attacks to actions intended to shield, favour, protect or impede military operations, while binding on States that are parties to API, does not reflect customary law.[125]

2 The focus of the Rule is on visible indicators of enemy status and will include national markings on military aircraft and other platforms. Consider a situation in which a State is planning to undertake an air attack against an adverse party's missile production facility that is defended by effective anti-air defences. The planners appreciate that if they apply the enemy's national and military markings to the aircraft and use call signs and other indications tending to show that the aircraft has enemy character, there is a greater chance of the attack aircraft reaching the target and conducting a successful attack. The use of the enemy military emblems will, however, breach the Rule.[126]

3 The authors take the view that, in the kind of context referred to in the previous paragraph, the words 'while visible to the enemy' should be interpreted somewhat broadly. The markings on the aircraft will be visible to the adversary in the likely event that the attacking aircraft is intercepted by enemy combat aircraft. In the view of the present authors, this would suffice for the marks to be regarded as 'visible to the enemy', irrespective of whether an intercepting aircraft is actually scrambled.

4 There is an important distinction between conduct that breaches the Rule – namely, the misuse of enemy visual emblems, insignia, etc. – and the use of lawful ruses, such as feigning enemy authorship of electronic or radio communications; using the enemy's signals, passwords, radio code signs and words of command; and pretending to communicate with non-existent troop formations. So, while, in the example given in paragraph 2, the use of the false flags and aircraft markings would breach the present Rule, the sending, say, of false communications from enemy commanders to air defence units instructing them not to fire on the aircraft undertaking the attack would be a lawful ruse, provided that the fake communications do not suggest a requirement to give, or an entitlement to receive, protection under LOAC.

5 If a party to the conflict is seeking to prevent or impede a nuclear attack by the adverse party, the present Rule will prohibit it from using enemy flags,

124 US DoD Law of War Manual, para. 5.23; UK Manual, para. 5.11; Canadian Manual, para. 607; German Manual, para. 473; AMW Manual, Rule 112(c); NIAC Manual, para. 2.3.5; ICRC Customary Law Study, Rule 62; Rome Statute, Article 8(2)(b)(vii).

125 The US DoD Law of War Manual, para. 5.23.1.3, finds the use of enemy flags, insignia, and military uniforms 'outside of combat' to be legitimate. See also Tallinn Manual 2.0, Commentary accompanying Rule 126, para. 2; Canadian Manual, para. 607.

126 Note that the aircraft will also, by showing false markings, not have belligerent rights.

military emblems, insignia or uniforms while doing so. Accordingly, the State seeking to prevent or impede the attack cannot paint its enemy's flag on the roof of expected targets, but is permitted to use ruses of the sort mentioned in the previous paragraph and in the Commentary accompanying Rule 49.

6 In the conduct of maritime operations, a warship – which, for these purposes, would include a submarine – may fly the flag of an enemy or neutral State, provided that it exhibits its true, national flag immediately before an armed engagement.[127] The term 'an armed engagement' would for these purposes include, for example, the firing of a nuclear armed missile or a conventional attack on a nuclear facility. So, before firing such a missile or undertaking such an attack, the submarine would be required to fly or otherwise show its correct national flag or military emblem. It is important to stress that this is not an outdated formality having no practical relevance in modern armed conflicts, in particular in nuclear operations at sea. It is not necessary for the showing of the true flag to be communicated to or noticed by the enemy or the (lawful) target. The reason for showing the true flag lies in the prohibition of privateering, which limited the exercise of belligerent rights to warships proper. Accordingly, the obligation makes it sufficiently apparent to the warships of neutral States that the attack is not a prohibited act of privateering.

7 The Rule will also have implications for the clothing worn by the crew of a military aircraft engaged in a nuclear attack or operation. During an airborne attack, the outer markings of the attacking aircraft satisfy the requirements of the Rule. If, however, in the event of being shot down, members of the crew plan to make use of enemy uniforms while undertaking attacks in the course of their attempts to escape, this action would breach the present Rule.

Improper Use of Indicators of Neutrality

Rule 53

It is prohibited to make use of flags, military emblems, insignia or uniforms of neutral or other States not party to the conflict.

1 The Rule is based on Article 39(1) of API and has customary law status. It applies in international armed conflicts.[128] The applicability of the Rule to

[127] San Remo Manual, para. 110.

[128] US DoD Law of War Manual, para. 5.24.1; UK Manual, para. 5.11; Canadian Manual, para. 606; German Manual, para. 473; AMW Manual, Rule 112(d); ICRC Customary Law Study, Rule 63. The exception to the Rule in naval warfare is discussed in the Commentary accompanying Rule 52, para. 6.

non-international armed conflicts is unclear. The reference to neutrality does not apply to such conflicts. The notion of States not being party to a non-international armed conflict does make sense, however, and it is unsettled whether the Rule applies to that extent.[129]

2 So, consider an adapted version of the scenario discussed in paragraph 2 of the Commentary accompanying Rule 52. The attacking State seeks to overcome the problem posed by the adversary's effective anti-air defences by applying to the aircraft the national and military markings of a neutral or non-party State and by using call signs and other indications tending to show that the aircraft undertaking the nuclear attack has neutral or non-party status. It does this in the belief that there is a greater chance of the attack aircraft reaching the target and conducting a successful attack. If the situation arises in the context of an international armed conflict, the use of the neutral nationality and military emblems will breach the present Rule. If the same situation were to arise in the context of a non-international armed conflict, it is unclear whether the Rule would apply.

3 Other aspects of the law of neutrality are addressed in Rules 65–8.

Zones

1 Military doctrine provides for zones to fulfil a number of military purposes. Exclusion zones may be established in international waters and in the superjacent airspace to such waters. An exclusion zone can be regarded as 'the three dimensional space beyond the territorial sovereignty of any State in which a Belligerent Party claims to be relieved from certain provisions of the law of international armed conflict, or where that Belligerent Party purports to be entitled to restrict the freedom of aviation (or navigation) of other States'.[130] A no-fly zone may be established in national airspace and, as the name implies, is a three-dimensional space in which a belligerent party restricts or prohibits aviation. The no-fly zone may be established in a party's own airspace or in the airspace of an adversary.[131] Neither an exclusion zone nor a no-fly zone constitutes a 'free-fire zone' in which an intruding aircraft or, in the former case, ship can be attacked on sight and without deliberation or precaution. During an armed conflict, the principles and rules on distinction, discrimination, proportionality and precautions apply within exclusion and no-fly zones, as they do outside them. 'Neutral, civilian and other protected

129 Tallinn Manual 2.0, Commentary accompanying Rule 127, para. 2.
130 AMW Manual, Commentary accompanying Section P, para. 3.
131 AMW Manual, Section P, para. 4.

objects or persons retain their protection under [LOAC] when they enter such zones, even if they have ignored the instructions issued by the party that established them.'[132]

2 If, during an armed conflict, a civilian aircraft or merchant vessel enters an exclusion zone or if a civilian aircraft flies within a no-fly zone, this may be an indication that the vessel or aircraft is a military objective. Equally, it may be the case, for example, that the crew of the vessel or aircraft is simply lost, that there is some kind of fault with the navigation systems or that the aircraft is in distress. The State that established the zone must not simply assume that the vessel or aircraft is in fact a military objective, but vessels and aircraft that have become military objectives can be made the object of attack. Appropriate steps must be taken to verify whether the vessel or aircraft is indeed making an effective contribution to military action and whether using force against it will, in the circumstances, be lawful.

3 If the intruding aircraft is a civilian airliner, it should be borne in mind that civilian airliners are civilian objects and that particular care must be taken when exercising the precautions required by Rules 39–46.[133] In case of doubt as to whether a civilian airliner has become a military objective, the civilian airliner must be presumed not to be making an effective contribution to military action, and thus not to be a military objective. This, however, applies only if the civilian airliner is normally exclusively dedicated to civilian purposes.[134] The crews of civilian airliners, irrespective of their State of registration, should avoid entering a no-fly or exclusion zone or the immediate vicinity of hostilities, but such aircraft do not lose their protected status merely by entering such zones.[135] Similar considerations apply in the case of merchant vessels.

4 A party to an armed conflict may therefore establish exclusion and no-fly zones (e.g. to prevent intrusions into the vicinity of nuclear weapon launch facilities or platforms). Such zones may need to be of a sufficient size to enable proper targeting decisions to be made before force is used. Moreover, while intrusion is not, per se, sufficient to characterise a civilian vessel or aircraft as a military objective, the apparently deliberate penetration of a zone by a vessel or aircraft, when considered in conjunction with other more specific information, may tend to help to

[132] Tallinn Manual 2.0, Commentary accompanying Section 9(B), para. 1, pp. 507–8.
[133] AMW Manual, Rule 58 and accompanying Commentary.
[134] AMW Manual, Rule 59 and accompanying Commentary.
[135] AMW Manual, Rule 60.

confirm that the merchant vessel or civilian aircraft is involved in some way in the conduct of military operations, such as an attack.

Persons and Objects Entitled to Specific Protection under the Law of Armed Conflict

LOAC grants general protection to civilians and civilian objects. However, there are also specific rules protecting certain classes of person and object. In some cases, those specific rules in effect grant a level of protection that does not differ from that accorded generally to civilians and civilian objects. Where that situation exists, the protection is referred to in this book as 'specific protection'. In other cases, the particular class of person or object is granted legal protection that exceeds that given generally to civilians and civilian objects. In those circumstances, the enhanced protection is referred to in this book as 'special protection'.

During periods of armed conflict, the parties to the conflict may reach special agreements that may either grant protection to persons or objects not otherwise protected by LOAC or grant to protected persons and/or objects protection which exceeds that granted by the applicable law. The Rules set forth below reflect the protection granted to the objects and persons referred to therein under LOAC. Agreements between the parties to the conflict cannot diminish that level of legal protection.[136] Such an inter-party agreement might of course provide that nuclear weapons shall in no circumstances be used by either party, might limit the circumstances in which such weapons might be employed or might prescribe agreed arrangements with a view to ensuring that no resort will be made by either side to such weapons. Such provision would have a protective effect going far beyond the specific and special protection afforded by the Rules in this Section.

Some classes of individual and object that enjoy specific or special protection under LOAC are not discussed in any detail in the following Rules. This does not mean that the protection the law gives such persons and objects is unimportant but, rather, that the provision in question is considered by the authors as being of limited relevance in the context of this book.

[136] GCI, GCII, GCIII, common Article 6; GCIV, Article 7; GCI, GCII, GCIII, GCIV, common Article 3; AMW Manual Rule 99 and accompanying Commentary; Tallinn Manual 2.0, 512, para. 2.

Medical and Religious Personnel, Medical Units and Transports

Rule 54

Medical and religious personnel, medical units and medical transports must be respected and protected and, in particular, may not be made the object of attack, including nuclear attack.

1 This Rule applies in international and non-international armed conflicts and is a rule of customary international law.[137]

2 During bombardments, 'all necessary steps must be taken to spare, as far as possible, ... hospitals, and places where the sick and wounded are collected, provided they are not being used at the time for military purposes'.[138]

3 Medical units comprise civilian or military establishments or units that are organised for medical purposes. The term therefore includes fixed or mobile units, hospitals, medical depots and medical and pharmaceutical stores, whether of a permanent or temporary nature. Medical transports encompass land, sea and air transportation of wounded, sick or shipwrecked persons, medical or religious personnel and equipment or medical supplies. Similar protections also apply to hospital ships, rescue craft and medical aircraft. Indeed, it should be borne in mind that medical aircraft may be being operated as flying clinics.

4 The 'respect' and 'protect obligations' are distinct duties. 'The duty to respect is breached by actions that impede or prevent medical or religious personnel, medical units, or medical transports from performing their medical or religious functions, or that otherwise adversely affect the humanitarian functions of medical or religious personnel, units or transports.'[139] It includes a prohibition on making the stated personnel, units or transports the object of attack, but does not extend to incidental effects, such as may arise as a result of an attack the object of which is a military objective.[140]

5 The 'respect' part of the Rule therefore prohibits making a hospital, medical clearance station, medical unit or medical transportation facility the object of an attack through the use of either a conventional or a nuclear weapon. However, if a nuclear attack is directed at a military objective such as the enemy's land-based missile launch facility, the mere fact that a medical unit is located nearby and will be destroyed will not cause this Rule to be

137 GCI, Articles 19, 24, 25, 35, 36; GCII, Articles 22, 24, 25, 27, 36–9 and Chapter 4 generally; GCIII, Article 33; GCIV, Articles 18–22; API, Articles 12, 15, 21–4, 26; APII, Article 9.

138 Hague Regulations, Article 27.

139 Tallinn Manual 2.0, Commentary accompanying Rule 131, para. 5; AMW Manual, Commentary accompanying Rule 71, para. 12.

140 Tallinn Manual 2.0, Commentary accompanying Rule 131, para. 5.

broken, although such incidental consequences must be taken into account when proportionality and precautions rules are being considered.

6 The 'protect' part of the Rule requires the taking of suitable precautions to ensure that others respect the protected facilities, transports and personnel.[141]

Identification

Rule 55

All feasible steps must be taken to ensure that the protected status of medical and religious personnel, medical units and medical transports is clearly indicated, although failure to do so does not deprive them of their protected status.

1 This is a customary law rule that applies in international and non-international armed conflicts.[142] The language 'all feasible steps' indicates that parties to the conflict must do everything that is practically possible to ensure that the persons and objects that are protected by this Rule are appropriately marked. What is appropriate will depend on the nature of the perceived threat. If that threat includes attack from the air, the emblem should be marked, to the degree possible, so that, if the medical facility itself can be seen, the protective emblem will also be apparent.

2 The distinctive emblems of the Red Cross, Red Crescent and Red Crystal will often be used as the means of indicating the protected status of the persons and objects referred to in this Rule. It is the medical or religious function being fulfilled by the medical or religious personnel, units and transports that confers protected status.[143] The use of the emblem is merely to facilitate identification of persons and objects that are entitled to that protected status.[144] If the personnel, units and transports referred to in this Rule do not display the protective emblem, this does not deprive them of their protected status.[145]

141 AMW Manual, Commentary accompanying Rule 71, para. 13.

142 Hague Regulations, Article 27(2); API, Article 18; APII, Article 12; GCI, Article 42; GCII, Articles 43, 44; GCIV, Articles 18, 20–2; US DoD Law of War Manual, para. 5.14.4; UK Manual, paras. 7.23–7.23.3; Canadian Manual, paras. 915–17; German Manual, paras. 635, 638; AMW Manual, Rule 72(a) and chapeau to Section K; NIAC Manual, Commentary accompanying para. 3.2. Note that supplementary electronic markings are provided for in API, Articles 8(m) and 18(5).

143 AMW Manual, Commentary accompanying Rule 72(c), para. 1.

144 API, Annex I, Article 1; APIII, preamble, para. 4.

145 AMW Manual, Rule 72(d).

Loss of Protection and Warnings

Rule 56

The protection to which medical and religious personnel, medical units and medical transports are entitled does not cease unless they commit, or are used to commit, outside their humanitarian function, acts harmful to the enemy. Protection may cease only after a warning has been given setting a reasonable time limit, and after such warning has remained unheeded.

1 This is a customary law rule that applies in both international and non-international armed conflicts.[146]

2 Acts are harmful to the enemy if they have the harmful purpose or effect of facilitating or impeding military operations. So, an act may be harmful by impeding enemy military operations or it may be harmful by enhancing the acting party's own military operations.[147] The Rule thus not only refers to acts that cause direct harm to the enemy (e.g. by directing attacks at the enemy) but also extends to activities that adversely affect military operations (e.g. by gathering military intelligence or corrupting military communications).[148]

3 Certain situations do not deprive the medical unit or transport of the protection afforded by Rule 55, namely:

> That the personnel of the unit or establishment are armed, and that they use the arms in their own defence, or in that of the wounded and sick in their charge.[149]
>
> That in the absence of armed orderlies, the unit or establishment is protected by a picket or by sentries or by an escort.[150]
>
> That small arms and ammunition taken from the wounded and sick and not yet handed to the proper service, are found in the unit or establishment.[151]
>
> That the humanitarian activities of medical units and establishments or of their personnel extend to the care of civilian wounded or sick.[152]

146 Hague Regulations, Article 28; GCI, Articles 21, 22; GCII, Articles 34, 35; GCIV, Article 19; API, Article 13; APII, Article 11(2); UK Manual, para. 7.13.1; Canadian Manual, paras. 447, 918; German Manual, paras. 613, 618–19; AMW Manual, Rule 74(a) and (b); NIAC Manual, para. 4.2.1; ICRC Customary Law Study, Rules 25, 28, 29.

147 Consider API and APII Commentaries, paras. 550, 4720; AMW Manual, Commentary accompanying Rule 74(a), para. 3.

148 Tallinn Manual 2.0, Commentary accompanying Rule 134, para. 2.

149 GCI, Article 22(1).

150 GCI, Article 22(2).

151 GCI, Article 22(3).

152 GCI, Article 22(5).

That members of the armed forces or other combatants are in the unit for medical reasons.[153]

4 If circumstances arise that justify ending the protected status of a medical unit or establishment in accordance with this Rule, a warning must be given setting forth the nature of the misuse that is occurring and stating, where appropriate, a reasonable time limit for the warning to be complied with. The warning may be communicated to the adverse party by electronic means, by radio or televised message, by press release or by other similar means. It may simply consist of an order to terminate the harmful activity within the specified period.[154]

5 Even if the warning is unheeded and an attack is to be undertaken, the principle of discrimination and the rules on proportionality and precautions in attack must be complied with.

6 So, consider the situation that might arise if State A has nuclear weapons and decides to disperse its holdings of the weapons. If its enemy, State B, finds out that a nuclear device is being stored within one of State A's hospital compounds, such action would fall outside the humanitarian function of the hospital and would, self-evidently, be harmful to State B. In such a scenario, the difficult decision confronting State B is whether it is feasible for it to set a time limit for compliance. Giving a warning with such a time limit will, potentially, give State A the opportunity to conceal the weapon elsewhere and may deprive State B of an opportunity to neutralise the nuclear weapon in some way. In such a situation, State B may be able to argue that the misuse of the medical facility is causing immediate and serious harm such that no reasonable time limit needs to be set for compliance. The alternative interpretation would be that it is the potential removal of the weapon to an unknown location, rather than the continued presence of the device in the hospital compound, that would cause immediate serious harm. Before undertaking an attack, the proportionality rule must be carefully applied and all appropriate precautions taken to minimise civilian casualties and damage and casualties and damage to specially protected persons and objects.

153 API, Article 13(2)(d).

154 AMW Manual, Commentary accompanying Rule 74(b), para. 2. As pointed out in paragraphs 3 and 4 of the Commentary accompanying Rule 74(b), the time limit must be reasonable, so as to give an opportunity for the relevant acts to be stopped or to allow for the removal of the wounded and sick from the medical facility before the attack takes place. Sometimes insisting on immediate compliance may be reasonable. It has been suggested that if the misuse is causing immediate serious harm, 'it will typically not be feasible to afford an opportunity for compliance' (Tallinn Manual 2.0, Commentary accompanying Rule 134, para. 6).

7 Loss of protection may also be the consequence of non-compliance with the conditions of protection, such as non-impartial assistance to victims. Such an activity would not be harmful to the enemy, so the aircraft or ship that is rendering such assistance may not be attacked but, for example, will lose its protection from capture.

8 If a medical establishment is being used for purposes that deprive it of its protection in accordance with this Rule, it is most unlikely that a nuclear weapon would be considered for a subsequent attack. The legal obligation to minimise civilian casualties and damage suggests that a precision munition that will limit its damaging effect as reliably as possible to the part of the compound that is actually being misused should be chosen. However, in the example given in paragraph 6, the target, a nuclear weapon, is of such a nature as to likely cause extensive collateral damage if attacked.

United Nations Personnel, Installations, Materiel, Units and Vehicles

Rule 57

It is prohibited to direct attacks, including nuclear attacks, against UN personnel for such time as the UN is not a party to the conflict and provided that they are entitled to protection as civilians. It is prohibited to direct attacks, including nuclear attacks, against materiel, installations, units and vehicles of the UN unless they are military objectives.

1 This Rule applies to international and non-international armed conflicts and has customary law status.[155] Article 7(1) of the UN Safety Convention provides: 'United Nations and associated personnel, their equipment and premises shall not be made the object of attack or of any action that prevents them from discharging their mandate.' UN personnel, materiel, installations, units and vehicles are permitted to display the UN emblem, and use of that emblem without the permission of the UN is prohibited (see Rule 51). However, when UN personnel take a direct part in hostilities or when UN materiel, installations, units or vehicles become military objectives, they lose their protection from being made the object of attack.[156]

155 Convention on the Safety of United Nations and Associated Personnel, New York, 9 December 1994 (UN Safety Convention), Article 7(1); Rome Statute, Article 8(2)(b)(iii) and 8(2)(e)(iii); UK Manual, paras. 14.9, 14.15; NIAC Manual, para. 3.3; ICRC Customary Law Study, Rule 33.

156 AMW Manual, Commentary accompanying Rule 98b, para. 2.

2 'United Nations personnel' comprise:

> (i) Persons engaged or deployed by the Secretary-General of the United Nations as members of the military, police or civilian components of a United Nations operation; (ii) Other officials and experts on mission for the UN or its specialized agencies or the International Atomic Energy Agency who are present in an official capacity in the area where a United Nations operation is being conducted.[157]

3 UN personnel are protected from attack so long as the UN is not a party to the conflict and so long as UN personnel do not take a direct part in the hostilities.[158] If the UN is a party to an international armed conflict, its military personnel who are engaged in the fighting become combatants and may be made the object of attack. UN personnel who are engaged in the provision or distribution of relief supplies or in peacekeeping duties will retain protected status.[159] Robust implementation of a peace enforcement mandate will not necessarily cause the UN to become a party to the conflict. Much will depend on the particular circumstances.

4 The protection afforded to UN materiel, units, installations and vehicles is contingent on them being entitled to the protection afforded to civilian objects by LOAC.[160] If they are being used to make an effective contribution to the military action of a party to the conflict, they become lawful targets.

5 While there are, therefore, certain circumstances in which UN personnel and their units, installations, materiel and vehicles may be lawfully attacked, the authors consider it to be most unlikely – indeed, almost inconceivable – that a nuclear attack against such targets would ever be lawful, let alone that it would realistically be contemplated by a responsible State. However if, for example, UN personnel, installations, materiel, units or vehicles bearing UN emblems were to be used by a party to the conflict to conceal or protect a nuclear weapon or to conceal or protect equipment associated with the use of nuclear weapons, the personnel, installations, materiel, units or vehicles that were being used in that way would be lawful targets and could be made the object of attack on that basis, subject to the rules on distinction, discrimination, proportionality and precautions.

157 UN Safety Convention, Article 1(a).

158 AMW Manual, Commentary accompanying Rule 98(b), para. 1.

159 AMW Manual, Commentary accompanying Rule 98(b), para. 5.

160 AMW Manual, Commentary accompanying Rule 98(c), para. 1.

Children

Rule 58

Conscripting or enlisting children into the armed forces or allowing them to take part in nuclear operations are prohibited.

This Rule is customary law and applies in both international and non-international armed conflicts. The term 'children' refers to persons under the age of fifteen years.

Journalists

Rule 59

Civilian journalists engaged in dangerous professional missions in areas of armed conflict shall be considered as civilians. They shall not be made the object of attack unless, and for such time as, they take a direct part in the hostilities.

1 This Rule is based on Article 79 of API. It applies in international and non-international armed conflicts and has customary law status.[161] Journalists, for the purposes of the present Rule, include reporters, cameramen, photographers and sound technicians.[162] The term will include persons who report for online media organisations, but it is unclear whether private persons who produce material for web blogs that are not associated with the established media will be included.[163]

2 API explains that journalists 'shall be protected as such under the Conventions and this Protocol, provided that they take no action adversely affecting their status as civilians … '.[164] Journalistic equipment, including recording equipment, cameras and computers, as well as all equipment directly associated with journalistic activities, will be classed as civilian objects and will retain protection as such, unless the equipment becomes a military objective (for the definition of military objective, see Rule 34 above). Journalists and their equipment enjoy specific protection, in that they are referred to explicitly in LOAC. They do not enjoy special protection, as the

[161] US DoD Law of War Manual, para. 4.24.2; UK Manual, para. 8.18; Canadian Manual, paras. 313, 441; German Manual, para. 515; NIAC Manual, para. 3.10; ICRC Customary Law Study, Rule 34.

[162] See United Nations Convention on the Protection of Journalists Engaged in Dangerous Missions in Areas of Armed Conflict, UN Doc A/10147 (1 August 1975), Annex I, Article 2(a), noted in Tallinn Manual 2.0, Commentary accompanying Rule 139, para. 4 and n. 1292.

[163] Tallinn Manual 2.0, Commentary accompanying Rule 139, para. 4

[164] API, Article 79(2).

level of protection they and their equipment have equates with that accorded to civilians and civilian objects.

3 Journalists lose their protection if and for such time as they take a direct part in hostilities. Journalistic investigation, collation of information and transmission of that information through broadcasting, print or other means are among the numerous routine activities of journalists. If, however, information in relation to one party to the conflict is obtained by a journalist secretively or by misrepresenting his or her identity or status with a view to communicating that information to the opposing party, such an activity might amount to espionage under LOAC.[165]

4 Consider, therefore, a situation in which a journalist receives information about the location of the nuclear weapons belonging to a party to the conflict, the preparedness of that party's nuclear forces, the command and control arrangements that party has made with regard to its nuclear force, the location of nuclear-armed submarines belonging to that party or the targets named on that party's nuclear strike list. If, while in that party's area of military operations, the journalist made any misrepresentation as to his or her identity or status as a journalist or acted secretively when obtaining that information, the mere act of obtaining the information may cause the journalist to be accused of spying and/or to be regarded as taking a direct part in the hostilities.[166]

Dams, Dykes and Nuclear Electrical Generating Stations

Rule 60

To avoid the release of dangerous forces and consequent severe losses among the civilian population, particular care must be taken when undertaking attacks, including nuclear attacks, against works and installations containing dangerous forces, namely, dams, dykes and nuclear electrical generating stations, and against military objectives located in the vicinity of such works and installations.

1 Article 56 of API and Article 15 of APII prohibit attacks against the works and installations referred to in this Rule, even where they qualify as military

165 Note that a civilian journalist will be subject to the domestic law applicable in the location where he or she is reporting and will therefore be subject to the definition of espionage applied there.

166 Note that while espionage does not breach LOAC, it is a crime under the criminal law of most countries and renders the spy liable to arrest, trial and, in the event of conviction, punishment.

objectives, if the attack may cause the release of dangerous forces and consequent severe losses among the civilian population. The API provision is subject to certain exceptions. While the two treaty provisions do not reflect customary law,[167] the more modest obligation in the current Rule is considered by the authors to have customary status.[168] However, States that are parties to API and APII will be bound by the treaty provisions.

2 To attack such works or installations using a nuclear weapon risks releasing two sets of dangerous forces – namely, the forces resident in the work or installation that is the target of the attack and the blast and nuclear fallout that the detonation of the nuclear weapon will release. Accordingly, a very high degree of care will be required, and in virtually all imaginable circumstances the use of a nuclear weapon against such a target would be unlawful. This is because it is accepted by all States, including those not parties to API and APII, that the prohibition of indiscriminate attacks (Rule 37) applies to all attacks, including those employing nuclear weapons. In most foreseeable circumstances, a nuclear attack on a work or installation of the sort referred to in this Rule can be expected to have indiscriminate effects. At any event, when considering which precautions are feasible, the attacker must take into account the severe dangers involved in such an attack and must accordingly maximise the precautionary measures that are taken and the care with which they are applied.

3 In deciding whether the consequent losses will be 'severe', a good faith assessment of all relevant and reasonably available information must be made.[169]

4 The Rule applies only to dams, dykes and nuclear electrical generating stations and to military objectives located in the vicinity of such works or installations. The Rule does not apply if the work or installation is used in regular, significant and direct support of military operations and if attacking it – say, using a conventional weapon – is the only feasible way of bringing that support to an end. If that is the case and if the work or installation is to be attacked, all feasible precautions must still be taken to avoid the release of the dangerous forces.

5 API provides for a mark to facilitate the identification of the objects that are protected by this Rule. The mark consists of a group of three bright orange circles placed on the same axis. This mark is specified in Article 16 of Annex

167 See US DoD Law of War Manual, paras. 5.13.1, 17.7.1.

168 See Tallinn Manual 2.0, Commentary accompanying Rule 140, para. 1.

169 Consider Tallinn Manual 2.0, Commentary accompanying Rule 140, para. 5.

I to API. The absence of such a mark does not deprive the work or installation of protection under the Rule.

Protection of Objects Indispensable to the Survival of the Civilian Population

Rule 61

It is prohibited to use nuclear weapons or substances to attack, destroy, remove or render useless objects indispensable to the survival of the civilian population, for the specific purpose of denying them for their sustenance value to the civilian population or to the adverse party.

1 This Rule is based on Article 54(2) of API, is a rule of customary law applicable in international armed conflicts and is a manifestation of the customary prohibition of starvation of civilians as a method of warfare. Where non-international armed conflicts are concerned, Article 14 of APII provides: 'Starvation of civilians as a method of combat is prohibited. It is therefore prohibited to attack, destroy, remove or render useless, for that purpose, objects indispensable to the survival of the civilian population . . . .'

2 The key element of the Rule is the purpose with which the activity is undertaken – namely, depriving the civilian population or the adverse party of the sustenance value of the items in question. Accordingly, military operations that are undertaken to achieve a different purpose but that have the effect of depriving the civilian population or the adverse party of the sustenance value of objects indispensable to survival will not breach this Rule (but may of course breach other Rules, for example, Rule 38 (proportionality)).

3 The treaty provisions give examples of items protected by the Rule – namely, foodstuffs; agricultural areas for the production of foodstuffs; crops; livestock; drinking water installations and supplies; and irrigation works. Other items may also be indispensable to the survival of the civilian population, such as medical supplies, clothing, bedding and means of shelter. What is in fact indispensable will depend on the circumstances, including the climate, geographical location and other factors. To come within the Rule, an object must be indispensable to survival, not simply beneficial.[170]

4 The Rule does not apply to objects that are exclusively used to sustain members of the armed forces or, if not as sustenance, then in direct support of military action. However, action must not be taken against such objects if it

170 Tallinn Manual 2.0, Commentary accompanying Rule 141, para. 4.

may be expected to leave the civilian population with such inadequate food or water as to cause it to starve or force it to move.[171]

5 Consider a decision to undertake a nuclear attack against an agricultural area for the specific purpose of destroying crops over a specified area and contaminating crops and water supplies over a wider area so that the civilian population will be deprived of food and water. Such an attack would breach this Rule. Alternatively, consider a nuclear attack the purpose of which is to destroy an industrial facility that is being used to manufacture the enemy's strategic strike missiles and other military equipment and ammunition. As a result of the attack it is to be expected that crops growing in neighbouring fields and water supplies in the vicinity will be rendered useless due to contamination. Because denial of objects indispensable to the survival of the civilian population was not the, or even a, purpose of the attack, this Rule will in this case not be breached (but consider other rules, such as Rule 38 (proportionality)).

Cultural Property

Rule 62

The parties to an armed conflict must respect and protect cultural property during nuclear operations. They may only use cultural property or its immediate surroundings for military purposes in cases where military necessity imperatively so requires. The parties to an armed conflict may only direct attacks against cultural property where military necessity imperatively so requires.

1 This Rule applies to both international and non-international armed conflicts and is a rule of customary law.[172]

2 The Hague Cultural Property Convention defines cultural property as

> movable or immovable property of great importance to the cultural heritage of every people, such as monuments of architecture, art or history, whether religious or secular; archaeological sites; groups of buildings which, as a whole, are of historical or artistic interest; works of art; manuscripts, books and other objects of artistic, historical or archaeological interest; as well as

[171] API, Article 54(3).

[172] Hague Regulations, Article 27; Hague Convention IX, Article 5; API, Article 53; APII, Article 16; Hague Cultural Property Convention, Article 4. See also US DoD Law of War Manual, para. 5.18, second para.; UK Manual, paras. 5.25–5.26.8, 15.18–15.18.3; Canadian Manual, paras. 111, 443; NIAC Manual, para. 4.2.2; ICRC Customary Law Study, Rules 38, 39; Rome Statute, Article 8(2)(b)(ix) and 8(2)(e)(iv).

scientific collections and important collections of books or archives or of reproductions of the property defined above.[173]

This definition is widely accepted as being comprehensive and as reflecting customary law.[174]

3 Parties to an armed conflict are required to respect and protect cultural property.[175] The former obligation requires that during military operations all practically possible measures be taken to avoid harm to cultural property.[176] The latter obligation requires that feasible protective measures be taken to safeguard cultural property against harm caused by others during military operations.[177]

4 Consider a nuclear attack against a military objective located near an archaeological site causing damage to the archaeological remains. If no consideration is given to the effect of the attack on the archaeological site and if a weapon with a reduced explosive footprint could have accomplished the military purpose of the attack, these may be relevant indicators to show that the duty to respect cultural property has not been complied with.

5 The use by a party to an armed conflict of cultural property for military purposes (e.g. to store equipment related to military nuclear operations) would constitute a breach of the second sentence of this Rule. The authors take the view that a decision to use cultural property for military purposes must be taken by the commander of a force of at least battalion size or equivalent.[178] The second sentence of the Rule applies also to the immediate surroundings of cultural property, because the use of those immediate surroundings for military purposes may be expected to expose the cultural property to the risk of damage or destruction in the event of an attack.[179] While the second sentence of the Rule refers to use for military purposes, it is the authors' view that any use of the cultural property or of its immediate surroundings for purposes that are likely to expose such property to the risk of damage or destruction should be avoided. Before a cultural object is used for military purposes, the emblem identifying its status as cultural property must be removed.

173 Hague Cultural Property Convention, Article 1(a). The definition also includes buildings and shelters for movable cultural property and centres containing a large amount of cultural property; see Article 1(b) and (c).

174 UK Manual, paras. 5.25, 5.25.2; AMW Manual, Rule 1(o).

175 Hague Cultural Property Convention, Articles 4, 2 respectively.

176 This duty goes wider than merely prohibiting attacks on cultural property. See UK Manual, para. 5.25.3; German Manual, para. 903; AMW Manual Rule 95(c).

177 AMW Manual, Rule 94; Tallinn Manual 2.0, Commentary accompanying Rule 142, para. 3.

178 In this regard, they share the view of the majority of the AMW experts; see AMW Manual, Commentary accompanying Section N(II)(i), para. 1.

179 AMW Manual, Commentary accompanying Rule 93(a), para 1.

6 In order to facilitate the identification and protection of cultural property in territory under their control, parties to the conflict should mark it with the internationally recognised emblem and should provide the enemy with appropriate information as to its location. If such measures have not been taken, this does not deprive the cultural property of its protected status during international armed conflicts.[180]

7 An attack may be directed at cultural property only if military necessity imperatively so requires.[181] So, if the military purpose can be achieved by taking some alternative action that does not involve attacking the cultural property, that alternative action must, other things being equal, be preferred. It is only if attacking the cultural property is imperatively required that it should be considered, subject to taking all required precautions with a view to avoiding, and in any event to minimising, the damage that the cultural property actually suffers. A decision to attack cultural property must be taken at an appropriate level of command; an effective advance warning should be given; and the attack should proceed only if the warning has gone unheeded.[182]

8 Notwithstanding the foregoing, the authors consider it unlikely – perhaps, inconceivable – that a responsible party to an armed conflict would actually consider using, let alone actually use, a nuclear weapon against cultural property 'of great importance to the cultural heritage of every people'.

The Natural Environment

The obligations that a State has in relation to the natural environment during times of armed conflict will vary depending on whether the State is a party to API, whether it is a party to the Environmental Modification Convention and whether, in the case of API, the State made a relevant statement on ratification of the treaty. As will be immediately evident, this situation results in differing legal obligations among States, and some of those differences have particular relevance to the use of nuclear weapons. In order to present the legal position

180 AMW Manual, Rule 94.

181 See Hague Cultural Property Convention, Articles 4(2), 11(2). The AMW Manual, Rule 95(b), applies this part of the Rule to the immediate surroundings of cultural property. The present authors do not believe, as a matter of *lex lata*, that an attack on a military objective in the immediate vicinity of cultural property is permissible only in the case of imperative military necessity. However, the expected destruction or damage to the cultural property must be carefully assessed and reflected in the proportionality assessment that is made, as is acknowledged by the authors of the AMW Manual in Rule 95(c) thereof.

182 AMW Manual, Rule 96.

as clearly as possible, the opening words of each of the Rules below will seek to make it clear which group of States is affected by that Rule.

Certain comments apply to both of the following Rules relating to the natural environment. For present purposes, there is no generally agreed definition of 'natural environment'.[183] However, it is clear that the use of the word 'natural' shows that the term does not include environmental features that are made by humans, and it is similarly clear that ecosystems will form part of the natural environment.[184] For practical purposes, it can be interpreted as meaning the biological environment in which the population is living, which would extend to fauna, flora and climatic elements.

Natural Environment: The Rule under API

Rule 63

For States that are parties to Additional Protocol I and that did not make a statement that applies to Articles 35(3) and 55 of that treaty, it is prohibited to employ methods or means of warfare which are intended, or which may be expected, to cause widespread, long-term and severe damage to the natural environment and thereby to prejudice the health or survival of the population.

1 As the opening language indicates, this Rule binds States that are parties to API and that made no statement in relation to Articles 35(3) and 55 of the treaty when becoming a party to it. The Rule blends the two provisions by adding the words 'and thereby to prejudice the health or survival of the population' at the end of the text. As to the meanings of means of warfare and methods of warfare, see Rule 69.

2 If the intention is to cause the prohibited environmental damage and if the relevant means or method is indeed employed, the Rule will have been breached, irrespective of whether the prohibited damage in fact materialises. The words 'which may be expected' are clearly intended to introduce a degree of objectivity into the treaty provision and thus into the present Rule. The terms 'widespread, long-term and severe' are not defined in API. The API Commentary observes:

> The time or duration required (i.e. long-term) was considered by some to be measured in decades. Some representatives referred to twenty or thirty years as being a minimum period. Others referred to battlefield destruction in

183 AMW Manual, Commentary accompanying Section M, para. 6; Tallinn Manual 2.0, Commentary accompanying Rule 143, para. 3.

184 AMW Manual, Commentary accompanying Section M, para. 6.

> France in the First World War as being outside the scope of the prohibition .... It appeared to be a widely shared assumption that battlefield damage incidental to conventional warfare would not normally be proscribed by this provision. What the article is primarily directed to is thus such damage as would be likely to prejudice, over a long term, the continued survival of the civilian population or would risk causing it major health problems.[185]

3 It should be noted that all three aspects – widespread, long-term and severe – must be present for the Rule to be broken. Accordingly, if a State to which this Rule applies were to use a nuclear weapon, thereby causing nuclear contamination that is spread far and wide, that will poison the environment for decades and that prejudices the survival and health of the civilian population, it will have breached this Rule.

Natural Environment: The Customary Law Rule

Rule 64

The following rules apply to all States, including those that are parties to API but that made a statement on ratification of the treaty excluding the application to nuclear weapons of the new rules introduced by the treaty. The natural environment is a civilian object except when a portion of it becomes a military objective. The use of a nuclear weapon to cause wanton destruction of the natural environment is prohibited. When planning, ordering or conducting nuclear operations, constant care must be taken to spare the natural environment.

1 A number of States made statements when ratifying API to the effect that the new rules introduced by the treaty will not apply for such States in relation to nuclear weapons. Articles 35(3) and 55 of API are widely recognised as being new rules introduced by API. Therefore, for States that made the relevant statements, Articles 35(3) and 55, and by extension Rule 63 of this book, do not apply to the use of nuclear weapons. This has the further effect that such States are bound only by the customary LOAC rules relating to the natural environment.

2 The provisions in the second, third and fourth sentences of this Rule bind all States. For States that ratified API without making a 'nuclear statement', this Rule applies in addition to Rule 63. For States that ratified subject to a nuclear statement and for States that are not parties to API, this Rule sets forth the law that protects the natural environment in times of armed conflict.

185 API Commentary, para. 1454.

The provisions of this Rule apply in international and non-international armed conflicts.[186]

3 When ratifying API, the United Kingdom made the following statement:

> It continues to be the understanding of the United Kingdom that the rules introduced by the Protocol apply exclusively to conventional weapons without prejudice to any other rules of international law applicable to other types of weapons. In particular, the rules so introduced do not have any effect on, and do not regulate or prohibit the use of, nuclear weapons.[187]

4 The rules referred to in this Rule apply to all States. That the natural environment is in principle a civilian object is widely accepted. As is the case with any other object, a portion of the natural environment may become a military objective if, by nature, location, purpose or use, it makes an effective contribution to military action such that its total or partial destruction, capture or neutralisation, in the prevailing circumstances, offers a definite military advantage.[188] The entire natural environment will never be a military objective and, if a part of it becomes a military objective, any attack, including a nuclear attack, must be directed at that part, must be reasonably limited to that part and must comply with the targeting law rules, so far as relevant, set forth in this Section. If an attack may be expected to cause incidental damage to the natural environment, that incidental damage must be considered when the proportionality of the planned nuclear attack is considered. Constant care must be taken to protect the natural environment in general.[189]

5 Wanton destruction of the natural environment is prohibited.[190] For this part of the Rule to be broken, the environmental destruction must be the result of a deliberate act undertaken maliciously, so the act must not be justifiable on the basis of military necessity.[191]

6 It would therefore be prohibited to use a nuclear weapon deliberately to target the natural environment in the knowledge that that part of the environment is not being used for military purposes, that it has not become a military objective and that the attack will not fulfil any military purpose. If a nuclear weapon is to be used to attack a military objective, the expected impact on the

186 AMW Manual, Commentary accompanying Section M, paras. 5, 9, 10; see also Tallinn Manual 2.0, Rule 143 and paras 1, 4, 5 of the accompanying Commentary.

187 Statement (a) made by the United Kingdom on ratification of API on 28 January 1998. Other NATO States made statements to similar effect.

188 See Rule 34 and API, Article 52(2).

189 See Rule 39 and API, Article 57(1).

190 Hague Regulations, Article 23(g); AMW Manual, Rule 88; ICRC Customary Law Study, Commentary accompanying Rule 43; Rome Statute, Article 8(2)(b)(iv) and 8(2)(e)(xii).

191 GCIV, Article 147; AMW Manual, Commentary accompanying Rule 88, para. 2.

natural environment must be included in the collateral damage part of the proportionality evaluation when the attack is being planned or considered. In deciding whether the use of a nuclear weapon is appropriate in particular circumstances or whether an attack on a nuclear weapon facility would be lawful, the legal duty to take constant care to spare civilian objects like the natural environment must be taken carefully into account. To direct an attack against part of the natural environment deliberately and knowing that it is not a military objective constitutes the war crime of intentionally directing an attack against a civilian object;[192] note that causing clearly excessive damage to the natural environment may, depending on the circumstances, also be a war crime.[193]

192 Rome Statute, Article 8(2)(b)(ii).
193 Rome Statute, Article 8(2)(b)(iv).

F

Neutrality

In this relatively brief Section, no attempt is being made to reproduce all of the rules of the law of neutrality. Rather, the purpose of the Section is merely to draw attention to some of those rules that are considered to be of greatest relevance to military operations involving nuclear weapons.

Neutrality law applies only during an international armed conflict. The law of neutrality and therefore the Rules of this Section do not apply to non-international armed conflicts.[1] Key rules of the law of neutrality are to be found in Hague Conventions V and XIII of 1907 and in customary law. The word 'neutral' refers to a State that is not a belligerent party to the conflict.[2] Neutral territory is therefore the 'land territory of neutral States, as well as waters subject to their territorial sovereignty (internal waters, territorial sea and, where applicable, archipelagic waters) and the airspace above those areas'.[3]

No declaration is required to establish neutral status. Rather, it is the simple fact of not being a belligerent party to the international armed conflict that suffices.[4] The law of neutrality does not apply if the UN Security Council has either (i) identified one or more belligerent parties as responsible for an unlawful resort to armed force in breach of Article 2(4) of the UN Charter or (ii) if the UN Security Council has taken binding preventive or enforcement measures under Chapter VII of the UN Charter. In such circumstances, a State that is not a party to the conflict cannot invoke the law of neutrality as justification for an act that is incompatible with its obligations under the UN Charter.[5] So, if the UN Security Council has determined the existence of

1 AMW Manual, Commentary accompanying Section X, para. 5.

2 San Remo Manual, para. 13(d).

3 Tallinn Manual 2.0, Commentary accompanying Part 20, para. 2. See also German Manual, paras. 1108, 1118; AMW Manual, Commentary accompanying Rule 166; San Remo Manual, para. 14.

4 UK Manual, para. 12.11.

5 AMW Manual, Commentary accompanying Rule 1(aa) and Rule 165.

a threat to the peace, a breach of the peace or an act of aggression under Article 39 of the UN Charter and has taken preventive or enforcement measures, the decisions of the Security Council are binding on member States and prevail over other treaty obligations.[6] Accordingly, States taking no part in the enforcement or preventive action are not permitted to hamper or impede action being taken in accordance with the binding UN Security Council decision and cannot rely on the impartial status of neutrals.[7]

Neutrality law governs the relationship between, on the one hand, States that are involved as parties to an international armed conflict and, on the other, States that are not party to the armed conflict. The primary purpose of the law of neutrality is to prevent an escalation of an international armed conflict. The parties to the conflict are obliged to respect the inviolability of neutral territory. To that end, the law of neutrality obliges the belligerent States to refrain from the exercise of any belligerent rights in neutral territory (which includes the territorial sea and, where applicable, archipelagic waters) and in neutral national airspace (which is the airspace above neutral territory and neutral sea areas). Neutral States are obliged to treat the belligerents impartially and to defend their neutral status. Strictly speaking, the law of neutrality, which protects the territorial sovereignty of neutral States, does not address the protection of neutral nationals or neutral aircraft and ships, whose status is to be determined under prize law (which can be ignored for present purposes).

Neutral Territory

Rule 65

Hostilities between parties to an international armed conflict, including nuclear operations, must not be conducted within or from neutral territory.

1 The basis for this Rule is Article 1 of Hague Convention V and Article 1 of Hague Convention XIII.[8] The Rule reflects customary law. Compliance with the Rule is vital if escalation of international armed conflicts is to be prevented.

2 The parties to an international armed conflict are not permitted to engage in hostilities in neutral airspace, on neutral territory, in neutral internal waters or in neutral territorial seas and archipelagic seas, if applicable. Similarly, they

6 UN Charter, Article 103.

7 AMW Manual, Commentary accompanying Rule 165, para. 2

8 See also the 1923 Draft Hague Rules of Aerial Warfare, Articles 39, 40; AMW Manual, Rule 166: Tallinn Manual 2.0, Rule 151.

may not fire off weapons while in such locations, even if the intended target is located outside neutral territory. The definition of neutral territory, given in the chapeau to this Section, does not include the Exclusive Economic Zone (EEZ). Accordingly, it is not prohibited to conduct hostilities within a neutral State's EEZ or in the airspace above a neutral State's EEZ.[9] There is, however, an obligation on the parties to the armed conflict to pay due regard to the rights of coastal States (e.g. in respect of exploration and exploitation of the EEZ's economic resources and the protection of the marine environment). This has been interpreted as an obligation to 'balance the military advantages anticipated as against any negative impact on the rights of Neutrals'.[10]

Prohibited Acts in Neutral Territory

Rule 66

In neutral territory the parties to an international armed conflict must not: commit hostile acts such as attacking or capturing persons or objects; establish bases of military operations; intercept, inspect, divert or capture vessels or aircraft; use neutral territory as a sanctuary; or undertake any activity that contributes to the war-fighting effort of either party to the conflict. Parties to such a conflict must not use neutral territory for the movement of troops, munitions of war or supplies or for the operation of military communication systems.

1 This Rule is based on Articles 2 and 3 of Hague Convention V, Articles 2 and 5 of Hague Convention XIII and Articles 39, 40, 42 and 47 of the Draft Hague Rules of Aerial Warfare of 1923. It is a rule of customary law.[11]

2 This Rule spells out the implications of the inviolability of neutral territory. If a party to an international armed conflict attacks, destroys or captures an enemy aircraft in neutral airspace, or attacks, destroys or captures a nuclear-armed enemy vessel (e.g. a submarine) in neutral waters or at a neutral port, this would be a clear breach of the Rule. Equally, if a party to such a conflict were, for example, to use an airfield on neutral territory as a base for aircraft that are being used for nuclear operations, or were to use a neutral port as the base from which a nuclear-armed submarine undertakes its patrols, this kind of activity would clearly breach this Rule.

3 The Rule also applies to overflights by military aircraft. So, if a nuclear-armed military aircraft of a party to an international armed conflict were to

9 San Remo Manual, paras. 34, 35.

10 AMW Manual, Commentary accompanying Rule 166, para. 3.

11 AMW Manual, Commentary accompanying Rule 167(a), para. 1.

overfly the territory of a neutral State – say, while on its way to the target of a planned attack, including a nuclear attack – the Rule will have been breached.[12] It follows from this that if a military aircraft belonging to a party to an international armed conflict enters neutral airspace (other than the airspace superjacent to straits used for international navigation or archipelagic sea lanes), the neutral must do everything in its power to prevent or terminate the violation of its neutrality.[13] If the intruding aircraft cannot be forced to land, it may be shot down. If the aircraft does land, the aircraft and its crew must be interned for the duration of the international armed conflict. Likewise, States that are party to an international armed conflict are prohibited from transporting equipment and supplies through neutral territory for use in connection with nuclear operations and from using apparatus on neutral territory for the purpose of communicating with nuclear forces, whether land-, sea- or air-based.

4 Belligerent warships may, however, continue to exercise the right of innocent passage in neutral territorial seas. That right does not, however, permit the launching, landing or taking-on-board of any aircraft or of any military device.[14] In addition, there is no violation of neutrality where a party to an international armed conflict uses a public, internationally and openly accessible network such as the Internet for military purposes, even if part of this infrastructure is situated within the territories of neutrals.[15]

5 It follows from the foregoing that parties to an international armed conflict must not attack persons or objects on neutral land, in neutral waters or in neutral airspace. They must not use those places as a base for undertaking military operations against targets, wherever those targets may be located. Moreover, they must not engage in the interception, inspection, diversion or capture of vessels or aircraft in neutral territory. Finally, they must not otherwise use military force or contribute to the war-fighting effort within neutral territory.[16]

12 Note, however, that a belligerent military aircraft in distress may be allowed to enter neutral airspace and to land on neutral territory. The neutral State, for its part, must require the aircraft to land – if need be, backing up the requirement with the use of suitable force – and must intern the aircraft and its crew for the duration of the conflict; see AMW Manual, Rule 172(a)(i). Belligerent military aircraft may also be permitted to enter neutral territory in order to capitulate; see AMW Manual, Rule 172(a)(iii). The capitulating military aircraft and its crew must likewise be interned for the duration of the conflict. If the aircraft commits a hostile act, it may be attacked; see AMW Manual, Rule 172(b).

13 Hague Convention XIII, Article 25; Draft Hague Rules of Aerial Warfare, Articles 42, 47; AMW Manual, Rule 170(c).

14 UNCLOS, Article 19(2).

15 Consider Hague Convention V, Article 8.

16 AMW Manual, Rules 171(a), (b), (c), (d).

6 As to activities that contribute to the war-fighting effort, it should be noted that a neutral 'is not bound to prevent the export or transit on behalf of a belligerent of aircraft, parts of aircraft, or material, supplies or munitions for aircraft'.[17] A neutral is, however, 'bound to use the means at its disposal: (1) to prevent the departure from its jurisdiction of an aircraft in a condition to make a hostile attack against a belligerent Power . . . '.[18]

Obligations of Neutrals

Rule 67

A neutral must not permit the acts referred to in Rule 66 to take place within its territory and must do everything it can to prevent or stop them.

1 This Rule is based on Article 5 of Hague Convention V and Article 42 of the Draft Hague Rules of Aerial Warfare. It is a rule of customary international law.[19] Central to the Rule, and to the law of neutrality, is the idea that if a State wishes to benefit from the advantages of neutrality and the protections it offers, the State must not permit misuse of its territory by the belligerent parties.

2 A neutral is required to use the means that are available to it to monitor activity on its territory, including its territorial sea and in its airspace, in order to become aware if a belligerent party is breaching its neutrality. The action that a neutral will, in practice, be able to take in this regard will depend on the relevant technical facilities that are available to it.[20]

3 The neutral State must use the means available to it to prevent or stop breaches of its neutrality.[21] Depending on the circumstances, those means may include the use of force. Such a use of force cannot be regarded as a hostile act by the neutral.[22] The degree of force used by the neutral must be limited to that which is required to 'repel the incursion and maintain its neutrality'.[23] These provisions reflect customary law.

4 If a neutral uses force to defend its neutrality, this cannot be regarded as an armed attack for the purposes of Article 51 of the UN Charter, with the

17 Draft Hague Rules of Aerial Warfare, Article 45.
18 Ibid., Article 46(1).
19 Consider San Remo Manual, para. 22.
20 AMW Manual, Rule 170(b) and the accompanying Commentary.
21 Hague Convention XIII, Article 8; Draft Hague Rules of Aerial Warfare, Articles 42, 47.
22 Hague Convention V, Article 10; Hague Convention XIII, Article 26; Draft Hague Rules of Aerial Warfare, Article 48.
23 AMW Manual, Rule 169. If the neutral uses force that exceeds what is required to terminate the violation of its neutrality, the affected belligerent may take countermeasures; see AMW Manual, Commentary accompanying Rule 169, para. 2.

consequence that the affected belligerent has no right to use force in self-defence.

5 Consider a situation in which a nuclear armed submarine belonging to a belligerent party to an international armed conflict is loitering within the territorial sea of a neutral State. The neutral State becomes aware of its presence and demands that the submarine move into international waters. The commander of the submarine refuses to leave the neutral's territorial sea. The neutral State would, in the absence of alternative, less destructive possible measures, be entitled, indeed required, to use force against the submarine in order to bring an end to the breach of its neutrality.

6 If a neutral State is unwilling or unable to take the measures necessary to terminate a violation of its neutral status, the opposing belligerent 'may, in the absence of any feasible and timely alternative, use such force as is necessary to terminate the violation of neutrality'.[24] In all other instances, the unjustified use of force against a neutral State by a belligerent will be contrary to Article 2(4) of the UN Charter and may trigger an international armed conflict between the belligerent and the neutral State.

7 The issue remains unresolved as to whether the law of neutrality applies in its entirety to a State that has declared itself neutral and that is a member State of a system of collective self-defence, such as NATO. For instance, during the 2003 Iraq War, the German government officially declared its neutrality, but it continued to allow the use of Allied military bases in Germany. While some take the position that membership of a system of collective self-defence modifies the law of neutrality, the present authors take the view that the use of military bases in neutral territory is in violation of neutrality.

Protection of Neutral Territory against Harmful Effects of Hostilities

Rule 68

In the conduct of military operations, including nuclear operations, the parties to an international armed conflict must take all feasible measures to avoid harmful effects on neutral territory.

1 Neither Hague Convention V nor Hague Convention XIII contains any specific provision corresponding to this Rule. Rather, the Rule follows from the general obligation to refrain from activities violating the rights of other States. It must not be confused with the obligation of belligerent States to pay

[24] AMW Manual, Rule 168(b). See also San Remo Manual, para. 22.

due regard to the rights enjoyed by neutral States in their EEZ, on their continental shelf or in high sea areas.[25]

2 The purpose of the Rule is to protect the territorial integrity of neutral States against harmful effects of hostilities. Accordingly, this obligation also applies, for example, to the radiation effects of a nuclear explosion. It is important to stress that it is not absolute. The term 'feasible' implies measures that are practicable or practically possible, taking all attendant circumstances into account, including military and humanitarian considerations. Accordingly, what is feasible has to be determined in the light of the circumstances of the concrete situation.

25 San Remo Manual, paras. 34, 35, 36.

G

Weapons Law as It Applies to Nuclear Weapons

In this Section we consider the application of the law of weaponry to nuclear weapons. At the outset, however, three qualifications are called for. First, in the opinion of many commentators, nuclear weapons are inherently unlawful, notwithstanding the application of particular weapons law rules. Second, such weapons have been the subject of an ICJ Advisory Opinion, discussed below in Section J, which acknowledged that their threat or use is likely to be unlawful in most circumstances. Third, a convention has been adopted, in the form of an arms control treaty, that, for participating States, will prohibit the use, possession, stockpiling and transfer of, and other activities associated with, such weapons; the convention's provisions will be examined in Section K. So it is against the background of these three qualifications that in this Section we consider how the principles and rules of weapons law apply to nuclear weapons.

There are important customary and treaty law rules that should be considered when making that assessment. Accordingly, our focus is on the law that applies to the means and methods of nuclear warfare (i.e. to the weapons and to the generic ways in which they would potentially be used), not on the law that regulates any particular intended, threatened or actual use of them. The latter aspect is addressed by the law of targeting and has been summarised in Section E.

It will be appreciated that weapons law includes numerous rules, some of which will have no relevance to nuclear weapons, and such irrelevant material has therefore been omitted from the present Section. The Section starts by considering the customary principles of weapons law, then addresses rules of general application and thereafter looks at compliance with weapons law, including the rules as to legal review of new means and methods of warfare. Treaties and other international arrangements that are concerned with arms reduction, or with the kinds or numbers of relevant weapons or platforms that a State is permitted to have or deploy, are briefly noted in Section K.

Means and Methods of Nuclear Warfare

Rule 69

For the purposes of this book, a 'means of nuclear warfare' comprises a nuclear weapon and its associated systems, whereas a 'method of nuclear warfare' consists of the tactics, techniques and procedures whereby nuclear hostilities are conducted.

1 The term 'means of warfare' refers to weapons and weapon systems. For the purposes of this Section, a weapon is an object, device or mechanism that is used, intended to be used or designed to be used to cause damage to an object and/or injury to a person in connection with an armed conflict. Accordingly, a nuclear means of warfare consists of the nuclear warhead, its delivery mechanism and all associated equipment and supporting systems that are required for the operation of the nuclear weapon. Typically, a nuclear weapon, in contrast to a nuclear means of warfare, will consist of the warhead and the other elements of the missile, rocket or bomb on board the weapon, including its fuel and the propulsion, guidance and associated equipment. The supplementary, off-board control and other systems that enable the nuclear weapon to perform its function will be the remaining parts of the nuclear means of warfare.

2 Methods of nuclear warfare consist of the ways in which nuclear hostilities are conducted and are distinct from the nuclear weapons and associated systems. Thus, while a specific short- to medium-range, limited-yield tactical nuclear weapon, together with its operating systems, would be a means of warfare, tactical, battlefield nuclear strike would be a method of warfare.

3 An important question arises in relation to the range of activities that States may undertake with regard to nuclear weapons. Not all such activities will necessarily qualify as methods of warfare. A threat to use a nuclear weapon during and in connection with an armed conflict, with the purpose of persuading the enemy to act, or refrain from acting, in a particular way, will so qualify. The maintenance in peacetime of a nuclear deterrent capability will not amount to a nuclear method of warfare, because no armed conflict is under way and because passive deterrence lacks a sufficient link with active hostilities. It should, however, be noted that acts that do not amount to nuclear attacks, as that term is defined in Rule 29, may nevertheless constitute methods of nuclear warfare.

Choice of Method and Means Not Unlimited

Rule 70

In any armed conflict, the right of the parties to the conflict to choose methods or means of nuclear warfare is not unlimited.

1 This Rule is based on Article 22 of the Hague Regulations and on Article 35(1) of API. It is a principle of the law of armed conflict (LOAC) that applies in international and non-international armed conflicts and that has customary law status.[1] It therefore binds all States.

2 The Rule implicitly recognises that there are different kinds of nuclear weapon and that the potential use of such a weapon may fall to be considered in diverse circumstances. The principle shows that it is international law that specifies that there are limits, the most stringent imaginable limits, on when such weapons may be employed, and indeed it is international law that determines what those limits are.

3 The limits on lawful use referred to in the previous paragraph may derive from general weapons law rules, from the application of targeting law rules or from weapons law rules specifically applicable to nuclear weapons.

Superfluous Injury and Unnecessary Suffering

Rule 71

It is prohibited to employ weapons, including nuclear weapons, that are of a nature to cause superfluous injury or unnecessary suffering.

1 This Rule has its origins in the preamble to the St Petersburg Declaration of 1868, subsequently developed in Article 23(e) of the Hague Regulations of 1899 and 1907. Its modern formulation, which is reflected in this Rule, is set forth in Article 35(2) of API. It is a LOAC principle that applies in both international and non-international armed conflicts. The principle has customary law status and therefore binds all States.[2]

2 The principle builds on the preceding principle embodied in Rule 70. It recognises that the infliction of injury and suffering is not inevitably unlawful. Injury or suffering may be necessary in order to achieve the

[1] The International Court of Justice noted that 'the established principles and rules of humanitarian law applicable in armed conflict' are imbued with an 'intrinsically humanitarian character ... which permeates the entire law of armed conflict and applies to all forms of warfare, those of the past, those of the present and those of the future'. ICJ Nuclear Opinion, para. 86.

[2] ICJ Nuclear Opinion, para. 78.

legitimate purpose of the armed conflict (i.e. the defeat of the enemy at the earliest possible moment with the minimum expenditure of life and resources). Nevertheless, a weapon or the method of using a weapon will be unlawful if it is of a nature to occasion additional injury or suffering for which there is no corresponding military purpose. This aspect is reflected in the use of the comparatives 'superfluous' and 'unnecessary'.

3 The practical application of the principle involves a consideration of alternative methods of achieving the generic kind of military advantage or military purpose for which the weapon will typically be used. All weapons can be misused in order to increase the amount of injury and/or suffering. The principle reflected in the present Rule is concerned with the degree of injury and/or suffering that is the inevitable consequence of the employment of the weapon in its intended or designed circumstances of use.

4 The fact that, when used as intended, a weapon will inevitably occasion the most serious injuries and/or the most grave suffering does not, per se, render such a weapon unlawful. If the generic purpose of that weapon is to achieve a military advantage of the greatest importance and if no alternative weapon exists that would achieve a similar generic military advantage while occasioning less injury and/or suffering, then the weapon system in question might comply with the principle.

5 Applying the principle to a nuclear weapon will involve the most careful application of these considerations. It would be legally wrong to assume that a nuclear weapon would necessarily breach the principle. It would, however, be likely to do so in most potential uses, and a weapon review of the kind referred to in Rule 75 should clearly articulate the circumstances in which its employment would not be legally permissible.

Applying the Indiscriminate Weapons Rule to Nuclear Weapons

Rule 72

It is prohibited to employ nuclear weapons that are indiscriminate by nature.

1 This Rule is based on Article 51(4)(b) and (c) of API. The prohibition of indiscriminate attacks is set forth in the first sentence of Article 51(4) of API. The present Rule is now recognised as a principle of customary international law that binds all States in respect of non-nuclear weapons and that applies in both international and non-international armed conflicts.

2 Sub-paragraphs (b) and (c) of Article 51(4) include within the definition of indiscriminate attacks the use of weapons and methods of warfare that cannot be directed at a specific military objective, or the effects of which cannot be limited as required by the Protocol, and which, in either such case, are of a nature to strike civilians, civilian objects and military objectives without distinction. These provisions have explicit application to weapons and methods of warfare and form the basis of the current Rule. The focus of these customary provisions, and of the Rule, is on the lawfulness of the weapon as such, not on whether a particular attack is indiscriminate.

3 It follows that, in any assessment of the lawfulness of a weapon (including a nuclear weapon), its ability, or otherwise, to engage a specific military objective and the feasibility of limiting its effects to such a military objective will be key considerations. This will involve a careful evaluation of each of the damaging and injurious effects of the weapon, including but not limited to: the extent of the blast effect and the degree of damage and injury likely to be caused by it; the quantity of nuclear fallout its detonation may be expected to generate; the likely spread of the damaging material; the likely effect of the damaging material on human health; whether the damaging/injurious effects can be limited or directed; and for how long the damaging/injurious effects will persist after the use of the weapon.

4 It follows that this Rule must be applied with great care when evaluating any nuclear weapon system. The NATO States that made nuclear statements of the kind referred to in the Commentary accompanying Rule 64 may consider that those statements apply to the present Rule, as the provisions reflected in Article 51(4)(b) and (c) had not been articulated as rules of law before the adoption of API in 1977. States adopting that view would regard sub-paragraphs 4(b) and (c) of Article 51 as constituting new rules introduced by API to which the nuclear statements made by those NATO States would apply. Accordingly, for such States, the present Rule would not apply to nuclear weapons. For States that are parties to API and that made no such statement when ratifying the treaty, the present Rule does apply to nuclear weapons. For all States, the prohibition of indiscriminate attacks, reflected in Rule 37, applies to all attacks, including nuclear attacks. So, while the weapons law point discussed in this paragraph may be legally interesting, it does not alter the fact that an indiscriminate nuclear attack will breach Article 51(4) and customary law.

The Natural Environment and Nuclear Weapons

Rule 73

A When employing nuclear means or methods of warfare, due regard should be had to the natural environment.

B It is prohibited for States that are parties to Additional Protocol I to use nuclear means or methods of warfare that are intended or that may be expected to cause widespread, long-term and severe damage to the natural environment.

C It is prohibited for States that are parties to the ENMOD Convention to engage in military or any other hostile use of environmental modification techniques having widespread, long-lasting or severe effects as the means of causing destruction, damage or injury to any other State that is a party to the Convention.

1 Lit. A of this Rule reflects the current state of customary law.[3] The word 'should' shows that the Rule represents best practice. It applies in both international and non-international armed conflicts. Having 'due regard' means that, when deciding on the acquisition as well as on the use of nuclear weapons, a State should take into account the impact of nuclear weapons, of nuclear weapon systems and of ways of undertaking nuclear hostilities. They should also incorporate environmental concerns into their policies and doctrine concerning nuclear weapons.

2 In this connection, it should be borne in mind that the natural environment is, in principle, a civilian object that must not be made the object of attack, and that incidental damage to it should be taken into account when the proportionality rule is being applied.

3 The term 'natural environment' is not defined in any LOAC provision. The UN Environmental Modification Convention refers to 'the dynamics, composition or structure of the Earth, including its biota, lithosphere, hydrosphere, and atmosphere, or of outer space'.[4] The present authors take the view that the *lex lata* interpretation of the natural environment includes the elements referred to in the ENMOD definition with the exception of outer space.

4 Lit. B is based on Articles 35(3) and 55 of API. It applies to States that are parties to API. However, a number of States ratified the treaty subject to declarations that excluded nuclear weapons from the scope of application of

3 AMW Manual, Rule 89 and accompanying Commentary.

4 Convention on the Prohibition of Military or Any Other Hostile Use of Environmental Modification Techniques, Geneva, 2 September 1976 (ENMOD Convention), Article II.

the new rules adopted in the treaty. Those new rules included Articles 35(3) and 55 of API. Accordingly, Lit. B will not apply to States that are parties to API and that made, and continue to be bound by, such a statement.

5 The terms 'widespread, long-term and severe' are cumulative (i.e. all three characteristics must apply for the Rule to be breached). The treaty text does not define the three criteria. The API Commentary observes that during the Diplomatic Conference that adopted the treaty long-term 'was considered by some to be measured in decades. Some representatives referred to twenty or thirty years as being a minimum period. Others referred to battlefield destruction in France in the First World War as being outside the scope of the prohibition.' The Commentary goes on to note that '[w]hat the article is primarily directed to is thus such damage as would be likely to prejudice, over a long term, the continued survival of the civilian population or would risk causing it major health problems'.[5]

6 It follows that Lit. B is breached only if the environmental damage is very serious. Consider, for example, a nuclear weapon that, when used as designed, can be expected to spread contaminating radiation over a wide area. If the contamination is of a sort that will persist over several decades, rendering the affected territory unusable by local populations, Lit. B is likely to be breached. However, the Rule refers to the expected or intended consequences of the attack. If the three criteria, or any one of them, is neither intended nor reasonably expected, Lit. B will not be breached.

7 The application of the rules in Lit. A and Lit. B can be summarised as follows: if a State is not a party to API, only Lit. A will apply; if a State is a party to API but made a nuclear statement, only Lit. A will apply; if a State is a party to API and did not make a nuclear statement, that State must apply both Lits. A and B when deciding on the acquisition or use of a nuclear weapon.

7 Lit. C is based on Article I(1) of the ENMOD Convention, which is not reflective of customary international law and therefore binds only those States that are parties to it.

8 Article II of the ENMOD Convention defines the term 'environmental modification techniques' as referring to 'any technique for changing – through the deliberate manipulation of natural processes – the dynamics, composition or structure of the Earth, including its biota, lithosphere, hydrosphere and atmosphere, or of outer space'. In short, the ENMOD Convention prohibits the use of the modified natural environment as a means of warfare (i.e. as a weapon). Arguably, the prohibition applies, for example, to the use of a nuclear device for the purpose of initiating an earthquake and/or a tsunami.

5 API Commentary, para. 1454.

Treaty on the Prohibition of Nuclear Weapons

Rule 74

States that are parties to the Treaty on the Prohibition of Nuclear Weapons must comply with the rules set forth in that treaty.

The provisions of the Treaty on the Prohibition of Nuclear Weapons are discussed in Section K.

Legal Review of Nuclear Weapons

Rule 75

A All States have an implied obligation to make sure that the nuclear weapons they acquire or use comply with the rules of international law that bind that State.

B States that are parties to Additional Protocol I are obliged, as part of the study, development, acquisition or adoption of a new means or method of nuclear warfare, to determine whether its employment would, in some or all circumstances, be prohibited by the Protocol or by any other rule of international law applicable to that State.

1 As to the meaning of weapons, means and methods of warfare, see Rule 69 and the accompanying Commentary. States that are not parties to API have an implied obligation to determine whether new nuclear or other weapons that they acquire or use comply with the international law rules that bind the State. Regrettably, there is insufficient compliance with this international law requirement to demonstrate a general practice of States. Accordingly, it cannot be said that there is a customary law rule. The requirement to conduct weapon reviews is, however, implied by the general obligation to comply with LOAC set forth in Article 1 common to the Geneva Conventions.[6]

2 The weapon review ought properly to be the subject of a detailed, formal assessment and will typically be prepared in writing and submitted to the military authorities responsible for the procurement of the weapon in question. The weapon review will consider the characteristics of the weapon; the generic circumstances of its intended use; the kinds of target it is anticipated the weapon will be used to engage; the expected effects of the weapon; the area

[6] Consider also API, Article 36; Convention Respecting the Laws and Customs of War on Land, The Hague, 18 October 1907 (Hague IV Convention), Article 3, second sentence; US DoD Law of War Manual, para. 6.2; UK Manual, paras 6.20–6.20.1; Canadian Manual, para. 530; German Manual, para. 405; AMW Manual, Rule 9; Tallinn Manual 2.0, Rule 110(a); and the mandatory terms in which weapons treaty obligations are expressed.

of its expected effects; the impact of the weapon on persons, objects and the natural environment; and all other relevant factors and details. The weapon review will apply the superfluous injury/unnecessary suffering principle; the indiscriminate weapons principle; LOAC environmental protection rules; and any weapons law rules that apply to nuclear weapons and that bind the State in question. The weapon review will identify whether the weapon's use would, in some or all circumstances, breach the international law obligations of the State.

3 Lit. B is based on Article 36 of API. It is a treaty law obligation that applies to all States that are parties to API. It goes beyond the obligation in Lit. A in that a legal review is required when the weaponisation of a nuclear technology is being studied and when a nuclear weapon system is being developed, as well as when a new nuclear weapon is being acquired. In addition, the treaty provision requires a review to be conducted when a new method of warfare is being adopted. Article 36 does not specify a particular procedure, system or technique for the conduct of such reviews, nor does it specify the form – written or oral – that the results of the review should take. However, a review of a new nuclear weapon or method of nuclear warfare should contain a detailed written assessment of all relevant legal aspects.

4 The fact that State A has already conducted a legal review of a nuclear weapon that it is supplying to State B does not exempt State B from its obligation to conduct its own review, applying the international law rules that bind State B.

Reprisals

Rule 76

Unless prohibited by conventional or customary law, a party to an international armed conflict may resort to reprisals in response to a prior violation of the law of armed conflict by the adversary, in order to induce the adversary to comply with its obligations under the law of armed conflict. A reprisal may not exceed the degree of the wrongful conduct it is designed to correct.

1 This Rule deals with reprisals in times of international armed conflict. On countermeasures taken in times of peace, see Rule 7 and the accompanying Commentary.

2 A reprisal is 'a response to an enemy's violation of the laws of war which would otherwise be a violation on one's own side'.[7] In other words, it is an act that would

[7] *United States of America* v. *William List et al. (The Hostage Case)*, Military Tribunal V, Judgment of 19 February 1948, in *Trials of War Criminals before the Nuremberg Military Tribunals under Control Council Law No. 10*, vol. XI (1950), 1230, 1248.

otherwise be unlawful were it not taken in response to a prior violation of LOAC by the adversary. Reprisals may not be taken in revenge or for punitive purposes; they may only serve the purpose of inducing the enemy to desist from violations of LOAC. Accordingly, a reprisal is a means of enforcing compliance with LOAC.[8]

3 A reprisal must not be confused with a retorsion. The latter consists of an act that is lawful but unfriendly, taken in response to prior conduct of another State. Accordingly, a reprisal by necessity involves a conduct that would be in violation of a given obligation under LOAC. A reprisal could therefore imply the use of a prohibited weapon or the unlawful use of a lawful weapon. For instance, the use of an illegal weapon could qualify as a reprisal if the enemy employs an unlawful weapon against a State party to the conflict and if the victim State, by way of reprisal, resorts to the use of a weapon which would be illegal for that State under either conventional or customary law. In this context, it is important to re-emphasise that nuclear weapons are not prohibited per se, other than for States that are parties to the Treaty on the Prohibition of Nuclear Weapons. Therefore, the employment of a nuclear weapon in response to prior unlawful conduct by the adverse party to an international armed conflict does not constitute a violation of LOAC, and the question of reprisals does not arise. As regards the use of a nuclear weapon, it may, however, qualify as a reprisal if that use is in violation of the rules and principles of targeting law and if it is designed to induce the adversary to cease the use of an illegal weapon or some other violation of LOAC.

4 Because reprisals involve a violation of LOAC, they are 'extreme measures to enforce compliance with the law of armed conflict'[9] and, therefore, subject to the following conditions:[10]

careful inquiry that reprisals are justified;
exhaustion of other means of securing the adversary's compliance with the law of war;
national-level authorisation for reprisal;
proportionality in reprisal; and
public announcement of reprisals.

8 US DoD Law of War Manual, para. 18.18; UK Manual, para. 16.16; German Manual, paras. 488ff., 1528.
9 UK Manual, para. 16.16.
10 US DoD Law of War Manual, para. 18.18. See also UK Manual, para. 16.17; German Manual, paras. 488, 489, 1528.

5 The requirement of proportionality has for a long time been a recognised condition under customary law.[11] According to the US Military Tribunal in Nuremberg, 'it is a fundamental rule that a reprisal may not exceed the degree of the criminal act it is designed to correct'.[12] Accordingly, and as rightly stated in the UK Manual, a 'reprisal must be in proportion to the original violation. Whilst a reprisal need not conform in kind to the act complained of, it may not significantly exceed the adverse party's violation either in degree or effect. Effective but disproportionate acts cannot be justified as reprisals on the basis that only an excessive response will forestall further violations.'[13] Hence, the unlawful use of a nuclear weapon may be justified as a reprisal if its effects are commensurate with the violation suffered and if the prohibitions of certain reprisals are observed.

6 There is general agreement that reprisals, while generally permissible, may never be directed against:

> the wounded, sick and shipwrecked;
> medical personnel and chaplains;
> medical units, establishments and transports;
> prisoners of war;
> protected persons and their property.[14]

In the light of the practice during the two World Wars,[15] these prohibitions are to be considered a major accomplishment brought about by the four 1949 Geneva Conventions.[16] Accordingly, any reprisal, whether by conventional or nuclear weapons, against the persons and objects listed in this paragraph is impermissible.

[11] See *Naulilaa Arbitration (Portugal* v. *Germany)*, Special Arbitral Tribunal, Award of 31 July 1928, (1927–8) 4 *Annual Digest of Public International Law Cases* 526.

[12] *USA* v. *List*, *supra* n. 7.

[13] UK Manual, para. 16.17. See also US DoD Law of War Manual, para. 18.18.2.4.

[14] UK Manual, para. 16.18.

[15] For instance, unrestricted submarine warfare and the establishment of war zones were justified as reprisals. Until the end of World War II, there was no prohibition of the execution of 'reprisal prisoners' in response to prior violations by the adversary. The US Military Tribunal in Nuremberg held that the right of 'killing … innocent members of the population as a deterrent to attacks upon its troops and acts of sabotage … has been recognized by many nations …. There has been complete failure on the part of the nations of the world to limit or mitigate the practice by conventional rule.' *USA* v. *List*, *supra* n. 7, at 1251. Accordingly, List and others were not held criminally responsible for having executed 'reprisal prisoners'. They were convicted because the reprisal prisoners had not been taken from areas where illegal acts had occurred and because the number of killed reprisal prisoners clearly exceeded the violation of the law of war by the enemy.

[16] For reprisals prohibited under the Geneva Conventions, see GCI, Article 14; GCII, Article 16; GCIII, Article 13; GCIV, Article 33.

7 The categories of persons and objects against whom reprisals are prohibited have been extended by API.[17] The API provisions on prohibited reprisals are not reflective of customary international law.[18]

8 In declarations made when ratifying API, some States reserved their right to resort to reprisals that would otherwise be prohibited under API. They include France[19] and Germany.[20] The clearest statement to that effect is the UK declaration, which reads as follows:[21]

> The obligations of Articles 51 and 55 are accepted on the basis that any adverse party against which the United Kingdom might be engaged will itself scrupulously observe those obligations. If an adverse party makes serious and deliberate attacks, in violation of Article 51 or Article 52 against the civilian population or civilians or against civilian objects, or, in violation of Articles 53, 54 and 55, on objects or items protected by those Articles, the United Kingdom will regard itself as entitled to take measures otherwise prohibited by the Articles in question to the extent that it considers such measures necessary for the sole purpose of compelling the adverse party to cease committing violations under those Articles, but only after formal warning to the adverse party requiring cessation of the violations has been disregarded and then only after a decision taken at the highest level of government. Any measures thus taken by the United Kingdom will not be disproportionate to the violations giving rise thereto and will not involve any action prohibited by the Geneva Conventions of 1949 nor will such measures be continued after the violations have ceased. The United Kingdom will notify the Protecting Powers of any such formal warning given to an adverse party, and if that warning has been disregarded, of any measures taken as a result.

17 API, Articles 51(6), 52(1), 53(c), 54(4), 55(2), 56.

18 See US DoD Law of War Manual, para. 18.18.3.4.

19 Declaration made by France on 11 April 2001 when ratifying API, para. 11: 'Le gouvernement de la République Française déclare qu'il appliquera les dispositions du paragraphe 8 de l'article 51 dans la mesure où l'interprétation de celles-ci ne fait pas obstacle à l'emploi, conformément au droit international, des moyens qu'il estimerait indispensables pour protéger sa population civile de violations graves, manifestes et délibérées des Conventions de Genève et du Protocole par l'ennemi.' Available at: https://ihl-databases.icrc.org/applic/ihl/dih.nsf/Notification.xsp?action=openDocument&documentId=DD316843AC252366C1256A3400487E4C.

20 Declarations made by Germany on 14 February 1991 when ratifying API, para. 6: 'The Federal Republic of Germany will react against serious and systematic violations of the obligations imposed by Additional Protocol I and in particular its Articles 51 and 52 with all means admissible under international law in order to prevent any further violation.' Available at: https://ihl-databases.icrc.org/applic/ihl/ihl.nsf/Notification.xsp?action=openDocument&documentId=3F4D8706B6B7EA40C1256402003FB3C7.

21 Declaration of 28 January 1998 made on ratification, available at: www.icrc.org/en/doc/resources/documents/article/other/57jp54.htm.

Accordingly, reprisals, including by the use of nuclear weapons, taken in accordance with the declaration are permissible by and against the United Kingdom if and to the extent that the above conditions are observed.

9 For the States that are parties to the Amended Protocol II to CCW and have not entered a reservation, it is 'prohibited in all circumstances to direct mines, booby-traps, and other devices, either in offense, defense or by way of reprisals, against the civilian population as such or against individual civilians or civilian objects.'[22]

[22] Amended Protocol II to CCW, Article 3(7).

H

Genocide, Crimes against Humanity and War Crimes as They Apply to Nuclear Operations

There can be no doubt that the international crimes of genocide, crimes against humanity and war crimes do not suddenly cease to have relevance simply because nuclear weapons are involved. Nuclear weapons might be the instrument, or one of the instruments, through which such crimes come to be committed. Equally, such crimes may be perpetrated against a nuclear-armed State. It is the purpose of the present Section to have a brief look at the crimes that appear to be of greatest relevance to a book concerned with nuclear weapons and associated operations, with a view to assessing how those crimes should be understood in that particular context. This Section is not intended to be a comprehensive treatment of international criminal law; neither does it comprise an in-depth consideration even of the crimes that are mentioned here. Rather, it is intended to give a general indication of the kinds of crime that might be relevant in the context of nuclear weapons.

The Section will briefly summarise the evolution of these crimes during the period since the end of World War II by referring to relevant provisions in the statute of the Nuremburg International Military Tribunal and in the statutes of three ad hoc tribunals. Recognising that the Rome Statute of the International Criminal Court was intended by its eminent negotiators and drafters to be based on generally accepted rules of customary law, particular attention will then be devoted to the terms in which some relevant crimes are defined in that treaty.

To add flesh to those somewhat bare definitions, the elements of the chosen Rome Statute crimes, also drafted by eminent experts, will be set forth, and the Section will conclude with a brief assessment of some of the important subsidiary provisions in the Statute dealing, for example, with modes of participation, defences and the mental element in crimes. Throughout, the purpose is to seek to identify where the threshold of criminality lies. It is well understood that many States, including numerous nuclear weapon-relevant

States, are not parties to the Rome Statute. Nevertheless, to the extent that the provisions discussed in this Section reflect customary law, it is hoped that the discussion will be useful.

Article 9 of the Rome Statute describes the function of the Elements of Crimes as being to 'assist the Court in the interpretation and application of' the crime provisions of the Statute (i.e. Articles 6, 7, 8 and 8bis). Article 21(1)(a) then requires the Court to apply in the first place the Statute, the Elements of Crimes and the Rules of Procedure and Evidence. In working out the meaning of any specific offence in its application to nuclear weapons, it is therefore vital that the relevant Elements of Crimes be properly taken into account.

In relation to some of the Rome Statute offences, examples are given of nuclear operations that might come within the scope of the provisions discussed. They are but examples; other nuclear-related circumstances may also give rise to the offences in question. Whether a particular circumstance actually does constitute such a crime will, inevitably, depend on the circumstances and on the available evidence.

H.1 CRIMES WITHIN THE JURISDICTION OF THE INTERNATIONAL MILITARY TRIBUNAL, NUREMBERG

The Charter of the Nuremburg International Military Tribunal[1] granted to the Tribunal the power to try and punish crimes against peace, war crimes and crimes against humanity. So far as is relevant to the present volume, crimes against peace were defined as 'planning, preparation, initiation or waging of a war of aggression, or a war in violation of international treaties, agreements or assurances, or participation in a common plan or conspiracy for the accomplishment of any of the foregoing'.[2] War crimes are described as 'violations of the laws or customs of war. Such violations shall include, but not be limited to, murder, . . ., wanton destruction of cities, towns or villages, or devastation not justified by military necessity'.[3] The Charter's definition of crimes against humanity includes 'murder . . . committed against any civilian population, before or during the war'.[4]

1 The Charter of the Nuremburg International Military Tribunal is annexed to the Agreement by the Government of the United Kingdom of Great Britain and Northern Ireland, the Government of the United States of America, the Provisional Government of the French Republic and the Government of the Union of Soviet Socialist Republics for the prosecution and punishment of the major war criminals of the European Axis, signed at London, on 8 August 1945 (IMT Charter).

2 IMT Charter, Article 6(a).

3 Ibid., Article 6(b).

4 Ibid., Article 6(c).

Certain general principles associated with international criminal law were set forth in the Charter. They deserve mention here. Article 6 provided that '[l]eaders, organisers, instigators and accomplices participating in the formulation or execution of a common plan or conspiracy to commit any of the foregoing crimes are responsible for all acts performed by any persons in execution of such plan'. Under Article 7, '[t]he official position of defendants, whether as Heads of State or responsible officials in Government Departments, shall not be considered as freeing them from responsibility or mitigating punishment'. Thirdly, '[t]he fact that the Defendant acted pursuant to order of his Government or of a superior shall not free him from responsibility, but may be considered in mitigation of punishment if the Tribunal determines that justice so requires'.[5]

So it can be seen that the notion of individual criminal responsibility was fully recognised in 1945.

H.2 CRIMES PROVISION IN THE STATUTES OF THE AD HOC TRIBUNALS

On 25 May 1993, the UN Security Council adopted Resolution 827/1993 and, with it, adopted the Statute of the International Criminal Tribunal for the Former Yugoslavia (ICTY), which was annexed to a report from the UN Secretary-General.[6] The Statute listed grave breaches of the 1949 Geneva Conventions, violations of the laws and customs of war, genocide and crimes against humanity as the offences over which the Tribunal would have jurisdiction. Of these, it is noteworthy, for the purposes of the present book, that violations of the laws and customs of war, listed in Article 3 of the Statute, included 'employment of poisonous weapons or other weapons calculated to cause unnecessary suffering' and 'wanton destruction of cities, towns or villages, or devastation not justified by military necessity'. Article 4 defined genocide as constituted by 'acts committed with intent to destroy, in whole or in part, a national, ethnical, racial or religious group'. The listed acts included 'killing members of the group' and 'causing serious bodily or mental harm to members of the group'. Article 5, under the heading 'Crimes against humanity', gave the Tribunal the power to prosecute listed crimes, which included murder, 'when committed in armed conflict, whether international or internal in character and when directed against any civilian population'.

5 Ibid., Article 8.

6 UNSC, Report of the Secretary-General Pursuant to Paragraph 2 of Security Council Resolution 808 (1993), UN Doc. S/27504 (3 May 1993).

On 8 November 1994, acting under Chapter VII of the UN Charter, the UN Security Council adopted Resolution 955 (1994) establishing the International Criminal Tribunal for Rwanda (ICTR), whose Statute was annexed to the Resolution.[7] The Statute grants the Tribunal the power to prosecute persons who committed genocide, crimes against humanity, violations of Article 3 common to the Geneva Conventions and of APII. Genocide, so far as relevant, is defined in exactly the same terms as under the ICTY Statute.[8] Article 3 of the ICTR Statute describes crimes against humanity as including, inter alia, murder 'when committed as part of a widespread or systematic attack against any civilian population on national, political, ethnic, racial or religious grounds'.

It was an agreement dated 14 August 2000 between the United Nations and the Government of Sierra Leone pursuant to UN Security Council Resolution 1315 (2000) that established the Special Court for Sierra Leone. Under the heading 'Crimes against humanity', Article 2 of the Statute of the Special Court grants the Court the power to prosecute persons who committed, for example, murder 'as part of a widespread or systematic attack against any civilian population'. Article 3 addresses violations of Article 3 common to the Geneva Conventions and of APII. Under the heading 'Other serious violations of international humanitarian law', Article 4 grants the Court the 'power to prosecute persons who committed the following serious violations of international humanitarian law'. The associated list of three offences includes '[i]ntentionally directing attacks against the civilian population as such or against individual civilians not taking direct part in hostilities'.[9]

H.3 INTERNATIONAL CRIMES PROVISION IN THE ROME STATUTE

The Rome Statute sets forth the offences over which the International Criminal Court has potential jurisdiction in Articles 6 ('Genocide'), 7 ('Crimes against humanity'), 8 ('War crimes') and 8bis ('Crime of aggression'). The ways of committing such crimes that seem to be of greatest potential relevance in connection with nuclear operations will be considered under the relevant headings below. Before looking at what appear to be the most relevant provisions, however, it is right to consider the declarations made by certain relevant States when becoming parties to the Rome Statute, and which States have yet to become parties to it.

7 Statute of the International Criminal Tribunal for Rwanda, 8 November 1994.
8 Ibid., Article 2(2)(a) and (b).
9 Statute of the Special Court for Sierra Leone, Article 4(a).

H.4 POSITIONS TAKEN BY STATES ON THE ROME STATUTE

H.4.1 *France*

Having asserted that the provisions of the Statute do not preclude France from exercising its inherent right of self-defence in accordance with Article 51 of the UN Charter, France then made a statement of direct relevance to nuclear weapons. The statement is as follows:

> The provisions of article 8 of the Statute, in particular paragraph 2(b) thereof, relate solely to conventional weapons and can neither regulate nor prohibit the possible use of nuclear weapons nor impair the other rules of international law applicable to other weapons necessary to the exercise by France of its inherent right of self-defence, unless nuclear weapons or the other weapons referred to herein become subject in the future to a comprehensive ban and are specified in an annex to the Statute by means of an amendment adopted in accordance with the provisions of articles 121 and 123.[10]

This statement therefore excludes, so far as France is concerned, the application to the possible use of nuclear weapons of all war crimes provisions under the Statute. That position would only change if a comprehensive ban of nuclear weapons is achieved. While the Treaty on the Prohibition of Nuclear Weapons was adopted on 7 July 2017, such a prohibition, it is suggested, can only be regarded as 'comprehensive' for the purposes of the French statement if all, or virtually all, States that currently possess nuclear weapons become parties to that treaty. Moreover, according to the terms of the statement, such weapons would need to be included in an annex adopted under Articles 121 and 123 of the Statute – a circumstance that is not likely to arise in the foreseeable future.

H.4.2 *United Kingdom*

On ratification of the Rome Statute, the United Kingdom made the following statement:

> The United Kingdom understands the term 'the established framework of international law', used in article 8(2)(b) and (e), to include customary international law as established by State practice and *opinio iuris*. In that

10 Interpretative declaration made by France on ratification of the Rome Statute on 9 June 2000, para. 2. UN Treaty Collection, Status of Treaties, Chapter XVIII, No. 10, viewed on 2 September 2021.

> context the United Kingdom confirms and draws to the attention of the Court its views as expressed, inter alia, in its statements made on ratification of relevant instruments of international law, including the Protocol Additional to the Geneva Conventions of 12th August 1949, and relating to the Protection of Victims of International Armed Conflicts (Protocol I) of 8th June 1977.[11]

This statement draws the Court's attention, inter alia, to the United Kingdom's nuclear statement made on ratification of API and is clearly intended to indicate to the Court that, so far as the United Kingdom is concerned, the Rome Statute, insofar as it reflects rules introduced by API, has no application to the use of nuclear weapons.[12] Arguably, it would be for the Court to determine whether a rule, reflected in a specific charge, was indeed introduced by API. This may be a complex issue. Article 8(2)(b)(iv) includes reference to environmental damage as part of the crime of excessive incidental death, injury or damage. Arguably, the characterisation of the natural environment as being, in principle, a civilian object was not a rule introduced by API, so the crime as expressed in Article 8(2)(b)(iv) would not be affected by the UK statement. An equally interesting question is whether the elaboration of the prohibition of indiscriminate attacks in the form of the proportionality rule in Article 51(5)(b) of API was a new rule for these purposes. Although sentiments similar to the proportionality rule were expressed in 1923 in Article 24(4) of the Draft Hague Rules of Aerial Warfare, the rule's first appearance in its modern form was in API. In some quarters, it may therefore be argued that, as a rule that is distinct from the general rule prohibiting indiscriminate attacks, the proportionality rule was indeed a new rule introduced by API and therefore inapplicable to nuclear weapons for those States that made statements to that effect, such as the United Kingdom. For such States, however, the prohibition of indiscriminate attacks does apply, and an attack that is expected to cause civilian deaths, injuries and/or damage that are excessive in relation to the anticipated military advantage is likely to be considered indiscriminate irrespective of the applicability or otherwise of the proportionality rule. What this does not of course change is the potential inapplicability of the offence under Article 8(2)(b)(iv) of API.

Japan became a party to the Rome Statute on 17 July 2007 without making a statement of the kind discussed above.

11 Declaration made by the United Kingdom on ratification of the Rome Statute on 4 October 2001, UN Treaty Collection, Status of Treaties, Chapter XVIII, No. 10, viewed on 2 September 2021.

12 See the UK statement (a) made on ratification of API on 28 January 1998 and reproduced in the Commentary accompanying Rule 64.

The following nuclear-relevant States and potentially nuclear-relevant States have not yet become parties to the Rome Statute: China, Democratic People's Republic of Korea, India, Iran, Israel,[13] Pakistan, the Russian Federation[14] and the United States.[15]

H.5 GENOCIDE

So far as relevant to the present discussion, genocide is defined in the Rome Statute as follows:

> For the purpose of this Statute, 'genocide' means any of the following acts committed with intent to destroy, in whole or in part, a national, ethnical, racial or religious group, as such:
>
> (a) Killing members of the group;
> (b) Causing serious bodily or mental harm to members of the group; . . . .[16]

While there are five ways in which the crime may be committed, the two listed methods would seem to be of most obvious relevance to nuclear weapon use and they will be considered here. For the first crime – killing members of the group – the elements are:

1 The perpetrator killed one or more persons.
2 Such person or persons belonged to a particular national, ethnical, racial or religious group.
3 The perpetrator intended to destroy, in whole or in part, that national, ethnical, racial or religious group, as such.
4 The conduct took place in the context of a manifest pattern of similar conduct directed against that group or was conduct that could itself effect such destruction.[17]

So, for a nuclear attack to amount to genocide by killing, the nuclear weapon would have to be aimed at members of a specific national, racial,

[13] In August 2002, Israel notified the UN Secretary-General that it had no intention of becoming a party to the Rome Statute and that its signature to the treaty text involves no legal obligations.

[14] In a communication dated November 2016 the Russian Federation informed the UN Secretary-General that it had no intention of becoming a party to the Rome Statute, noting that, in accordance Article 18(a) of the Vienna Convention on the Law of Treaties of 1969, it was no longer obliged by the fact of having previously signed the Statute to refrain from acts that would defeat its object and purpose.

[15] In a communication dated May 2002, the United States informed the UN Secretary-General that it had no intention of becoming a party to the Rome Statute and that its signature to the treaty text involves no legal obligations.

[16] Rome Statute, Article 6.

[17] Elements of Crimes, Article 6(a) (footnote omitted).

ethnical or religious group and the attacker must intend to destroy either the whole of that group or at least a part of it – almost certainly a substantial part. In addition, either this kind of attack must be associated with a clear pattern of similar behaviour also targeting the same group, or the attack alone must have had the capability of achieving that outcome (i.e. destroying the whole or a significant part of the group). Depending on the nature, extent and level of geographical concentration of the relevant group, it is conceivable that an attack using a nuclear weapon with a sufficiently large footprint of effect may indeed have the capacity to destroy a substantial part of such a group.

Similar conduct might, for these purposes, consist of other nuclear attacks or, it is suggested, might include other bombardments aimed at the group but not necessarily involving the use of nuclear weapons. If the nuclear attack did not take place in the context of other similar conduct, the language of the fourth element suggests that it suffices that the nuclear attack is capable of having that effect, regardless of whether or not that effect actually materialised. It is suggested, therefore, that clear evidence of a genocidal intent is required to support such a charge.

However, if evidence of genocidal intent is absent, the available evidence may support other charges under the Statute.

The second offence, causing serious bodily or mental harm to members of the group, comprises the following elements:

1 The perpetrator caused serious bodily or mental harm to one or more persons.[18]
2 Such person or persons belonged to a particular national, ethnical, racial or religious group.
3 The perpetrator intended to destroy, in whole or in part, that national, ethnical, racial or religious group, as such.
4 The conduct took place in the context of a manifest pattern of similar conduct directed against that group or was conduct that could itself effect such destruction.[19]

It will be noted that elements 2, 3 and 4 are identical to the corresponding elements of genocide by killing. They do not therefore need further discussion here. In the nuclear context, consider, for example, the use of a dirty bomb to direct nuclear contamination, and thus grave levels of sickness, at members of

[18] A footnote indicates that '[t]his conduct may include, but is not necessarily restricted to, acts of torture, rape, sexual violence, or inhuman or degrading treatment'. Such activities, when combined with certain nuclear-related operations such as of the kind mentioned in the discussion of this offence, might, if taken together, amount to this form of genocide.

[19] Elements of Crimes, Article 6(b).

a specific national, ethnical, racial or religious group. Such an act would potentially come within the scope of this offence if, but only if, the remaining elements of the crime are present. Alternatively, using a dirty bomb that, for example, causes severe sickness among some members of such a group, while also engaging in other activities that cause mental harm to other members of the same group, may collectively have a sufficient effect to come within the scope of the offence, again provided that the other three elements of the crime are present.

Certain elements apply when considering both of these offences. The language 'in the context of' can apply to the initial acts in what becomes an emerging pattern of activity, while 'manifest' is an objective qualification, suggesting that it suffices if, viewed objectively, there was a clear pattern of genocidal action going on. The third introductory element under Article 6 of Elements of Crimes states as follows:

> Notwithstanding the normal requirement for a mental element provided for in article 30, and recognizing that knowledge of the circumstances will usually be addressed in proving genocidal intent, the appropriate requirement, if any, for a mental element regarding this circumstance will need to be decided by the Court on a case-by-case basis.

This rather emphasises the point made earlier that the factual circumstances of each case will be of critical importance. In the opinion of the present authors, the cases in which nuclear-related operations form part of, or constitute, genocidal conduct are likely to be relatively rare. Nevertheless, the possibility of such conduct taking place cannot be excluded, so it is thought to have been useful to refer to these provisions, largely for completeness.

H.6 CRIMES AGAINST HUMANITY

For the purposes of the Rome Statute, and thus of the International Criminal Court, crimes against humanity comprise any one of certain listed acts 'when committed as part of a widespread or systematic attack directed against any civilian population, with knowledge of the attack'.[20] Of the listed acts, the one of potential relevance in the nuclear context is the crime against humanity of murder. Article 7(2) then explains some of the important terms. So, 'attack directed against any civilian population' involves 'a course of conduct involving the multiple commission of [the listed acts] against any civilian

[20] Rome Statute, Article 7(1).

population, pursuant to or in furtherance of a State or organizational policy to commit such attack'.[21]

The elements of the crime against humanity of murder are as follows:

1 The perpetrator killed one or more persons.
2 The conduct was committed as part of a widespread or systematic attack directed against a civilian population.
3 The perpetrator knew that the conduct was part of or intended the conduct to be part of a widespread or systematic attack against a civilian population.[22]

The Introduction to Article 7 of Elements of Crimes notes that crimes against humanity 'are among the most serious crimes of concern to the international community', that they 'entail individual criminal responsibility' and that they 'require conduct which is impermissible under generally applicable international law'. There must be 'participation in and knowledge of a widespread or systematic attack against a civilian population'. The Introduction explains, however, that 'the last element should not be interpreted as requiring proof that the perpetrator had knowledge of all characteristics of the attack or the precise details of the plan or policy of the State or organization'. Intent in the last element is satisfied 'if the perpetrator intended to further such an attack', meaning, the authors assume, a widespread or systematic attack. 'Attack directed against a civilian population' means a course of conduct involving the commission of multiple acts specified in Article 7(1) of the Rome Statute, such as murder, against a civilian population in furtherance of a State or organisational policy. The policy aspect presupposes the active encouragement or promotion by a State or an organisation of an attack against a civilian population.

Here again, therefore, an isolated nuclear attack that erroneously attacks a civilian population centre is not going to amount to a crime against humanity. The required course of conduct and the knowledge required by the third element will both be lacking. However, a nuclear attack against a civilian population centre that is, for example, accompanied by other acts that are directed against the same civilian population may, taken together, satisfy the widespread or systematic attack requirement, may be indicative of a policy to commit such an attack and, if accompanied by the requisite intent and knowledge, might constitute the offence.

21 Rome Statute, Article 7(2)(a).
22 Elements of Crimes, Article 7(1)(a) (footnote omitted).

H.7 WAR CRIMES

Article 8(2)(b) of the Rome Statute lists a considerable number of war crimes associated with international armed conflicts. To come within the jurisdiction of the International Criminal Court on the basis of this provision, the offences must be 'serious violations of the laws and customs applicable in international armed conflict, within the established framework of international law'.[23] While a number of the acts listed in Article 8(2)(b) are capable of being relevant in the context of nuclear operations, the following may be of greatest relevance.

H.7.1 *War Crime of Attacking Civilians*

This war crime consists of '[i]ntentionally directing attacks against the civilian population as such or against individual civilians not taking direct part in hostilities'.[24] The elements of this crime are:

1. The perpetrator directed an attack.
2. The object of the attack was a civilian population as such or individual civilians not taking direct part in hostilities.
3. The perpetrator intended the civilian population as such or individual civilians not taking direct part in hostilities to be the object of the attack.
4. The conduct took place in the context of and was associated with an international armed conflict.
5. The perpetrator was aware of factual circumstances that established the existence of an armed conflict.[25]

Certain points should be made. It is clear that making peaceable civilians the object of an attack is a clear breach of the distinction principle and that this prohibition applies also to the use of nuclear weapons. It will be for the Court to determine, by reference to the evidence, who in fact 'directed the attack'. Imagine a situation in which the head of the government of a nuclear-capable State directs that a nuclear attack be launched against a specific target. It will be at least arguable that it is the head of government who directed the attack, and that the military unit and its commander that actually fired the missile did not direct the attack. If the object of the attack was civilian persons who were taking a direct part in the hostilities, the second element of the offence will not have been satisfied. However, if the object of the attack was non-participating

23 Rome Statute, chapeau to Article 8(2)(b).

24 Rome Statute, Article 8(2)(b)(i).

25 Elements of Crimes, Article 8(2)(b)(i).

civilians, the second element will indeed be made out. The object of the attack, for these purposes, will be the persons whom the attack is intended to kill, injure or disable.

For the offence to be proved, it must be shown that the accused person intended to make the civilian population or individual civilians not taking part in the hostilities the object of the attack. If, for example, a commander of a nuclear armed submarine receives instructions to fire a nuclear missile at geographical co-ordinates that are communicated to him or her, the third element of the crime will be proved against that commander only if the evidence shows that that commander intended to make peaceable civilians or the civilian population the object of the attack. If, for example, the commander did not and could not know the civilian nature of the persons represented by the transmitted co-ordinates, it follows that the commander cannot have formed the required intent and, on that basis, the presence of the third element will not have been established.

There may be occasions when a commander of a nuclear-armed platform such as a submarine or aircraft is unaware that a state of armed conflict is already in existence. That said, the firing of a nuclear weapon will, if no armed conflict previously existed, bring about such a state of affairs.

If, however, during an international armed conflict a senior military commander or political leader directs a nuclear attack intending that peaceable civilians or the civilian population shall be the object of the attack, that senior military commander or political leader may well have committed this war crime.

H.7.2 *War Crime of Attacking Civilian Objects*

This war crime consists of '[i]ntentionally directing attacks against civilian objects, that is, objects which are not military objectives'.[26] The elements of this crime are:

1 The perpetrator directed an attack.
2 The object of the attack was civilian objects, that is objects which are not military objectives.
3 The perpetrator intended such civilian objects to be the object of the attack.
4 The conduct took place in the context of and was associated with an international armed conflict.

[26] Rome Statute, Article 8(2)(b)(ii).

5 The perpetrator was aware of factual circumstances that established the existence of an armed conflict.[27]

Making civilian objects the object of attack is clearly contrary to the principle of distinction, irrespective of the kind of weapon that is used to undertake the attack. To the extent that these elements use the same language as those relating to the previous war crime, they will have the same meaning, and thus will have the same significance for nuclear operations.

Objects are military objectives if they satisfy the definition in Article 52(2) of API (as to which, see Rule 34 in Section E). Accordingly, dual-use objects are military objectives. If objects fulfilling the definition of military objectives were intended by the accused person to be the object of the attack, this offence was not committed. If the object of the attack included both military objectives and civilian objects, it is not clear whether this offence is committed. The use of the definite article 'the' at the beginning of the second element might imply that the offence is only made out if the object of the attack consisted exclusively of civilian objects. That, it is suggested, is a matter on which the Court will have to rule, probably on a case-by-case basis. Importantly, if incidental damage was unintentionally caused to civilian objects, this offence will not have been committed.

H.7.3 *War Crime of Excessive Incidental Death, Injury or Damage*

This war crime consists of '[i]ntentionally launching an attack in the knowledge that such attack will cause incidental loss of life or injury to civilians or damage to civilian objects or widespread, long-term and severe damage to the natural environment which would be clearly excessive in relation to the concrete and direct overall military advantage anticipated'.[28] The elements of this crime are:

1 The perpetrator launched an attack.
2 The attack was such that it would cause incidental death or injury to civilians or damage to civilian objects or widespread, long-term and severe damage to the natural environment and that such death, injury or damage would be of such an extent as to be clearly excessive in relation to the concrete and direct overall military advantage anticipated.
3 The perpetrator knew that the attack would cause incidental death or injury to civilians or damage to civilian objects or widespread, long-term and severe damage to the natural environment and that such death, injury or damage would be of such an extent as to be clearly excessive in

[27] Elements of Crimes, Article 8(2)(b)(ii).
[28] Rome Statute, Article 8(2)(b)(iv).

relation to the concrete and direct overall military advantage anticipated.

4 The conduct took place in the context of and was associated with an international armed conflict.

5 The perpetrator was aware of factual circumstances that established the existence of an armed conflict.[29]

This offence is the war crime that corresponds to attacks that breach the proportionality rule as set forth in Article 51(5)(b) of API and as referred to in Article 57 of the same treaty.

Whereas the first element of the first two war crime offences referred to the perpetrator *directing* an attack, the first element in this offence refers to the perpetrator *launching* the attack. The launching of an attack would seem to involve the person who actually initiates the forceful act, as opposed to the perhaps more senior individual who gives directions that the attack is to take place. Three significant concepts are added to the Article 51(5)(b) wording. The first is that the offence can be committed by causing excessive damage to the natural environment. If, however, part of the natural environment has become a military objective, damage to that part would not be 'incidental' for the purposes of this offence. Moreover, the status of Articles 35(3) and 55 of API as new rules introduced by the treaty, to which the nuclear statements of NATO States referred to in the Commentary to Rule 64 apply, would suggest that, certainly so far as nationals of those States are concerned, this offence cannot, arguably, be committed through damage caused by a nuclear weapon to the natural environment, irrespective of whether or not the part of the natural environment that is involved has become a military objective.

The second added concept is that the incidental damage to civilians, civilian objects or the environment must be 'clearly' excessive. This suggests the existence of a margin of appreciation. The offence will not have been committed if the expected incidental injury and damage were only somewhat greater than the anticipated military advantage. The disparity must be such, it is suggested, that no reasonable decision-maker would have decided to proceed with the attack.

The third added concept is the reference to 'overall' military advantage. This seems likely to be an oblique reference to a statement made by a number of States when ratifying API to the effect that, when applying the proportionality rule, it is the military advantage anticipated from the attack considered as a whole that must be considered.[30]

29 Elements of Crimes, Article 8(2)(b)(iv) (footnotes omitted).

30 Consider, for example, the statement made by the United Kingdom on ratification of API on 28 January 1998, para (i). See similar statements by Australia, Germany, Italy and the

The third element makes it clear that the perpetrator must know that the attack will cause excessive incidental injury and damage. Suspicion, or indeed any state of mind other than knowledge, will be insufficient, but knowledge can no doubt be inferred if the facts known to the accused make the excessiveness obvious.

The proportionality rule is of course concerned with the decision that is made in advance to undertake an attack. This must be borne in mind when interpreting the elements. So, the first element requires that the attack be actually launched. The second element, with its awkward wording about 'was such that it would', must, it is suggested, mean that the nature and circumstances of the attack, taking into account the information that was reasonably available to the perpetrator at the time when deciding to undertake the attack, were such as to make it clear that the attack would cause incidental death, injury and damage that would be clearly excessive in comparison to the anticipated military advantage.

In the nuclear context, therefore, it is highly likely that if a nuclear weapon is fired, the pilot of the relevant nuclear-armed aircraft or the commander of the relevant nuclear-armed submarine would be the person, or at least would be among the persons, who would be treated as having launched the attack. It will, in relation to the second element, then be a question of fact whether the circumstances of the attack were indeed such that it would be expected to cause incidental death or injury to civilians or damage to civilian objects or widespread, long-term and severe damage to the natural environment that is clearly excessive when compared with the concrete and direct overall military advantage that the attack is anticipated to yield. The state of mind of the pilot or commander then comes into play when we consider the third element. This element requires the pilot or commander to know that the attack would cause excessive incidental death, injury or damage of the sort referred to in the offence. If the pilot or commander has not been informed of the circumstances in the target area, it would seem unlikely that he or she is in any position to know those things. Clearly if a pilot or commander, while preparing to execute such a mission, receives information that causes him or her to suspect that the incidental injury or damage may prove to be excessive, they ought to postpone the attack and seek further information. However, it must be emphasised that for the war crime to be made out, knowledge as to the excessiveness of the incidental injury or damage is what is required, and doubt or suspicion are not sufficient. So, if, for example, during a pre-mission

Netherlands and the statement made by France on ratification of the Rome Statute on 9 June 2000, para. 5.

briefing it becomes clear to the pilot of a nuclear strike mission that the incidental injury or damage will be excessive in relation to the anticipated military advantage, the mission should be called off.

H.7.4 *War Crime of Employing Poison or Poisoned Weapons*

The war crime consists of '[e]mploying poison or poisoned weapons'.[31] The elements of this crime are:

1 The perpetrator employed a substance or a weapon that releases a substance as a result of its employment.
2 The substance was such that it causes death or serious damage to health in the ordinary course of events, through its toxic properties.
3 The conduct took place in the context of and was associated with an international armed conflict.
4 The perpetrator was aware of factual circumstances that established the existence of an armed conflict.[32]

The open question in relation to this crime is whether the nuclear contamination that is released as a result of the detonation of a nuclear weapon is to be regarded as a poison for the purposes of Article 8(2)(b)(xvii). It is clear that the explosion of a nuclear weapon does indeed release radiation and radioactive debris. It is equally clear that exposure to radioactivity can, depending on the degree and duration of such exposure, cause illness and/or death. It would be arguable that it is the toxic properties of the radioactive debris and radiation that, 'in the ordinary course of events', cause death or serious damage to health. It remains to be seen whether the Court will conclude that the use of a nuclear weapon in the context of an international armed conflict amounts to a breach of Article 8(2)(b)(xviii) of the Rome Statute.

If, as the authors believe, those negotiating the Rome Statute and its Elements of Crimes intended the provisions to reflect customary law, it is difficult to imagine that the interpretation put forward in the previous paragraph can indeed be correct. After all, the most important global military powers possess nuclear weapons and have established doctrine setting forth the (very limited) circumstances in which they would use them. It is highly unlikely that those powers consider that a decision to resort to the use of nuclear weapons will, automatically, amount to a war crime of employing

[31] Rome Statute, Article 8(2)(b)(xvii).
[32] Elements of Crimes, Article 8(2)(b)(xvii).

poison or poisoned weapons. If that assumption is correct, it is difficult to see how characterising nuclear weapons as 'poison or poisoned weapons' can properly be regarded as reflecting the general practice of States accepted as law.

H.7.5 *War Crime of Employing Weapons, Projectiles or Materials or Methods of Warfare Listed in the Annex to the Statute*

The war crime consists of '[e]mploying weapons, projectiles and material and methods of warfare which are of a nature to cause superfluous injury or unnecessary suffering or which are inherently indiscriminate in violation of the international law of armed conflict, provided that such weapons, projectiles and materials and methods of warfare are the subject of a comprehensive prohibition and are included in an annex to this Statute . . .'.[33] At the time of writing, no weapons, projectiles or material or methods of warfare have been included in an annex to the Statute. This is therefore an offence which is not yet complete and cannot therefore yet be made the subject of a charge.

The Introduction to Article 8 of Elements of Crimes explains that war crimes must be interpreted within the established framework of the law of armed conflict. In relation to the last two elements of each crime, it is also noted, inter alia, that there is no requirement for a legal evaluation as to the existence or nature of the armed conflict. However, the factual existence of a situation of armed conflict is of course an essential requirement for the commission of a war crime.

While the negotiators may have intended that the Rome Statute should reflect customary law and thus reflect rules and crimes that, respectively, bind and apply to all States, it is worthy of note that, at the time of writing, two P5 States are parties to the Statute – namely, France and the United Kingdom – while the remaining P5 States – namely, China, the Russian Federation and the United States – are not. Other nuclear weapon-relevant States that are not parties to the Statute include India, Iran, Israel, North Korea and Pakistan.

[33] Rome Statute, Article 8(2)(b)(xx).

I

Published National Doctrines of Nuclear Weapon States

The following paragraphs cannot be a comprehensive compilation of the relevant doctrine of all nuclear weapon-capable States. The aim of this Section is simply to draw attention to some of the statements that some relevant States have made about nuclear weapons, in order to clarify, so far as possible, State views on what the law is.

I.1 FRANCE

The *Manuel de droit des conflits armés*[1] notes that a nuclear weapon is a non-conventional weapon that uses the energy generated by nuclear fusion or fission. The *Manuel* makes brief and general reference to the Treaty on the Non-Proliferation of Nuclear Weapons (NPT), to the Comprehensive Nuclear-Test-Ban Treaty and to measures addressing outer space, the deep ocean, Antarctica and nuclear-free zones. The *Manuel* comments that nuclear weapons are not specifically and absolutely prohibited by international law but are subject to the law of armed conflict, which limits the methods and means of combat, prohibiting weapons of a nature to have indiscriminate effects and those that cause superfluous injury or unnecessary suffering.[2] After drawing attention to the ICJ Nuclear Opinion, the *Manuel* observes that a policy of deterrence is accordingly possible in certain circumstances.

1 Ministère de la Défense, Manuel de droit des conflits armés [Legal Handbook on Armed Conflicts] (2012).

2 Ibid. at 21: 'Cela pose évidemment problème pour la politique de dissuasion nucléaire.' [That clearly poses a problem for nuclear deterrence policy.]

I.2 UNITED KINGDOM

The UK Manual of the Law of Armed Conflict devotes a page to the issue. It asserts that there 'is no specific rule of international law, express or implied, which prohibits the use of nuclear weapons. The legality of their use depends upon the application of the general rules of international law, including those regulating the use of force and the conduct of hostilities.'[3] In a footnote the reader is directed to Chapter 5 of the Manual dealing with the conduct of hostilities. That chapter includes a description of the indiscriminate attacks rule that does not exclude the application of the rule to nuclear weapons. Paragraph 6.17 makes the point that the rules on the use of force and on the conduct of hostilities cannot be applied in isolation from the factual context to imply a general prohibition. In an associated footnote, an example of such an impermissible argument is given – namely, 'the argument that attacks with nuclear weapons are necessarily indiscriminate'.[4] While, according to the Manual, nuclear weapons 'fall to be dealt with by reference to the same general principles as apply to other weapons', rules introduced by API apply exclusively to conventional weapons and do not have any effect on or regulate nuclear weapons.[5]

Referring to some of the findings in the ICJ Nuclear Opinion, the Manual notes that '[t]he threshold for the legitimate use of nuclear weapons is clearly a high one' and comments that '[t]he United Kingdom would only consider using nuclear weapons in self-defence, including the defence of its NATO allies, and even then only in extreme circumstances'.[6]

The Manual points out that the United Kingdom has given a unilateral assurance that it will not use or threaten to use nuclear weapons against States that are parties to the NPT. The Manual then notes as follows: 'In giving this assurance, the UK has emphasised the need for universal adherence to and compliance with the NPT, and noted that this assurance would not apply to any state in material breach of those non-proliferation obligations.'[7] The United Kingdom also noted that 'while there is currently no direct threat to the UK or its vital interests from States developing capabilities in other weapons of mass destruction, for example chemical and biological, the UK

[3] UK Manual, para. 6.17, first two sentences.

[4] UK Manual, para 6.17 n. 83.

[5] UK Manual, para. 6.17, quoting the statement made by the United Kingdom on ratification of API and noting the nuclear weapons statements made by Belgium, Canada, Germany, Italy, the Netherlands and Spain on ratification, and by the United States on signature, of API.

[6] UK Manual, para 6.17.1 (footnote omitted).

[7] UK Manual, para 6.17.2.

reserved the right to review this assurance if the future threat, development and proliferation of these weapons make it necessary'. The Manual noted that similar assurances had been given to Belarus, Kazakhstan, Ukraine and, in treaty form, to Latin American, African and South Pacific States that were parties to treaties establishing nuclear weapon-free zones in those regions.[8]

I.3 UNITED STATES

Section 6.18 of the US DoD Law of War Manual addresses nuclear weapons.[9] It starts with a clear statement that '[t]here is no general prohibition in treaty or customary international law on the use of nuclear weapons'. This assertion is stated to be consistent with a Written Statement of the Government of the United States of America dated 20 June 1995 and evidently associated with the proceedings of the International Court of Justice that gave rise to the ICJ Nuclear Opinion. While the Manual states that nuclear weapons are lawful weapons for the United States, it recognises that the law of war governs the use of nuclear weapons, as it does conventional weapons. 'For example, nuclear weapons must be directed against military objectives. In addition, attacks using nuclear weapons must not be conducted when the expected incidental harm to civilians is excessive compared to the military advantage expected to be gained.'[10]

In a footnote, attention is drawn to a report by the Secretary of Defense entitled 'Report on Nuclear Employment Strategy of the United States Specified in Section 491 of 10 U.S.C.', dated June 2013. That guidance evidently makes it clear that all plans must be consistent with the fundamental principles of the law of armed conflict. The plans will, reportedly, apply the principles of distinction and proportionality and will seek to minimise collateral damage to civilian populations and civilian objects. The report apparently makes it clear that the United States will not intentionally target civilian populations or civilian objects.[11]

The Manual then draws attention to US policy on the use of nuclear weapons, noting that 'the United States has stated that it would only consider

8 UK Manual, para. 6.17.2.

9 It should be borne in mind that the Manual is issued with the authority of the US Department of Defense and does not necessarily reflect the views of the US government as a whole; see Introduction to the Manual.

10 US DoD Law of War Manual, para. 6.18 (footnotes omitted).

11 US DoD Law of War Manual, para 6.18 n. 412, also citing the Written Statement of the Government of the United States of America dated 20 June 1995 and E. R. Cummings, 'The Role of Humanitarian Law', 25 September 1982, III (1981–8) *Cumulative Digest of United States Practice in International Law* 3421, 3422.

the use of nuclear weapons in extreme circumstances to defend the vital interests of the United States or its allies and partners', adding that it 'will not use or threaten to use nuclear weapons against non-nuclear-weapon States that are party to the Nuclear Non-Proliferation Treaty and in compliance with their nuclear non-proliferation obligations'.[12] The Manual then draws attention[13] to the nuclear statements made by a number of States on ratification of API and referred to above in the discussion of the United Kingdom's doctrinal position, commenting that it was US understanding when participating in the negotiations leading to the adoption of API that the rules on the conduct of hostilities established by the Protocol were not intended to have any effect on, and do not regulate or prohibit, nuclear weapons.[14]

The final paragraph on the subject is short but important and will be quoted in full. It reads:

> **Authority to Launch Nuclear Weapons.** The authority to launch nuclear weapons generally is restricted to the highest levels of government. The domestic law and procedures concerning nuclear weapons employment are beyond the scope of this manual.[15]

Such procedures are of course highly classified and the provisions they contain are beyond the intended scope of this book. However, it is interesting and highly significant – for example, in relation to the question of potential criminal liability – that the US DoD Law of War Manual specifies that the authority to launch is governmental in nature and, accordingly, is not a matter for an individual military commander.

12 US DoD Law of War Manual, para. 6.18.1.

13 US DoD Law of War Manual, para. 6.18.2.

14 See, in particular, the statement made by the United States, 1125 UNTS 434, cited in US DoD Law of War Manual, para. 6.18.3 n. 418.

15 US DoD Law of War Manual, para. 6.18.4.

J

The ICJ Advisory Opinion

In this Section, the analysis in the Nuclear Weapon Advisory Opinion of the International Court of Justice (ICJ)[1] will be reviewed. Given that the Opinion was issued approximately a quarter of a century ago, the purpose of the Section is to consider whether, if the issue were to come back before the Court now, the same or a similar Opinion could be expected. Accordingly, we will consider the elements of the ICJ Nuclear Opinion that are of greatest relevance to the discussion in this book. The specific purposes are to assess whether the Court might be expected to analyse the issues in a similar way and whether it might be expected to reach similar overall conclusions.

It was the General Assembly of the United Nations that requested an opinion from the Court pursuant to Resolution 49/75 K, which was adopted on 15 December 1994. In the preambular paragraphs of the Resolution, the General Assembly drew attention to numerous resolutions dating from 1961 to 1991, in which it had declared that the use of nuclear weapons would violate the UN Charter and be a crime against humanity. The question posed by the General Assembly was: 'Is the threat or use of nuclear weapons in any circumstance permitted under international law?'[2]

Having concluded that it had the authority to deliver an opinion on the question posed,[3] the Court considered the question by referring, in turn, to a number of bodies of law or legal propositions. It addressed the suggestion that the use of nuclear weapons would violate the right to life as guaranteed by Article 6(1) of the International Covenant on Civil and Political Rights (ICCPR). The Court noted that ICCPR protection does not cease in times

[1] *Legality of the Threat or Use of Nuclear Weapons* (Advisory Opinion of 8 July 1996) [1996] ICJ Rep. 226 (ICJ Nuclear Opinion).

[2] ICJ Nuclear Opinion, para. 1.

[3] ICJ Nuclear Opinion, para. 19.

of war other than by derogation in accordance with Article 4; that the right to life cannot be derogated from and applies in hostilities; that the test of what is an arbitrary deprivation of life in breach of the ICCPR falls to be determined by applicable *lex specialis* (i.e. LOAC, the law of armed conflict); and that whether a particular loss of life through use of a certain weapon in warfare is an arbitrary deprivation of life can be decided only by reference to the law applicable in armed conflict, and not deduced from the terms of the ICCPR itself.[4]

The questions that arise are whether, twenty-five years on, the ICJ would apply the same reasoning, and if not, what reasoning it would apply and with what implications for the lawfulness of the possession and use of nuclear weapons and of nuclear deterrence policies. In subsequent cases the ICJ has adopted a more nuanced approach. In the *Palestinian Wall* case, for example, the Court reaffirmed that, subject to any permissible derogation that a State might make, human rights protections do not cease during armed conflict. The Court identified three possible circumstances. Some situations may be exclusively matters for LOAC, others may be exclusively matters for human rights law and yet others may have to be considered by reference to both bodies of law. The issues concerning the Palestinian Wall fell, in the opinion of the Court, into the last of these three categories.[5] Thereafter, in the case of *Democratic Republic of the Congo* v. *Uganda*, the ICJ characterised LOAC and human rights law as complementary.[6]

The authors conclude that, were the legality of nuclear weapons to come back before the Court, it would likely apply the *Palestinian Wall* case approach and determine that both LOAC and human rights law must be considered in determining the issue. The LOAC aspects that would be of most significance would be those that were discussed in the 1996 Advisory Opinion, subject to a few additional points made below.

Where human rights law is concerned, the right to life, and specifically the ICCPR right not arbitrarily to be deprived of life, is likely, in the view of the authors, to weigh heavily on the minds of the judges. The possibility of the Court finding that the characteristics of a nuclear explosion – the blast, the fallout and the casualties and damage it is likely to occasion – would be difficult to reconcile with the ICCPR right to life cannot be entirely excluded. Such a finding would likely sit uncomfortably with the

4 ICJ Nuclear Opinion, para. 25.

5 *Legal Consequences of the Construction of a Wall in the Occupied Palestinian Territory* (Advisory Opinion of 9 July 2004) [2004] ICJ Rep. 136, para. 106.

6 *Case Concerning Armed Activities on the Territory of the Congo (Democratic Republic of the Congo* v. *Uganda)* (Judgment of 19 December 2005) [2005] ICJ Rep. 116, paras. 178–80, 216–17.

practice of the States that possess and maintain nuclear weapon capabilities. Whether that State practice aspect would influence the Court in its human rights law deliberations is unclear.

The Court went on to review the prohibition of genocide in the Genocide Convention[7] and concluded, as reflected in Section H, that the requisite intent would need to be established.[8] The treatment of genocide in the Rome Statute involves requirements as to intent similar to those noted by the Court, so there is no reason to believe that a different conclusion in that regard would be reached today.

The Court then examined the rules protecting the natural environment, specifically Article 35(3) of API, the Environmental Modification Convention and two principles taken from environmental law. Recognising 'the general obligation of States to ensure activities within their jurisdiction and control respect the environment of other States or of areas beyond national control', the Court did 'not consider that the treaties in question could have intended to deprive a State of the exercise of its right of self-defence'.[9] However, the Court did conclude that States 'must take environmental considerations into account when assessing what is necessary and proportionate in pursuit of legitimate military objectives'. One assumes these include, but are not necessarily limited to, self-defence.[10] So the Court found no explicit prohibition of the use of nuclear weapons on the basis of environmental law, but noted there are environmental factors to consider in the context of implementing LOAC.[11] Were the same issue to come before the Court again, Articles 35(3) and 55 of API would again be addressed, alongside more recently adopted provisions of environmental law. The inclusion in the Rome Statute of reference to environmental damage in the proportionality-based war crime mentioned in Article 8(2)(b)(iv) may be seen as simply reflecting the conclusion reached in paragraph 33 of the Opinion. However, one cannot help thinking that increasing global concerns linked to notions of global warming, climate change, rising sea levels and related issues will cause the Court to reflect perhaps a little more thoroughly on the legal acceptability, or otherwise, of the use of a kind of weapon that may be expected to render significant areas of land essentially useless for very long periods of time. It would seem appropriate for the hypothetical modern-day Court to consider the categorisation of the

[7] Convention on the Prevention and Punishment of the Crime of Genocide, Paris, 9 December 1948.
[8] ICJ Nuclear Opinion, para. 26.
[9] ICJ Nuclear Opinion, paras. 29, 30.
[10] ICJ Nuclear Opinion, para. 30.
[11] ICJ Nuclear Opinion, para. 33.

natural environment as, in principle, a civilian object and to assess whether, in the modern context, the use of a nuclear weapon could be equated with the infliction of wanton destruction. An act is wanton if it involves intent and malice. While the modern-day Court would be unlikely to conclude that all potential uses of nuclear weapons would satisfy those twin tests, it would be interesting to receive the Court's views as to the circumstances in which the tests are likely to be satisfied.

The Court's view, expressed in paragraph 34, was that the UN Charter law on the use of force, LOAC rules on the conduct of hostilities and any relevant treaty law dealing with nuclear weapons constitute the most directly relevant applicable law. Perhaps nowadays, as discussed above, certain provisions of human rights law would be added to that list.

The Court assessed the key characteristics of nuclear weapons as being the immense quantities of heat and energy they produce and the powerful and prolonged radiation they release, rendering such weapons 'potentially catastrophic'. The assertion that their destructive power 'cannot be contained in either space or time',[12] and in particular the long-term potential effects of ionising radiation, clearly weighed heavily with the judges and formed the baseline against which their lawfulness in *ad bellum* and *in bello* terms was analysed by the Court.[13]

J.1 APPLYING JUS AD BELLUM

Famously, the Court observed that the prohibition of the use of force in Article 2(4) of the UN Charter, the recognition of the inherent right of self-defence in Article 51 and forceful Security Council action under Article 42 'apply to any use of force, regardless of the weapons employed'.[14] As the Court pointed out, the Charter 'neither expressly prohibits, nor permits, the use of any specific weapon, including nuclear weapons'. Here, maybe, the Court was starting to lay down the basis for its subsequent, and controversial, *non liquet* finding. That Article 2(4)'s prohibition applies to nuclear weapons is not controversial and would no doubt feature with suitable prominence in any revised Opinion. The existing Opinion states that the proportionality limitation on lawful self-defence[15] cannot exclude the use of nuclear weapons in all circumstances, but that such a proportionate use must also comply with LOAC. This view would

[12] ICJ Nuclear Opinion, para. 35.
[13] ICJ Nuclear Opinion, para. 36.
[14] ICJ Nuclear Opinion, para. 39.
[15] See Rule 12 in Section C; ICJ Nuclear Opinion, para. 42.

probably be repeated in any updated Opinion, while noting that the nature of nuclear weapons and the profound risks, including escalation, associated with their use must be borne in mind by States when addressing proportionality.[16]

The Opinion goes on to consider threats contrary to Article 2(4) of the UN Charter, observing that 'States sometimes signal that they possess certain weapons to use in self-defence against any State violating their territorial integrity or political independence', and suggesting that '[i]f the envisaged use of force is itself unlawful, the stated readiness to use it would be a threat prohibited under Article 2, paragraph 4'.[17] Perhaps the fact that China, France, India, Pakistan, the Russian Federation, the United Kingdom and the United States all appear, according to their practice, to adopt, to a greater or lesser extent, a policy of deterrence that contemplates *in extremis* the use of nuclear weapons should cause the Court, in any revised Opinion, to ask itself whether the cited sentence from paragraph 47 really reflects a general practice of States accepted as law and, if it does not, whether it has a proper place in such an Opinion. The present authors would suggest that a threat in breach of Article 2(4) must involve a somewhat more directed and specific expression that must be communicated explicitly, or impliedly through conduct. The interpretation of 'threat' now being put forward would, arguably, also be more readily coherent with the final sentence of paragraph 47.

Continuing with the deterrence theme, the Court recognised that, to be effective, a deterrence policy 'necessitates that the intention to use nuclear weapons be credible'.[18] It is certainly right that a threat to use force directed against the territorial integrity or political independence of a State or against the purposes of the United Nations breaches Article 2(4). It is also right that a threat to use force in purported self-defence that breaches the requirements as to proportionality and/or necessity would also be unlawful. However, the real point that paragraph 48 arguably fails properly to tease out is that the mere maintenance of a capability, without more, appears generally not to be considered by States, in their general practice, as constituting an unlawful threat.

J.2 NUCLEAR WEAPONS UNDER THE LAW OF ARMED CONFLICT

Having pointed out that international law does not specifically authorise the use of any weapon in general or in specified circumstances, the Court explains

16 ICJ Nuclear Opinion, para. 43.
17 ICJ Nuclear Opinion, para. 47.
18 ICJ Nuclear Opinion, para. 48.

that 'the illegality of the use of certain weapons as such does not result from an absence of authorization but, on the contrary, is formulated in terms of prohibition'.[19] That reference to the essentially prohibitive terms in which most of LOAC is expressed remains true today and would need to be reflected carefully in any revised Opinion.

The Court then looked at whether nuclear weapons should be treated in the same way as poisoned weapons, drawing attention to the prohibition of the latter in the Hague Regulations of 1899,[20] in Article 23(a) of the 1907 Hague Regulations and in the Geneva Gas Protocol.[21] As the Court correctly pointed out, the term 'poison or poisoned weapons' is not defined in the Hague Regulations, but has not been treated by the parties to the listed instruments as referring to nuclear weapons. This consideration of the conduct of States by reference to nuclear weapons would also seem to be applicable to notions of nuclear deterrence in the manner suggested above. It seems most unlikely that, in an updated Opinion, the Court would depart from that position, as the general practice of States has not significantly changed.[22]

The Court noted that, at the date of delivery of its Advisory Opinion, no treaty of general prohibition of the same kind as the chemical and biological conventions had been adopted. More recently, the Treaty on the Prohibition of Nuclear Weapons, discussed in Section K, has been adopted and has now come into force. It is not at present clear what influence, if any, the existence of that treaty would have on the deliberations of the judges, were the issue to come back before the Court. The authors rather suspect that, until nuclear weapon States, and States nearing the development or acquisition of nuclear weapons, start to become parties to the Convention, its influence will be somewhat limited. In the ICJ Nuclear Opinion, the Court grouped relevant treaties into those dealing with acquisition, manufacture and possession of nuclear weapons; those concerned with their employment; and, finally, treaties addressing nuclear weapon testing. The Opinion then addresses the numerous treaties that establish nuclear weapon-free zones, non-proliferation obligations or similar restrictive arrangements and shows how

19 ICJ Nuclear Opinion, para. 52.

20 Regulations Respecting the Laws and Customs of War on Land, Annex to Hague Convention II, 29 July 1899.

21 Protocol for the Prohibition of the Use in War of Asphyxiating, Poisonous or Other Gases, and of Bacteriological Methods of Warfare, Geneva, 17 June 1925.

22 ICJ Nuclear Opinion, paras. 54–6. Clearly, the adoption of the Treaty on the Prohibition of Nuclear Weapons, discussed in Section K, clarifies the position of certain States, but the point being made here is that the generality of State practice, including that of States that retain nuclear weapons, has not altered materially.

these texts are variously interpreted by supporters and critics of the lawfulness of a resort to nuclear weapons in appropriately grave circumstances.

The Court, rather presciently, suggested that those treaties could 'be seen as foreshadowing a future general prohibition of the use of such weapons', adding that 'they do not constitute such a prohibition by themselves'.[23] The present authors agree and would merely add that the Treaty on the Prohibition of Nuclear Weapons (TPNW), which at the time of writing has been ratified by fifty-two States and is now in force,[24] also does not reflect binding customary law.[25] Specifically, the Court did not view the treaty arrangements that it addressed 'as amounting to a comprehensive and universal conventional prohibition on the use, or the threat of use, of [nuclear] weapons as such'.[26] The present authors do not believe this view would necessarily be affected by the TPNW, unless and until nuclear weapon States start to become parties to the convention. In this context it is worth mentioning that the fifty-two States that are parties to the TPNW at the time of writing do not include China, France, India, Israel, Pakistan, the Russian Federation, the United Kingdom, the United States or any NATO member States.

It was at this point in the judgment that the Court assessed whether customary international law included a prohibition on the threat or use of nuclear weapons, referring to the *Continental Shelf* case for this purpose.[27] Evidently, the argument had been made that a customary rule prohibiting the use of nuclear weapons already existed, based on 'a consistent practice of non-utilization of nuclear weapons by States since 1945'[28] and an implied *opinio juris*. The Opinion juxtaposes that thought with the notion of deterrence, where the right to use such weapons in self-defence is reserved in the case of 'an armed attack threatening . . . vital security interests'.[29] The argument goes that it is merely fortuitous that such circumstances have not arisen. The Court felt unable to find an *opinio juris* linked to the non-recourse to nuclear weapons over what was then a period of fifty years. If the Court were to reconsider this aspect today, it would probably be unlikely to reach a different conclusion, despite the continuation of the practice for a further quarter of a century.[30]

23 ICJ Nuclear Opinion, para. 62.
24 www.icrc.org (viewed 30 January 2021).
25 See ICJ Nuclear Opinion, para. 62.
26 ICJ Nuclear Opinion, para. 63.
27 *Continental Shelf (Libyan Arab Jamahiriya/Malta)* (Judgment of 3 June 1985) [1985] ICJ Rep. 13, para. 27.
28 ICJ Nuclear Opinion, para. 65.
29 ICJ Nuclear Opinion, para. 66.
30 See ICJ Nuclear Opinion, para. 67.

The Court considered a sequence of relevant UN General Assembly resolutions, including Resolution 1653 (XVI) of 24 November 1961 essentially condemning nuclear weapons, but could not find an associated customary prohibition. It did, however, recognise a widespread desire for a decisive step to be taken towards nuclear disarmament.[31] As has already been noted, the TPNW discussed in Section K certainly represents a significant step in the desired direction. How decisive it may be expected to prove will be assessed in that Section.

So, having failed to find a rule, conventional or customary, the Court turned its attention to the principles and rules of international humanitarian law and to neutrality law. After briefly charting the evolution of international humanitarian law (IHL), the Court famously recognised certain IHL principles – namely, distinction and superfluous injury/unnecessary suffering – while also taking into account the Martens Clause as set forth in Article 1(2) of API.[32] Importantly, the Court asserted that if a weapon's use would not meet IHL requirements, a threat to use it would also breach IHL.

More generally, the Court considered that IHL principles and rules indicate the normal conduct and behaviour expected of States and shared the majority view among States and writers that IHL applies to nuclear weapons. The Opinion pointedly asserts that the intrinsically humanitarian character of the principles of IHL 'permeates the entire law of armed conflict and applies to all forms of warfare and to all kinds of weapons, those of the past, those of the present and those of the future'.[33] The language that is used in this part of the judgment is somewhat convoluted and risks being misinterpreted. Read literally, the sentence is stating that the humanitarian character permeates IHL as a whole and that this humanitarian character applies to all forms of warfare. That would appear to be a nonsense and is not, it is assumed, what the learned judges were trying to say. Rather, this oft-cited passage has been widely interpreted as signifying that the principles and rules themselves apply to past, present and future weapons. It is likely that any revised ICJ Opinion would make that point somewhat less ambiguously, no doubt citing in support, inter alia, Article 1 common to the Geneva Conventions and Article 36 of

[31] ICJ Nuclear Opinion, para. 73.

[32] As given in Article 1(2), the clause states: 'In cases not covered by this Protocol or by other international agreements, civilians and combatants remain under the protection and authority of the principles of international law derived from established custom, from the principles of humanity and from the dictates of public conscience.' The text is cited in the ICJ Nuclear Opinion, para. 78.

[33] ICJ Nuclear Opinion, para. 86.

API, as well as the Martens Clause and the national positions noted later in paragraph 86 of the judgment.

The principle of neutrality is then considered, and the Court readily finds the principle to be fundamental and to apply, subject to the relevant UN Charter provisions, to all international armed conflicts irrespective of the weapons used. Weighing the competing views and arguments against the foregoing principles and rules, the Court pointed out that those advocating legality have not indicated the circumstances that might justify the use of a low-yield nuclear weapon, even supposing such low-yield use were to be feasible. The Court therefore could not determine whether such a use would be potentially lawful. Of course, were the issue to come back before the Court, more specific evidence would need to be forthcoming on the existence, foreseen circumstances of use, likely characteristics and impact of such a limited-yield weapon. Notwithstanding such factors, the likelihood of nuclear escalation following such a limited-yield nuclear attack would, in all probability, influence the Court to conclude that such use would, in most if not all circumstances, be unlawful.[34]

The Court expressed the opinion that the use of nuclear weapons seems scarcely reconcilable with LOAC rules, but could not 'conclude with certainty that the use of nuclear weapons would necessarily be at variance with' IHL principles and rules 'in any circumstances', and in this context cited the right of every State to resort to self-defence 'when its survival is at stake'.[35] This *non liquet* part of the judgment has been roundly criticised from a number of perspectives, and judges reconsidering these issues would be less than human were they not to take those criticisms into account. However, the basis for that part of the finding lies in the preceding analysis in the earlier paragraphs of the Opinion and, as the foregoing discussion tends to suggest, while there are certainly additional points that would likely be made in a revised Opinion, it is by no means certain that the ultimate conclusion would necessarily be radically different.

In the closing paragraphs of the Opinion, the Court drew attention to diverse authorities that, taken together, place an obligation on States to pursue negotiations to achieve effective measures towards nuclear disarmament.[36] In Section K, the TPNW will be examined and evaluated to see whether it may be the vehicle whereby this objective can be achieved.

34 Consider ICJ Nuclear Opinion, para. 94.

35 ICJ Nuclear Opinion, para. 96, largely re-stated in para. 97.

36 ICJ Nuclear Opinion, para. 103.

In its concluding findings, the Court decided by thirteen votes to one to comply with the request for an advisory opinion. It then found, unanimously, that '[t]here is in neither customary nor conventional international law any specific authorization of the threat or use of nuclear weapons' and, by eleven votes to three, that '[t]here is in neither customary nor conventional international law any comprehensive and universal prohibition of the threat or use of nuclear weapons as such'. Unanimously, the Court opined that '[a] threat or use of force by means of nuclear weapons that is contrary to Article 2, paragraph 4, of the United Nations Charter and that fails to meet all of the requirements of Article 51, is unlawful'. Also unanimously, it found that '[a] threat or use of nuclear weapons should also be compatible with the requirements of the international law applicable in armed conflict, particularly those of the principles and rules of international humanitarian law, as well as with specific obligations under treaties and other undertakings which expressly deal with nuclear weapons'.

Then came the *non liquet* part of the judgment. By seven votes to seven and by the casting vote of the president, the Court found:

> It follows from the above-mentioned requirements that the threat or use of nuclear weapons would generally be contrary to the rules of international law applicable in armed conflict, and in particular the principles and rules of humanitarian law;
>
> However, in view of the current state of international law, and of the elements of fact at its disposal, the Court cannot conclude definitively whether the threat or use of nuclear weapons would be lawful or unlawful in an extreme circumstance of self-defence, in which the very survival of a State would be at stake.

Finally, the Court stated, unanimously, that '[t]here exists an obligation to pursue in good faith and bring to a conclusion negotiations leading to nuclear disarmament in all its aspects under strict and effective international control'.[37]

The foregoing analysis of the judgment leads the authors to consider that, while the details of the language used and the voting numbers might well differ, there can be no certainty that, were the matter to come back before the Court, there would necessarily be a different overall outcome. While the right to life might attract a greater focus, while environmental impact may be seen as even more important and while the TPNW may have some influence on the judicial analysis, it seems likely that the absence of a general practice of States

37 ICJ Nuclear Opinion, para. 105(2).

recognised as law indicating a customary prohibition would cause the judges to hesitate before finding definitive illegality. An argument that treaties and other State documents might support a finding of illegality would, in the end, have to be weighed against the actual practice of the numerous most powerful States in the world in their maintenance of their nuclear capabilities and of their associated deterrence policies. In such a legal contest, it is the clear opinion of the authors that it is the nuclear conduct of States that will, in the end, be decisive.

K

Nuclear Disarmament and Arms Control

Nuclear disarmament and arms control law encompasses a variety of multilateral, regional and bilateral agreements. The multilateral counter-proliferation regime can be considered a fairly successful effort. It aims to prevent the proliferation of nuclear weapons beyond recognised nuclear-weapon States (China, France, Russian Federation, the United Kingdom and the United States) and is supplemented by a verification regime under the auspices of the International Atomic Energy Agency (IAEA) and by two informal arrangements. It does not apply to States that are not parties to the NPT, such as India, Israel, the Democratic People's Republic of Korea (North Korea) and Pakistan. A further problem is the involvement of non-State actors in the proliferation of nuclear weapons materiel and technologies. Therefore, the proliferation of nuclear weapons can often be prevented only if the UN Security Council is able to agree on binding resolutions, including on (non-military) enforcement measures. In addition to the non-proliferation regime, States have agreed, at a multilateral level, on the prohibition of the testing and/or emplacement of nuclear weapons in certain areas and, at a regional level, on nuclear weapon-free zones. The most ambitious step some States have taken so far is the adoption of the Treaty on the Prohibition of Nuclear Weapons in 2017.

K.1 BILATERAL TREATIES BETWEEN THE UNITED STATES AND THE RUSSIAN FEDERATION/FORMER USSR

The former USSR/the Russian Federation and the United States have, since 1969, agreed on a number of bilateral treaties and other measures to limit and reduce their strategic and intermediate nuclear arsenals, delivery and strategic defence systems. From the outset, those agreements served a twofold purpose: (1) the establishment of a binding regime of mutual control in order to prevent the outbreak of (nuclear) war; and (2) the preservation of the multilateral non-proliferation regime through the taking of credible steps towards nuclear disarmament. As far as strategic offensive arms[1] are concerned, it suffices to mention:

the SALT I process, which resulted in the adoption of the ABM Treaty[2] and of the SALT I Interim Agreement[3] on 26 May 1972;
the SALT II Agreements of 1979,[4] which were not ratified by the US Senate;
the START I Agreement of 1992;[5]
the START II Agreement of 1993,[6] which did not enter into force;
the START III process of 1997, which ended without results because its success had been linked to the entry into force of the START II Agreement;
the 2002 SORT,[7] which remained in force until 31 December 2012; and
New START of 2010.[8]

The SALT I Interim Agreement and its Protocol expired on 3 October 1977. The ABM Treaty was denounced by the United States as of June 2002. The reduction obligations under START I were fulfilled in December 2001 (i.e.

1 The term 'strategic offensive arms' applies to nuclear warheads deployed by strategic nuclear delivery vehicles (SNDVs). SNDVs are inter-continental ballistic missiles (ICBMs) with a range exceeding 5,500 kilometres, strategic bombers, warships (including strategic submarines) and cruise missiles, including air- and sea-launched cruise missiles (ALCMs, SLCMs).

2 Treaty on the Limitation of Anti-Ballistic Missile Systems (Russia–United States of America), signed 26 May 1972, entered into force 3 October 1972, 944 UNTS 13.

3 Interim Agreement between the United States of America and the Union of Soviet Socialist Republics on Certain Measures with Respect to the Limitation of Strategic Offensive Arms (SALT I Interim Agreement), signed 26 May 1972, entered into force 3 October 1972, 944 UNTS 3.

4 Treaty between the United States of America and the Union of Soviet Socialist Republics on the Limitation of Strategic Offensive Arms (SALT II), done 18 June 1979, never entered into force, 18 (1979) ILM 1138.

5 Treaty between the United States of America and the Union of Soviet Socialist Republics on the Reduction and Limitation of Strategic Offensive Arms, signed 31 July 1991, entered into force 5 December 1994, 16 (1991) *United Nations Disarmament Yearbook*, 450.

6 Treaty on Further Reduction and Limitation of Strategic Offensive Arms (Russia–United States of America), signed 3 January 1993, entered into force 14 April 2000, reprinted in *SIPRI Yearbook 1993: Armaments, Disarmament and International Security* (Oxford University Press, 1993) 576.

7 Treaty between the Russian Federation and the United States of America on Strategic Offensive Reductions, done 24 May 2002, entered into force 1 June 2003, 2350 UNTS 415.

8 Treaty between the United States of America and the Russian Federation on Measures for the Further Reduction and Limitation of Strategic Offensive Arms, signed 8 April 2010, entered into force 5 February 2011, 50 (2011) ILM 342.

four years prior to the agreed date of expiration). Accordingly, the only agreement on the reduction and limitation of strategic offensive arms is New START.[9] New START would have expired on 5 February 2021 but, in January 2021, the parties agreed on an extension of its duration for an additional five years. The only agreement between the two States on nuclear weapons deployed by ground-launched ballistic and cruise missiles with ranges of between 500 and 5,500 kilometres (i.e. by intermediate- or short-range missiles) is the Intermediate-Range Nuclear Forces (INF) Treaty, from which the United States withdrew as of 2 August 2019.

The agreement on an extension of the duration of New START is to be considered an important accomplishment. However, this does not necessarily imply that the current bilateral regime on the reduction and limitation of strategic offensive nuclear arms will survive or even improve. The non-nuclear-weapon States' continuing compliance with the NPT is, therefore, far from being a given. Moreover, the lack of a binding legal regime on intermediate- and short-range missiles has certainly adversely affected security in Europe. Apart from these considerations, however, it may be doubted whether bilateral approaches to nuclear disarmament and arms control are nowadays suitable methods of enhancing nuclear security. In the twentieth century, the bilateral agreements between Russia and the United States were necessary steps in the right direction. The United States and the USSR/Russian Federation were the States with the biggest nuclear arsenals, and the nuclear arsenals of China, France and the United Kingdom were not important enough to be included in a nuclear disarmament regime. However, in the twenty-first century, the number of recognised and non-recognised nuclear-weapon States has risen from five to nine, with the nuclear capabilities of China, India and Pakistan having reached a considerable level. If those States remain outside of a binding regime on strategic and non-strategic nuclear weapons, the States that do not possess nuclear weapons and that are parties to the treaty may legitimately wonder whether their promise not to engage in nuclear activities for other than peaceful purposes continues to be beneficial for them.

K.2 MULTILATERAL TREATIES AND ARRANGEMENTS

The first category of multilateral and potentially universal treaties deals with the prohibition of nuclear weapon tests, either in a comprehensive manner or

9 For a summary of the obligations under NEW START, see U.S. Department of State, 'New START Treaty Aggregate Numbers of Strategic Offensive Arms: Fact Sheet' (1 April 2021), www.state.gov/new-start-treaty-aggregate-numbers-of-strategic-offensive-arms/.

in given areas.[10] Under the treaties of the second category, it is prohibited to emplace nuclear weapons in a given area or space. Multilateral treaties of the latter category apply to the seabed[11] and to outer space, including the moon and other celestial bodies.[12] The third category includes regional treaties on nuclear weapon-free zones[13] that are binding only on the States that are parties to them and that have no impact on the activities of nuclear-weapon States in the regions covered by such agreements. Also worthwhile mentioning in this context is the Open Skies Treaty.[14] The fourth category addresses the problem of nuclear terrorism.[15]

K.2.1 *The Nuclear Non-Proliferation Treaty and Related Instruments*

The fifth category deals with the non-proliferation of nuclear weapons, with the NPT[16] forming the cornerstone of the international non-proliferation regime. The NPT imposes complementary obligations on nuclear-weapon

10 Treaty Banning Nuclear Weapon Tests in the Atmosphere, in Outer Space and Under Water (PTBT), opened for signature at London, Moscow and Washington 8 August 1963, entered into force 10 October 1963, 125 parties; Comprehensive Nuclear-Test-Ban Treaty (CTBT), adopted 10 September 1996, opened for signature at New York 24 September 1996, 170 parties; Antarctic Treaty, signed at Washington 1 December 1959, entered into force 23 June 1961, 54 parties. Article V of the Antarctic Treaty prohibits 'any nuclear explosions in Antarctica'.

11 Treaty on the Prohibition of the Emplacement of Nuclear Weapons and Other Weapons of Mass Destruction on the Seabed and the Ocean Floor and in the Subsoil Thereof, opened for signature at London, Moscow and Washington 11 February 1971, entered into force 18 May 1972, 94 parties.

12 Treaty on Principles Governing the Activities of States in the Exploration and Use of Outer Space, Including the Moon and Other Celestial Bodies, opened for signature at London, Moscow and Washington 27 January 1967, entered into force 10 October 1967, 110 parties; Agreement Governing the Activities of States on the Moon and Other Celestial Bodies, opened for signature at New York 18 December 1979, entered into force 11 July 1984, 18 parties.

13 Treaty for the Prohibition of Nuclear Weapons in Latin America and the Caribbean (Treaty of Tlatelolco), opened for signature at Mexico City 14 February 1967, entered into force for each State individually, 33 parties; South Pacific Nuclear-Free Zone Treaty (Treaty of Rarotonga), opened for signature at Rarotonga 6 August 1985, entered into force 11 December 1986, 13 parties; Treaty on the Southeast Asia Nuclear Weapon-Free Zone (Bangkok Treaty), opened for signature at Bangkok 15 December 1995, entered into force 27 March 1997, 10 parties; African Nuclear Weapon-Free Zone Treaty (Pelindaba Treaty) opened for signature at Cairo 11 April 1996, entered into force 15 July 2009, 41 parties; Treaty on a Nuclear Weapon-Free Zone in Central Asia (CANWFZ), opened for signature at Semipalatinsk 8 September 2006, entered into force 21 March 2009, 5 parties.

14 Treaty on Open Skies, opened for signature at Helsinki 24 March 1992, entered into force 1 January 2002, 34 parties.

15 International Convention for the Suppression of Acts of Nuclear Terrorism, opened for signature at New York 14 September, entered into force 7 July 2007, 117 parties.

16 Treaty on the Non-Proliferation of Nuclear Weapons (NPT), opened for signature at London, Moscow and Washington 1 July 1968, entered into force 5 March, 191 parties. Pursuant to

States (Article 1) and non-nuclear-weapon States (Article II). The obligations in Article I are as follows:

> Each nuclear-weapon State Party to the Treaty undertakes not to transfer to any recipient whatsoever nuclear weapons or other nuclear explosive devices or control over such weapons or explosive devices directly, or indirectly; and not in any way to assist, encourage, or induce any non-nuclear-weapon State to manufacture or otherwise acquire nuclear weapons or other nuclear explosive devices, or control over such weapons or explosive devices.

The complementary obligations in Article II are in the following terms:

> Each non-nuclear-weapon State Party to the Treaty undertakes not to receive the transfer from any transferor whatsoever of nuclear weapons or other nuclear explosive devices or of control over such weapons or explosive devices directly, or indirectly; not to manufacture or otherwise acquire nuclear weapons or other nuclear explosive devices; and not to seek or receive any assistance in the manufacture of nuclear weapons or other nuclear explosive devices.

While all States continue to enjoy the right 'to develop research, production and use of nuclear energy for peaceful purposes' (Article IV), non-nuclear-weapon States are obliged to conclude safeguards agreements with the IAEA 'with a view to preventing diversion of nuclear energy from peaceful purposes to nuclear weapons or other nuclear explosive devices' (Article III).

Verification of the parties' compliance with their obligations under the NPT could be considerably facilitated by the proposed Fissile Material Cut-Off Treaty, which would impose restrictions on nuclear-weapon States with regard to the production of highly-enriched uranium and plutonium.[17] However, the UN Conference on Disarmament has not yet arrived at a sufficient consensus.

To a certain extent, the NPT and the IAEA safeguards agreements are supplemented by two informal arrangements – the Zangger Committee[18] and the Nuclear Suppliers Group (NSG).[19] The former is an informal group of 39 States that have agreed to implement safeguards and guidelines for the export of source or special fissionable material and of equipment or material

Article X(2), the Review and Extension Conference decided, on 11 May 1995, that the NPT would continue to be in force indefinitely.

17 For an overview, see UN Institute for Disarmament Research, 'A Fissile Material Cut-off Treaty: Understanding the Critical Issues', UNIDIR/2010/4, https://unidir.org/files/publications/pdfs/a-fissile-material-cut-off-treaty-understanding-the-critical-issues-139.pdf.

18 For an overview, see www.zanggercommittee.org.

19 For an overview, see www.nuclearsuppliersgroup.org.

especially designed or prepared for the processing, use or production of special fissionable material. The NSG is an informal group of 48 nuclear supplier States that seek to contribute to the non-proliferation of nuclear weapons through the national implementation of guidelines for nuclear exports.

K.2.2 *The Treaty on the Prohibition of Nuclear Weapons*

The sixth category of multilateral treaties – dealing with the prohibition of nuclear weapons and aiming at the total elimination of such weapons – is the Treaty on the Prohibition of Nuclear Weapons (TPNW).[20] The TPNW entered into force on 22 January 2021, ninety days after the fiftieth State ratified, accepted, approved or acceded to the Treaty.[21] At the time of writing, the TPNW had been ratified by fifty-two States and signed by eighty-six States (which do not include China, France, India, Israel, Pakistan, the Russian Federation, the United Kingdom, the United States or any other NATO member States).

According to the preamble, the signatory States have been guided not only by the wish to prevent the 'catastrophic humanitarian consequences' resulting from an intentional or accidental use of nuclear weapons[22] but also by 'the ethical imperatives for nuclear disarmament'[23] and by legal considerations under both *jus ad bellum*[24] and *jus in bello*.[25] The references to *jus in bello* indicate that, according to the States already parties and, in due course, future member States, 'any use of nuclear weapons'[26] would be contrary to the basic principles of international humanitarian law,[27] including the Martens Clause.[28] However, the exact content of those principles to which the Treaty negotiators were referring remains unclear. The prohibition of indiscriminate attacks, including the prohibition of excessive collateral damage (principle of

20 UN Doc. A/CONF.29/2017/8 of 7 July 2017.

21 TPNW, Article 15.

22 Ibid., preambular paras. 2, 3, 4, 6.

23 Ibid., preambular para. 5. Those 'ethical imperatives' are complemented by concerns about the 'world's human and economic resources' being diverted for armaments (preambular paras. 12, 14), about the preservation of indigenous peoples (preambular para. 7) and about the 'equal participation of both women and men' (preambular para. 22).

24 Ibid., preambular paras. 12, 13.

25 Ibid., preambular paras. 8, 9, 10.

26 Ibid., preambular para. 10.

27 Ibid., preambular para. 9: no unlimited right in the choice of methods or means of warfare; principle of distinction; prohibition of indiscriminate attacks; proportionality; precautions in attack; prohibition of superfluous injury and unnecessary suffering; protection of the natural environment. Interestingly, the preamble refers to the 'rule of distinction'.

28 Ibid., preambular para. 11.

proportionality), and the obligation to take precautions in attack are but specifications of the principle (not rule!) of distinction. The overall object of the TPNW is, on the one hand, to preserve the NPT,[29] the CTBT,[30] the regional agreements on nuclear weapon-free zones[31] and the peaceful uses of nuclear energy[32] and, on the other hand, to arrive at 'general and complete disarmament'[33] through the adoption of a 'legally binding prohibition of nuclear weapons …, including the irreversible, verifiable and transparent elimination of nuclear weapons'.[34] The underlying reason for the adoption of the treaty is discontent with the steps that have so far been taken by nuclear weapon States to fulfil the promise given under the NPT – namely, 'to achieve at the earliest possible date the cessation of the nuclear arms race and to undertake effective measures in the direction of nuclear disarmament'.[35] The signatory States are disappointed with the 'slow pace of nuclear disarmament',[36] and they indirectly accuse nuclear weapon States of not complying with the 'obligation to pursue in good faith and bring to a conclusion negotiations leading to nuclear disarmament in all its aspects under strict and effective international control'.[37]

Accordingly, the legitimacy of the considerations that guided the signatory States cannot, in principle, be doubted, although they seem to provide evidence of a certain educationally and morally pretentious attitude on the part of the signatory States. However, the legal assessments contained in the preamble will not necessarily be shared by other States. Firstly, the promise made under the NPT is part of the preamble, not of the operative provisions of the NPT. Secondly, it is rather difficult, if not impossible, to prove the existence of a legal obligation to enter into a comprehensive agreement on nuclear disarmament. Thirdly, the illegality of 'any use of nuclear weapons' under the law of armed conflict can hardly be based on a consensus of States to that effect.

The TPNW applies to nuclear weapons and to other nuclear explosive devices. That distinction is rather artificial, if the definition of nuclear weapons adopted in the present book is taken into consideration. Accordingly, a 'nuclear explosive device' will regularly qualify as a 'nuclear weapon'. Obviously, the distinction has been adopted with a view to bringing within

29 Ibid., preambular para. 18
30 Ibid., preambular para. 19.
31 Ibid., preambular para. 20.
32 Ibid., preambular para. 21.
33 Ibid., preambular para. 16.
34 Ibid., preambular para. 15.
35 NPT, preambular para. 8.
36 TPNW, preambular para. 14.
37 Ibid., preambular para. 17.

the scope of the TPNW the entire spectrum of nuclear weapons, including those designed for tactical purposes.

The material obligations established by the TPNW are far-reaching and quite ambitious. Reservations are not permitted.[38] While it would go too far to characterise those obligations as unreasonable, they are likely to be acceptable to only a comparatively small number of States. Nevertheless, the likelihood of the Treaty attracting those States whose interests are specially affected is rather low. Accordingly, it may well be doubted whether it will ever crystallise into customary international law. More worrying is the prospect that TPNW will add to the fragmentation of international law, thereby weakening the existing legal (and non-legal) regime of nuclear disarmament and arms control.

The substantive obligations are set forth in Article 1 in the following, arms control terms:

> 1. Each State Party undertakes never under any circumstances to:
>
> (a) Develop, test, produce, manufacture, otherwise acquire, possess or stockpile nuclear weapons or other nuclear explosive devices;
> (b) Transfer to any recipient whatsoever nuclear weapons or other nuclear explosive devices or control over such weapons or explosive devices directly or indirectly;
> (c) Receive the transfer of or control over nuclear weapons or other nuclear explosive devices directly or indirectly;
> (d) Use or threaten to use nuclear weapons or other nuclear explosive devices;
> (e) Assist, encourage or induce, in any way, anyone to engage in any activity prohibited to a State Party under this Treaty;
> (f) Seek or receive any assistance, in any way, from anyone to engage in any activity prohibited to a State Party under this Treaty;
> (g) Allow any stationing, installation or deployment of any nuclear weapons or other nuclear explosive devices in its territory or at any place under its jurisdiction or control.

Much of the language here is of a sort previously used in the Chemical Weapons Convention, the Biological Weapons Convention and in other arms control treaties. Certain points should, however, be made. Lit. (a), (b), (c) and (d) will not pose insurmountable problems for non-nuclear-weapon States, because they are in part reflective of such States' obligations under the NPT and general international law. This certainly holds true for the prohibition in Lit. (a) to '[d]evelop, test, produce, manufacture, otherwise acquire,

[38] TPNW, Article 16.

possess or stockpile nuclear weapons or other nuclear explosive devices'. Read in conjunction with lit. (g), the prohibition of stockpiling does not include the presence of nuclear weapons and other explosive devices on the territory of a party if they are under the control of another State. The prohibitions of transferring or receiving the transfer of nuclear weapons or other nuclear explosive devices or of control over such weapons under lit. (b) and (c) differs from the NPT obligations insofar as they are not limited to inter-State relations, but apply to 'any recipient' and to any direct or indirect transfer or reception of such transfer. The prohibition of the use, or threat of use, of nuclear weapons and nuclear explosive devices may be understood as being reflective of the prohibition of the use of force under Article 2(4) of the UN Charter and under customary international law. It is important, however, to bear in mind that the prohibition of the threat of the use of such weapons is limited to the threatening of an illegal use. At first glance, the obligations under lit. (e) and (f) seem to be redundant and duplicative of those under lit. (b) and (c). There are, however, considerable differences. Firstly, the prohibitions under lit. (e) and (f) apply to the involvement only of individuals, not of States. Secondly, lit. (b) and (c) are limited to the physical transfer of weapons prohibited under the Treaty or of control over such weapons. Lit. (e) and (f) apply to 'any activity' prohibited under the Treaty – in particular, to the development of nuclear weapons and nuclear explosive devices. Against the background of the role the notorious Dr Khan[39] played in the transfer of the expertise required for the development and production of nuclear weapons, these prohibitions seem to be reasonable and necessary, if the obligations under the treaty are to be taken seriously. Finally, the obligation under lit. (g) is the most problematic for those non-nuclear-weapon States that have chosen to profit from the nuclear umbrella of a nuclear weapon State. For instance, NATO member States could not become parties to the TPNW without severely shattering NATO's nuclear deterrence policy, which requires nuclear weapons to be stationed, installed or deployed in the territory of NATO member States that are non-nuclear-weapon States.

According to Article 2, a party must, within thirty days of the TPNW's entry into force for that State, submit a declaration to the Secretary-General of the United Nations. The declaration must disclose whether the State owned, possessed or controlled nuclear weapons or nuclear explosive devices and

39 For a brief assessment, see Carnegie Endowment for International Peace, 'The A.Q. Khan Network and Its Fourth Customer' (23 January 2012), https://carnegieendowment.org/2012/01/23/a.q.-khan-network-and-its-fourth-customer-event-3505</int_u>.

eliminated its nuclear weapons programme and all nuclear weapons-related facilities prior to entry into force of the Treaty for that State (para. 1, lit. (a)); whether it owns, possesses or controls any such weapons or devices (para. 1, lit. (b)); and whether there are any such weapons or devices in its territory or in any place under its jurisdiction or control that are owned, possessed or controlled by another State (para. 1, lit. (c)). Such declarations are transmitted by the Secretary-General of the United Nations to the States that are already parties to the Treaty (para. 2).

Article 3 applies to those parties to which paragraphs 1 and 2 of Article 4 do not apply – that is, to those States that, after 7 July 2017, did not or ceased to own, possess or control nuclear weapons or other nuclear explosive devices. In other words, the provision applies to recognised non-nuclear-weapon States (or former nuclear weapon States). Article 3 is closely linked to the objective of preambular paragraph 18 to preserve and strengthen the verification regime of the NPT. Accordingly, non-nuclear-weapon States are obliged, 'at a minimum', to adhere to their existing IAEA safeguards obligations (para. 1) and to conclude with the IAEA comprehensive safeguards agreements, if they have not yet done so (para. 2). Such a non-nuclear-weapon State is obliged to start negotiations to that effect within 180 days from the entry into force of the TPNW and to ensure that the comprehensive safeguards agreement enters into force 'no later than 18 months from the entry into force of this Treaty for that State'.

Paragraphs 1–3 of Article 4 apply to parties that, after 7 July 2017, eliminated their nuclear weapon programmes, 'including the elimination or irreversible conversion of all nuclear-weapons-related facilities' (para. 1). It also applies to parties that continue to own, possess or control nuclear weapons and other nuclear explosive devices (para. 2). It is unclear whether those parties that have eliminated their nuclear weapon programmes but not yet irreversibly converted their nuclear-weapons facilities belong to either of these two categories. This is a deficiency of the Treaty. Arguably, such States are under at least an implicit obligation to convert their nuclear weapons-related facilities to purposes that do not involve nuclear weapons. Still, the wording seems to suggest that the obligations under Article 4(1) come into operation only if the conversion has been completed.

States to which Article 4(1) applies are obliged to co-operate with the international authority designated pursuant to Article 4(6) 'for the purpose of verifying the irreversible elimination' of their former nuclear weapon programmes and, within 180 days from the entry into force of the TPNW, to enter into negotiations with the IAEA aimed at the conclusion of a safeguards agreement 'sufficient to provide credible assurance of the non-diversion of declared nuclear material from peaceful nuclear activities and of the absence of undeclared nuclear material or activities in that State Party as a whole'. Such an agreement shall enter into force no later than eighteen months from the TPNW's entry into force for the State concerned. The safeguard agreement must be maintained 'at a minimum'. At first glance, the obligation seems to be clear. However, the actions required of the authority under Article 4(1) do not include verification of the 'elimination or irreversible conversion of all nuclear-weapons-related facilities' and the reporting thereof to other States parties to the Treaty. Moreover, it begs the question why parties that have eliminated their nuclear weapon programmes are excluded from the obligation under Article 3(2) to enter into comprehensive safeguards agreements with the IAEA. One possible explanation could be the intent to give such States an incentive to become parties by subjecting them to less strict obligations. In the light of the obligations of nuclear-weapon States under paragraphs 2 and 3, however, the missing reference to an irreversible conversion of all nuclear weapon-related facilities would rather seem to be due to a drafting error or to the unfounded belief that those States that have eliminated their nuclear weapon programmes will necessarily also irreversibly convert their nuclear weapons-related facilities. The fact that, according to Article 4(6), the authority's competence includes verification of the elimination or irreversible conversion may, therefore, be taken account of in determining the obligations and authorities under Article 4(1). Still, this would not entirely solve the problem, if the provision of Article 4(1) is considered a *lex specialis* that prevails over Article 4(6).

According to Article 4(2), a party that, after 7 July 2017, has not eliminated its nuclear weapon programmes and that continues to own, possess or control nuclear weapons or other nuclear explosive devices is obliged to 'immediately remove them from operational status, and destroy them as soon as possible but not later than a deadline to be determined by the first meeting of States Parties, in accordance with a legally binding, time-bound plan for the verified and irreversible elimination of that State's nuclear weapon programme, including the elimination or irreversible conversion of all nuclear-weapons-related facilities'. No later than sixty days after the entry into force of the TPNW for that State, the plan must be submitted to the other parties or to the competent international authority designated pursuant to Article 2(6), and the latter, after negotiations with the State in question, 'shall submit it to the subsequent meeting of States Parties or review conference, whichever comes first, for approval in accordance with its rules of procedure'. Accordingly, the authority has no power to verify compliance with the said obligations, but is limited to a procedural role. A State to which Article 4(2) applies is, according to paragraph 3, also obliged to conclude a safeguards agreement with the IAEA with the same content and within the same timeframe as provided for in paragraph 1.

Article 4(4) applies to States to which paragraphs 1 to 3 do not apply – that is, to non-nuclear-weapon States that have on their territories or in places under their jurisdiction or control nuclear weapons or nuclear explosive devices that are owned, possessed or controlled by another State. Such territorial States are required to 'ensure the prompt removal of such weapons, as soon as possible but not later than a deadline to be determined by the first meeting of the States Parties'. That obligation is not entirely coherent. On the one hand, it requires such States to ensure 'prompt' removal, which is to be understood as an obligation to take the necessary steps without undue delay. On the other hand, the obligation is to be complied with 'as soon as possible' but not later than the deadline to be determined. Moreover, the parties may determine the deadline without consulting the State that owns, possesses or controls the nuclear weapons. The potential for such an obligation to result in a dilemma for the States bound by paragraph 4 is obvious. The deployment of nuclear weapons on their territory may be the subject of a (bilateral or multilateral) treaty which may not be terminated easily or only after a given period of time.

All former and current nuclear weapon States, and States to which paragraph 4 applies, are obliged to 'submit a report to each meeting of States Parties and each review conference on the progress made towards the implementation' of their obligations under Article 4(1)–(4), 'until such time as they are fulfilled'.

The powers of the competent international authority or authorities to be designated by the parties in accordance with Article 4(6) are limited to the negotiation and verification of the obligations under paragraphs 1, 2 and 3. As stated above, it is not entirely settled whether they include verification of the elimination or irreversible conversion of all nuclear-weapons-related facilities by States to which paragraph 1 applies. Where such a designation has not been made for former or current nuclear weapon States falling under paragraphs 1 or 2, the UN Secretary-General is obliged to 'convene an extraordinary meeting of States Parties to take any decisions that may be required'.

The obligation of each party under Article 5(1) to 'adopt the necessary measures to implement its obligations under this Treaty' would, as such, not be difficult to fulfil, because it would be subject to the States' discretion to determine which measures of national implementation are 'necessary'. However, according to Article 5(2), the States are also obliged to 'take all appropriate legal, administrative and other measures, including the imposition of penal sanctions, to prevent and suppress any activity prohibited . . . under this Treaty undertaken by persons or on territory under [their] jurisdiction or control'. While that obligation is designed to effectively enforce the obligations under Article 1(e) and (f), and while it is based on well-established jurisdictional concepts, it deeply impacts on parties' sovereignty. This may prevent signatory and other States from eventually becoming parties, because the prohibition of reservations also applies to Article 5.

Article 6 on victim assistance and environmental remediation may have similar deterring effects. The far-reaching obligations under paragraph 1 to provide assistance to victims (i.e. those persons who are affected by the use or testing of nuclear weapons) applies with regard to individuals under a party's jurisdiction. Accordingly, it applies to that State's nationals and to those who are on its territory. The reference to 'applicable international humanitarian law and human rights law' seems to identify the legal bases of the obligation. Of course, international humanitarian law would be applicable in times of international or non-international armed conflict only. However, it would oblige States to provide assistance to all victims of armed conflict, not merely to those under their jurisdiction. The reference to human rights law may be correct, but some States – in particular, those in regions without an advanced regional human rights regime – may take the position that they are obliged to provide medical care, but not to provide 'age- and gender-sensitive assistance' or 'rehabilitation and psychological support', nor to provide for 'social and economic inclusion'. The obligation under paragraph 2 to take the necessary and appropriate measures towards the environmental remediation of areas contaminated as a result of activities related to the testing or use of nuclear weapons is limited to the State that has jurisdiction or control over such areas. This begs the question of why the State that has caused the said contamination is not included. The obligation placed by Article 7(6) on a State that has used or tested nuclear weapons is limited to the provision of 'adequate' assistance to the affected State, but it does not include an independent requirement for that State to render assistance to victims or to decontaminate the affected areas. Moreover, the question of whether, in a given case, the assistance is 'adequate' may be a source of considerable dispute.

Article 7 on international co-operation and assistance goes well beyond the known co-operation clauses in other treaties. Whereas the obligation under paragraph 1 to 'cooperate with other States Parties to facilitate the implementation' of the TPNW may be considered of minor practical relevance, Article 7's provisions on international assistance may be considered as quite progressive. According to paragraph 2, each party has a right to seek and receive assistance from other parties, unless that is not feasible. The obligations under paragraphs

3 and 4 of providing technical, material and financial assistance to parties affected by nuclear weapons use or testing, and to victims of such use or testing is limited to States that are 'in a position to do so'. The right to provide assistance through the international organisations and institutions enumerated in paragraph 5 is declaratory and dependent on the consent of the organisation or institution. As already stated, the obligation of States having used or tested nuclear weapons under paragraph 6 is limited to the provision of assistance to the affected State.

As seen, the TPNW is poorly drafted, at least insofar as parts of the preamble and Article 4 are concerned. Compliance with the treaty will not be overly difficult for those parties that are not present or former nuclear weapon States and if they are not affected by the use or testing of nuclear weapons. Such non-nuclear-weapon States may merely show some hesitancy with regard to the obligation under Article 3 (2) to conclude with the IAEA a comprehensive safeguards agreement. It is highly questionable, however, whether present or former nuclear-weapon States will ever be willing to become parties. While they might, in theory, be prepared to accept the obligations under Article 4(1)–(3), it is rather doubtful whether they would also accept the obligations under Article 7 on international co-operation and assistance. As long as nuclear deterrence is considered necessary not only by nuclear-weapon States but also by those States that have chosen to be protected by a nuclear umbrella, the prospects of the TPNW acquiring universal adherence as envisaged in Article 12 are rather low.

K.3 UNSC RESOLUTIONS ENFORCING THE NON-PROLIFERATION REGIME

K.3.1 *Resolution 1540*

UN Security Council Resolution 1540 (2004)[40] imposes on member States of the UN, in an abstract and general manner, a number of far-reaching obligations with regard to the prevention and suppression of the proliferation of weapons of mass destruction, including nuclear weapons and their delivery systems, by non-State actors.[41] Resolution 1540 also established the so-called 1540 Committee, which monitors its implementation.[42]

40 UN Doc. S/RES/1540 of 28 April 2004.

41 Ibid., operative paras. 1–3.

42 Ibid., operative para. 4.

More than 150 States are taking part in the Proliferation Security Initiative (PSI) that was announced by President G. W. Bush on 31 May 2003 and which is designed to increase their practical capabilities in preventing and suppressing proliferation activities by non-State actors and, when permissible under international law, by State actors.

Resolution 1540 should be seen as a milestone, because it subjects the UN member States to clear obligations which, if properly implemented, would prove an effective tool in the prevention and suppression of the proliferation by non-State actors of weapons of mass destruction, including their delivery systems. Of course, proper monitoring of its implementation is dependent upon the political will of the five permanent Council members to extend the mandate of the 1540 Committee.

K.3.2 *Specific Resolutions*

Apart from the power to establish general and abstract obligations incumbent on UN member States, the UN Security Council is in most instances likely to be limited in its ability to respond to nuclear threats by States. It may, however, consider using its powers under Chapter VII of the Charter. In this regard, the Council has so far adopted enforcement measures against two States: the Democratic People's Republic of Korea (North Korea) and Iran.

Democratic People's Republic of Korea (North Korea): After North Korea announced its withdrawal from the NPT, the UN Security Council urged it to reconsider that step.[43] After the test launch of ballistic missiles, the Council imposed the first sanctions and set up a Sanctions Committee.[44] The North Korean nuclear test of 25 May 2009 led to expanded sanctions and to the establishment of a Panel of Experts that was to assist the Sanctions Committee.[45] The mandate of the Panel of Experts was last extended in March 2020.[46] Further North Korean nuclear tests, including the launch of ballistic missiles, were condemned by the Council, which imposed additional sanctions.[47] However, despite the continuing preparedness of the permanent Council members to remain seized of the North Korean issue, the possibility

43 S/RES/825 of 11 May 1993.

44 S/RES/1695 of 15 July 2006; S/RES/1718 of 14 October 2006.

45 S/RES/1874 of 12 June 2009.

46 S/RES/2515 of 30 March 2020.

47 S/RES/2087 of 22 January 2013; S/RES/2094 of 7 March 2013; S/RES/2270 of 24 March 2016; S/RES/2321 of 30 November 2016; S/RES/2356 of 2 June 2017; S/RES/2371 of 5 August 2017; S/RES/2371 of 5 August 2017; S/RES/2375 of 11 September 2017; S/RES/2397 of 22 December 2017.

cannot be excluded that permanent Council members will fail to take the necessary steps to fully implement the Council's resolutions.

Iran: In 2006, the Security Council called upon Iran 'to take the steps required by the IAEA Board of Governors in its resolution GOV/2006/14, which are essential to build confidence in the exclusively peaceful purpose of its nuclear programme' and demanded that 'Iran shall suspend all enrichment-related and reprocessing activities, including research and development, to be verified by the IAEA'.[48] In the following years, the Security Council established a Sanctions Committee and imposed a variety of sanctions on Iran's trade and individuals.[49] After the United States' withdrawal from the Joint Comprehensive Plan of Action[50] which aims at ensuring the exclusively peaceful nature of Iran's nuclear programme, the Security Council failed to adopt any further resolutions on Iran's nuclear programme, and it remains to be seen whether any future draft resolution will obtain the required votes.

K.4 FINAL OBSERVATIONS

The current non-proliferation regime is considerably advanced, and it has proven successful for the last decades. However, withdrawal from the NPT in accordance with its Article X(1) is always a feasible option if a member State 'decides that extraordinary events, related to the subject matter of this Treaty, have jeopardized the supreme interests of its country'. While the Security Council may oblige a withdrawing State to continue to comply with its obligations under the NPT, as in the case of North Korea, and take non-military enforcement measures against that State if it does not act accordingly, this will not necessarily contribute to a strengthening of the international non-proliferation regime. This negative assessment also holds true for Security Council action against member States of the NPT.

Ratification of the TPNW by a representative number of States, including those whose interests are specially affected, could contribute to nuclear security and, eventually, to the total elimination of nuclear weapons and other nuclear explosive devices. As seen, there is little prospect of such a development. Accordingly, stabilisation in the area of nuclear security could be best accomplished if (1) the United States and the Russian Federation were to preserve New START and return to the INF arrangements;

48 S/RES/1696 of 31 July 2006.
49 S/RES/1737 of 23 December 2006; S/RES/1747 of 24 March 2007; S/RES/1929 of 9 June 2010.
50 Agreed upon by Iran and the P5 + 1 (i.e. the five permanent members of the Security Council plus Germany and the European Union), Vienna 14 July 2015.

(2) other nuclear weapon States could be brought under the existing nuclear disarmament and arms control regime; (3) non-recognised nuclear weapon States were to acquire recognition under the NPT; and (4) the non-proliferation regime under the NPT and Resolution 1540 were effectively implemented insofar as recognised non-nuclear-weapon States are concerned.

L

Implications of International Law for Nuclear Command, Control and Communications

At the start of this Section we should remind ourselves of the overarching purpose of a nuclear command, control and communications (NC3) system. It must be designed to ensure that the threat or use of nuclear weapons is an absolutely last resort; that every less violent alternative to their use is pursued; that the resort to nuclear weapons is indeed prevented; and that confusion, ambiguity, uncertainty, mis-communication and any other factor that may lead to strategic misunderstanding is, as far as possible, prevented. All nuclear weapon-armed States must employ NC3 systems that are similarly effective in achieving these goals. A parallel, and arguably equally important, objective of an NC3 system should be to try to make sure that all involved in nuclear weapon operations fully understand the rules of international law that apply to their activities and actually implement those rules in all of their actions relating to nuclear weapons.

In the following paragraphs, the authors offer thoughts on some of the matters that should, in their view, be addressed in an NC3 mechanism – which, for these purposes, can be taken to comprise the instructions, directives, guidance, training, laws, documents, orders and other elements that, taken together, constitute NC3 arrangements. The Rules and Commentaries in the earlier Sections of this book will, it is hoped, assist States to identify the international law provisions that are of greatest relevance when drawing up or revising their NC3 mechanisms. In the following paragraphs, some of the matters that are considered by the present authors to be of greatest importance are teased out in the hope that this will be useful for those tasked with such a revision.

In Section A we concluded that, to be effective, NC3 measures must be rigorous, robust and sufficiently secure to ensure that nuclear weapons will not be used outside the most exceptional, compelling and strictly lawful of circumstances. The NC3 architecture must be so designed that nuclear weapons are only ever used as an absolutely last resort; that every possible step to prevent and avoid their use is taken; that the precautionary NC3 procedures that are in place will prevent the resort to nuclear engagement; and that confusion, ambiguity, uncertainty, miscommunication or any other source of reduced clarity are weeded out. There is a mutual interest among States to be sure that all other nuclear-capable States have in place the best possible NC3 systems that are designed to achieve the same objectives and that all such States can feel mutual confidence in each other's NC3 systems. We also noted that NC3 processes must be designed such that, were nuclear weapons ever actually to be employed, they would not have an adverse impact on third-party, neutral States.

It is clear from Section B that wider NC3 arrangements must include legislation that prescribes the nuclear weapon-related activities that are prohibited; that criminalises those prohibited acts; that provides for arrangements that are necessary to secure nuclear sites and equipment, as well as the associated information relating to nuclear weapons; and that implements other required arrangements. The legal basis for this requirement rests in the sovereign rights and responsibilities of States. Accordingly, nuclear weapon-capable States must make sure that their legal arrangements enable them potentially to take legal action in all cases where international law gives them jurisdiction to do so. This means that such legal arrangements must extend to ships, aircraft or other platforms over which the State has flag-State or State-of-registration jurisdiction. Such legal arrangements must also be so designed that sovereign immunity, where applicable, is respected.

The detailed NC3 provisions must have the effect that the nuclear weapon capabilities of States situated on their territory or under their exclusive control, including their NC3 systems themselves along with the associated equipment and information, are not used in peacetime for activities that adversely and unlawfully affect other States. This again implies the need for suitable legislation; for the issuing of appropriately clear orders and instructions throughout the relevant chains of command and management; and for the maintenance of proper discipline so that the laws, orders and instructions will in fact be complied with. If such activity adversely and unlawfully affecting another State were to take place, all means at the disposal of the nuclear weapon-capable State must be so organised as to put an end to the activity promptly. Information that nuclear weapon-related equipment is being used in State A adversely and unlawfully to affect State B must be acted on swiftly and the NC3 arrangements must facilitate this.

Underpinning the NC3 architecture, there should be a recognition that the State will be responsible for all activity that breaches international law and that is attributable to the State. So proper disciplinary and other arrangements must apply to the armed forces; to internal security, customs, intelligence and other relevant State agencies; and proper control must be exercised among all persons that are acting on the instructions of, or under the direction or control of, the State while carrying out nuclear weapon-related duties. This includes military, civilian and State agency personnel and contractors' employees. Because State responsibility may also extend to the activities of groups or individuals involved in a non-international armed conflict where the relevant State is providing material assistance, the NC3 arrangements should stipulate the security arrangements designed sufficiently to safeguard nuclear weapons and their related materials, equipment and data.

NC3 documentation should reflect certain core international law obligations of the State, such as to refrain from the threat or use of force contrary to the UN Charter. This implies the inclusion of clear instructions within the documentation and an explanation of what 'threats' for these purposes comprise. Such instructions should be expressed as applying to all persons who have the authority to make statements on behalf of the State or to decide on the taking of nuclear weapon-related action.

It seems to the present authors that it would be useful for States in peacetime to consider, in advance as it were, the kinds of nuclear weapon-related event or situation that they would classify, respectively, as a use of force contrary to Article 2(4) of the UN Charter or as an armed attack. States should consider specifying the criteria they would regard as relevant to such determinations, with a view to reflecting these in strategic-level, probably classified, doctrine. Such doctrine might also, usefully, set forth national policy on the response options to particular kinds and degrees of nuclear operation amounting to an armed attack or the use or threat of force.

The military doctrine of all States should recognise that NC3 systems of a State are likely to be regarded by it – and, indeed, by other States – as being part of its critical national infrastructure, such that disabling and damaging interference with such systems is likely to be classed by the victim State as an armed attack. This implies the need for great caution in undertaking certain intrusive operations involving the nuclear weapon systems of nuclear weapon-capable States, and the present authors believe that this need should be reflected in both doctrine and practice.

The Commentary accompanying Rule 11 sets forth the legal controversy over the right of a victim State to take forceful action by way of extraterritorial self-defence. The opportunity to formulate a policy on that topic may well be limited or non-existent in the immediate aftermath of a relevant nuclear weapon-related incident. The present authors therefore consider that each nuclear weapon-capable State should develop internal, probably classified, strategic doctrine addressing this and related issues for inclusion in the NC3 documentation.

It would be sensible for States to include, either in their classified strategic doctrine or in their publicly available LOAC manuals, a statement of the national view as to whether force in self-defence can be employed lawfully to address an imminent armed attack and, if so, in which circumstances where nuclear weapons and their associated systems are concerned. The points made in the Commentary accompanying Rule 13 are, it is hoped, helpful in formulating the national view. Where NC3 documents address the taking of collective self-defence action, they should draw attention to the requirement for a prior request from the assisted State and to the need for any collective defensive action to comply with the terms of the request. The provisions dealing with action in self-defence generally should also allocate responsibility for submitting a timely report to the UN Security Council, as noted in Article 51 of the UN Charter and in Rule 15.

NC3 documents and instructions must be consistent with the differing international law rules that apply to the range of nuclear operations throughout the spectrum of conflict. Thus, the rules applicable in international and non-international armed conflicts must be distinguished from those that apply in peacetime, and those states of affairs must be explained with clarity. Moreover, the danger that an unauthorised act involving nuclear weapon systems (e.g. undertaken by a member of the armed forces) could cause a State to become involved in an international armed conflict reinforces the extreme importance of proper discipline and of clear, unambiguous instructions and lines of authority.

Section E suggests that it would be wise to include within NC3 arrangements an explanation of the differing situations confronting members of the armed forces and civilians (including civil servants and contractors' employees) who take a direct part in nuclear operations. Such guidance will need to differentiate between peacetime and armed conflict and will draw upon points made in the Commentaries accompanying Rules 21 and 22. The guidance will necessarily clarify what activities the State considers amount to direct participation in nuclear-related hostilities and the time periods during which a person is to be regarded as so participating. It is hoped that the Commentary accompanying Rule 28 provides helpful information to States on the matters to be considered. In the view of the present authors, civilians whose duties would, in the event of armed conflict, be likely to involve direct participation in nuclear-related hostilities should be made aware of the potential legal consequences for them of such participation.

It would be useful for States to express, preferably publicly, whether they regard unmanned maritime systems and vessels that otherwise fulfil the relevant requirements as constituting warships and, thus, as having belligerent rights, including the right to participate in nuclear operations. So, for example, before unmanned maritime platforms are developed and deployed for maritime patrols involving the carrying of nuclear weapons, the present authors regard it as essential that the deploying State make its legal interpretation on this topic publicly known. The Commentary accompanying Rule 23 explains the relevant issues.

A State's NC3 arrangements that regulate the conduct of nuclear operations during an armed conflict will, of necessity, distinguish between those activities that constitute attacks and nuclear operations that fall below the attack threshold, noting that non-violent operations that have no adverse effect on the enemy are not subject to the principle of distinction. However, most nuclear operations will cause death, injury, damage and/or destruction, so the distinction principle will apply and will need to be explained in terms informed by Rules 30–6. The NC3 documentation should specify the persons and objects that can lawfully be made the object of attack and those that must not, and should draw attention to the point made in paragraph 2 of the Commentary accompanying Rule 34.

More generally, it is most important that all of the Rules applying the principle of distinction to persons and objects, in particular Rules 25–47, are properly set forth in the NC3 documents and instructions. While this might in part be achieved by the inclusion of a 'legal annex', the Rules should also properly inform the content of other, substantive and procedural parts of the NC3 text. So, for example, while the legal annex might state and explain the definition of military objective in Rule 34, the other substantive NC3 provisions should also reflect that definitional Rule, the Commentary relating to it, paragraph 2 of the Commentary accompanying Rule 35 and Rule 36 with its accompanying Commentary. A legal annex that does not inform the substance of the NC3 arrangements is of limited value. An NC3 regime that in its entirety is coherent with applicable legal rules is, in the opinion of the present authors, what is required.

There might be merit in stating in the NC3 documentation, or perhaps in a more generally applicable national LOAC text, the relevant State's view as to the US position on war-supporting or war-sustaining objects.[1] Complex issues do, however, arise in connection with the prohibition of indiscriminate attacks. The precise terms of the rule, as it applies to a particular State, will

[1] See Commentary accompanying Rule 34, para. 8.

depend on the factors mentioned in the Commentary accompanying Rule 37. Accordingly, a State should consider its own position under applicable treaty law and should then draft the relevant part of its NC3 instructions and guidance accordingly. States should also consider the kinds of circumstance that can render a nuclear attack indiscriminate and should mention this in the instructions and guidance, which will draw attention to the proportionality rule,[2] explaining the procedures that the State employs in order to ensure that nuclear attack decision-making complies with the Rule. The very nature of nuclear attack operations and of their likely consequences makes it essential that the rules on indiscriminate attacks and proportionality are explained with utmost clarity and applied with the greatest care. This point therefore applies with equal force to the implementation of the rules on precautions in nuclear attack and against the effects of nuclear attacks.[3]

A clear priority will therefore be for the NC3 mechanism clearly to set forth the precautionary measures referred to in Rules 39–47 that the particular State acknowledges are required by international law as it applies to that State, noting the points made in the narrative preceding Rule 39. Having stated the constant care obligation as given in that Rule, the documentation should then specify the persons and activities to which, and the times when, the duty applies. How such care is in practice to be exercised should, where appropriate, be spelt out, and procedural mechanisms designed to enhance that care should be devised and implemented. These will include, among other things, the arrangements under which targets are selected and verified; the procedures for assessing expected collateral damage and anticipated military advantage and for comparing them; the technique for programming target co-ordinates into the missile guidance system; whether a controller is able to divert and disable the warhead at all times up to the point of detonation; and the ways in which orders from senior commanders are communicated to the pilot of a nuclear weapon-armed aircraft or the commander of a nuclear weapon-armed submarine.

The constant care duty requires that these and related arrangements be effective in ensuring that nuclear weapons are only ever used in lawful circumstances as a very last resort and that every possible precaution is taken to avoid or minimise collateral damage. While Rules 39–47 set forth the precautionary rules that apply to the use of nuclear weapons, arguably all possible precautions should be taken, including all of the precautions given in

2 Rule 38.

3 Rules 39–47.

Article 57 of API, whether as a matter of law or, in some cases, as a matter of policy.

On a matter of detail, note should be taken of the points made in paragraphs 2–4 of the Commentary accompanying Rule 40 regarding the persons who are required to take specific precautions in attack. It is in order to implement the precautions referred to in Rule 43 that States must devise and employ a suitable collateral damage estimate process so that the proportionality rule can be properly applied.

As paragraph 3 of the Commentary accompanying Rule 43 illustrates, pilots of nuclear-armed aircraft and commanders of nuclear-armed submarines rely on their superiors making lawful decisions based on a proper consideration of the law and of all relevant and reasonably available information. This does, of course, presuppose that those superiors are seeking to make rational and lawful decisions. Profoundly complex issues would arise if, say, an unstable individual were to occupy the supreme command position in a State that has nuclear weapons ('the madman with the codes'). The analysis in the Commentary accompanying Rules 40 and 43 presupposes the stability and rationality of supreme commanders and assumes that they are seeking to act within the law. If, hypothetically, a pilot of a nuclear-armed aircraft or the commander of a nuclear-armed submarine were to receive an order to fire a nuclear weapon and if the supreme commander of the State is known to be unstable, irrational or reckless, or to have evil intent, it would seem to the present authors that the pilot or submarine commander can no longer assume that the orders he has received are lawful and proper. In such a circumstance, the pilot or submarine commander is under an obligation to verify the lawfulness of the order he or she has received. If unable to do so, he or she should decline to implement that order. It is appreciated that this will place that individual in a most difficult position and is likely to amount to a potential breach of his or her service disciplinary code.

Accordingly, it is most important that the NC3 arrangements that are put in place give pilots and submarine commanders ample assurance that the nuclear weapon-related orders that they receive have been thoroughly reviewed to ensure their compliance with applicable law.

Rules 48–68 should, it is suggested, be incorporated into the training of relevant personnel, and the Rules themselves should also feature in the legal annex mentioned earlier.

Nuclear weapons, like any other weapon, are regulated by the principles and rules of weapons law. While the detail of the weapon review obligations of States differs depending on whether or not the particular State is a party to API, the present authors suggest that any State that is studying, developing or acquiring a nuclear weapon should conduct a full weapon review, in which the factors discussed in Rules 70–73 and 75 and in the Commentaries accompanying those Rules are properly considered. This is a legal obligation for each State, and States that have ratified the TPNW must also ensure that any action they take in respect of nuclear weapons complies with their obligations under that Treaty.

FINAL REMARKS

It is hoped that the comments made in this Section, and indeed in the rest of the book, help States to develop and maintain NC3 provisions, arrangements and policies that achieve the purposes outlined in Section A and in the opening paragraphs of this Section. The dire potential consequences of a nuclear mistake, or indeed of most nuclear weapon-related incidents, mean that it is now of vital importance that the NC3 processes of all nuclear weapon-equipped States must achieve and maintain the very highest standards. In a sense, the duty to do NC3 properly is the corollary of the perceived security that derives from nuclear deterrence. The perceived security and the duty sit together. States cannot have the perceived benefit without complying with the duty. If the guidance in this short book helps States to comply with that duty, the goal which the authors set themselves will have been achieved.

Index

www.ingramcontent.com/pod-product-compliance
Lightning Source LLC
LaVergne TN
LVHW011813200926
848484LV00005B/1169

* 9 7 8 1 3 1 6 5 1 1 4 2 8 *